Robin Williams **DVD** Design Workshop

John Tollett + David Rohr

with Robin Williams

Published by Peachpit Press
Berkeley • California

Robin Williams DVD Design Workshop
John Tollett and David Rohr with Robin Williams

Copyright ©2004 John Tollett, David Rohr, and Robin Williams

Peachpit Press
1249 Eighth Street
Berkeley, California 94710
510.524.2178
510.524.2221 fax

Find us on the World Wide Web at www.peachpit.com
Peachpit Press is a division of Pearson Education

All original illustrations, art, and design
 ©2004 John Tollett or David Rohr

Cover design and production by John Tollett
Interior design and production by John Tollett and David Rohr
Index by Laura Egley Taylor
Editing by Nancy Davis
Prepress by Hilal Sala

ISBN
0-321-13628-4

10 9 8 7 6 5 4 3 2 1

Printed and bound in the United States of America

Contents

3 Designer's Toolbox 31

DVD hardware and software overview

4 Video & Audio Overview 51

Essential hardware and software

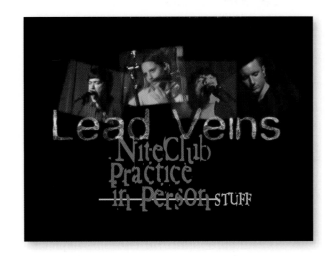

Section Two

DVD menu design: structure, style, design and production guidelines, usability, and video compositing

11 Designing with Motion Graphics 169

Use video compositing techniques to create motion menus

Section Three

DVD planning, encoding, authoring, testing, and duplication vs. replication

12 Professional DVD Showcase 181

Menu design inspiration

13 Create a Plan 225

Planning and information architecture

14 Encoding 233

Compressing video and audio for DVD

Section Four

Extra stuff

Acknowledgments

Designers

The Pavement: Kristen O'Sullivan, Lloyd Shaer

Finishing Post: Mark Harwood

La F@KTORY: Marek Doszla

Stanford Design: Ron Stanford

MPL Media: Scott Long

Additional support

Tiz Beretta

Mark Kimonedes

Michael Schwartz

Heyday Satoh

Atsuko Shimizu

Clay Williard

Kansas (Phil Ehart)

Panorama Point: Andy Alsop, Alisa Smith

Software companies

Sonic: Paul Lefebvre

Adobe: Jill Devlin

Apple: Jerry Hsu

Ahead

Canopus

CinemaCraft

Discreet

Innobits

Pegasys

Pinnacle

Primera Technology, Inc.

Roxio

TriLab Productions

Stage Tools MovingPicture

Ulead

Businesses

Route 66 Sandwich Shop, Santa Fe

Bonanza Creek Ranch, Santa Fe

Training

Bruce Nazarian

Friends in personal menu examples

40th Birthday: Roni Rohr, Rich and Fran Powers, Rich and Al Feit, Mary Jane Rohr, Annabelle Smith, Joan Wren

1950s and '60s Home Movies: Mathias Rohr, Julius Rohr

Biking Across Kansas: Sherry McKee, Mark Levine, Charlie Summers, Denise Duerksen, Donna Allen

Bonanza Creek Ranch: Imogene Hughes

Burns Supper: Ross Carter, Nick Lawrence, Andrew, Jim Wallace

Clan Tynker: The Whippos: Elijah, Marygold, Rebekah, Sarah, Sam, and Santiago Carrillo

Danny Wilding: Danny Wilding

Durango to Quray: Tom Brimacombe

Hands On Community Art: Betsy Millard

The Lead Veins: Greg Epman, Caitlin Love, Jimmy Thomas (Williams), Stevan Wintermeyer

Ozark Folk Music: Ed Stilley

Recital and Yearbook: Scarlett Williams

Return to Bhaktapur: Robin Williams

Ritmo del Alma: Domino and Keyana

Scarlett in Concert: Scarlett Williams

Whatta Year: Scarlett Willams

Looking for Mary: Dana Evans, Jim'Bo Norrena, Laura Egley Taylor, Robin Williams

Journey through Nepal: John Tollett

Various example graphics: Amy Rohr, Matthew Rohr, Leonard Feit

Editing and production support

Nancy Davis, Laura Taylor, Hilal Sala

Special thanks

From John:

Thanks to David Rohr for the original book idea and his contributions of design, technical knowledge, and friendship.

From David:

A heartfelt thanks to my pal John for investing his vast talent and enthusiasm into this book. It's been a real privilege to partner with him to explore yet another design frontier. I give my love and appreciation to Roni, Matthew, and Amy, for their constant support and endurance throughout this long project.

From John and David:

Special thanks to Ada DeAguero and the Ritmo del Alma flamenco dance troupe, Danny Wilding, and Clan Tynker, for their gracious cooperation, inspiration, and enthusiasm for this project.

A giant thank you to the designers who submitted DVD designs and spent considerable time and energy obtaining permissions to reproduce their beautiful work in this book.

Also, many thanks to Nancy Davis for being more than a great editor, Hilal Sala for great production assistance, and to Nancy Ruenzel for giving us this opportunity.

And extra special thanks to Robin for her suggestions, guidance, editing, inspiration, and expert project supervision.

From Robin:

Thanks to John and Dave for a great job!

Dive into DVD!

The future of design is here.

The advent of digital desktop video design and production and the overwhelming consumer acceptance of the DVD format as a video delivery medium have resulted in an explosion of affordable, powerful hardware and software tools that enable all of us, both professional and amateur designers, to create, edit, and produce multimedia projects of amazing sophistication. We suggest you dive right in to DVD, not only for the fun and personal satisfaction you'll get from creating and delivering video projects, but also for the potential profit of being a DVD producer. You may never work on a Hollywood movie, but there are many opportunites and potential clients out there just waiting to learn how DVD projects can benefit their business and help their organization. This book is for anyone who needs a concise overview of the DVD process, explained from a designer's point of view.

What to expect from this book

This book is an introduction to the world of DVD design and production, with an emphasis on menu design. We hope to interest you in using the DVD format to communicate ideas in a creative way. There are other books twice this size that go into greater detail about the technical aspects of DVD, but we've attempted to present the most critical information in a simple, non-technical way so you won't be intimidated or have your eyes glaze over reading through a technical manual. This book provides an overview of the main elements of DVD, tells you what equipment you need, and what you need to know to produce your first DVD projects. We hope it also gets you excited about chasing that creative urge for which designers are known. DVD-specific design instructions and tips are presented along with advice on issues to consider when designing DVD menus. We're convinced that you'll decide, as we have, that DVD can offer more creative satisfaction than any other design path you've followed.

Also included are overviews of some of the most popular software used for video and audio editing, encoding, and DVD-authoring. We've attemped to provide a general sense of the various programs and how user-friendly they are so you'll have an idea of what's available as you make choices for the hardware and software you'll need to be a DVD designer.

What you shouldn't expect

▼ This book does not pretend to be a software manual for any of the video and authoring programs that are showcased. Since each software program mentioned requires one or more manuals, our intent is to provide a very general overview.

▼ We've avoided showing a preference for a particular platform, Mac or PC. Both platforms have advantages and many DVD authors are most productive when using both platforms.

▼ Skip this book if you're already familiar with DVD design and production and you're looking for in-depth technical information about the process, features, or functions of DVD. Our goal is to give a comprehensive DVD overview.

What you'll learn

We've squeezed a lot of information into this book to provide a comprehensive overview of DVD, as well as related issues and disciplines. You'll learn about:

▼ The functions and features of DVD technology.

▼ Design concepts specific to DVD menu planning and creation.

▼ Menu design. In addition to menu examples throughout the book, we include examples of projects ranging from home movies to Hollywood movies (Chapters 5 and 12).

▼ NLE software options. NLE (non-linear editor) software enables you to edit movies on your computer (Chapter 4).

▼ DVD-authoring software options. You'll be amazed at how many applications are available (Chapter 15).

The creative potential of working with motion video, audio, and video-compositing effects makes DVD design an exciting, fascinating, and satisfying field for both amateur and professional designers. Today's affordable hardware and software provide creative tools and production power that until recently was beyond our reach.

A super-simple DVD overview

DVD development can seem complex unless you have a clear idea of what's involved. Unless you're familiar with the process, you may be confused about things such as the difference between using *NLE software to edit a movie* and using *authoring software to author a DVD*. To avoid confusion, we offer this super-simple overview of the process before you dive in:

Step one: Content creation and asset acquisition

You must have content (usually movies) to put in a DVD project. Either someone gives you movie footage to use, or you shoot it yourself. During this first step you *collect all the assets* that you'll need for your project—video, audio, photos, etc.

Step two: Editing

Unless someone provides *edited* movies to use in your DVD project, you'll use *NLE software (non-linear editing) to edit the video* into finished movies, then save the edited movies in a format that DVD-authoring software requires.

Step three: DVD authoring and multiplexing

Using *DVD-authoring software,* you'll *assemble* the final assets into a DVD project. Authoring software is a tool for integrating edited content (audio, video, slideshows) with menus you design, and provides an interface that makes it easy for you to create links between menus and content. After assembling a DVD project, the authoring software prepares it for reproduction, a process called *multiplexing.* Multiplexing re-assembles the files into a structure and format required to *reproduce* the project on DVD discs.

Step four: Duplication or replication

Reproduce copies of your project on DVD discs and amaze the world (Chapter 17).

Section One

*DVD basics, hardware requirements,
and software overviews*

Sarah, from the Clan Tynker DVD

You might be a DVD designer if . . .

▼ you use the word "mux" a lot.

▼ you ever muxed anything on purpose.
   Or accidentally.

▼ you're deciding whether to duplicate or replicate.

▼ you rent DVDs to see the menus.

▼ you've studied lots of multiple-camera-angle DVDs
   that aren't X-rated.

DVD Basics

DVD *is your next design frontier*

Okay. We'll admit it. We're all fired up about the new creative possibilities of the DVD format. "Hollywood" DVDs have been around for a while, but only recently have ordinary people like us been able to think about creating our own. The recent availability of affordable DVD hardware and software opens up a whole new world of interactive design and communication with video. Once the domain of high-end specialists, DVD creation (or authoring) is now within the grasp of people with creative ideas but modest budgets.

DVD is a great format for regular non-Hollywood types who want to express their creativity with video. The most obvious benefit of consumer DVD is that we now have a reliable way to archive all those home video tapes lying around. Editing your home movies and saving them to DVD might just be convenient enough so you and your family will actually watch some of that old footage from time to time.

Beyond home movies, the list of uses includes independent films, event videos (weddings, parties, etc.), business presentations, artist portfolios, family genealogy and much more. We will show examples of these and other possibilities in Chapter 5.

Before you create a DVD, you must first understand a few basic concepts on how they're put together. This chapter will guide you through the origins of DVD and highlight the features that have made it so popular. Most importantly, we'll tell you why you should jump onto the DVD bandwagon and head out for new and exciting creative territories.

The Meaning of DVD

While it may seem obvious to some, we won't take it for granted that everyone on planet Earth knows the meaning of the letters DVD. DVD originally stood for *Digital Video Disc* or *Digital Versatile Disc*, but these days, no one really cares about that—it's now just plain ol' DVD. Like its technical ancestor, the CD (compact disc), DVD has become an extremely popular consumer video format, rapidly replacing the familiar VHS video tape.

Physically, a DVD disc is the exact same size as a CD, but it contains many times more digital information. A single-sided consumer disc can contain up to 4.37 gigabytes (GB) of digital data. You can certainly use a DVD disc to backup computer files, but it's so much more than a super-sized CD.

A Popular Format

DVD has, in a very short time, become the preferred way to distribute film and video to the masses. It's compact, easy to use, and can deliver hours of video content with killer picture quality—no wonder it's had the fastest adoption rate of any consumer format in history. Forget about records, eight-track tapes, cassettes, VHS, or CDs. While each of these earlier formats found favor with the public, none was embraced as quickly as the DVD.

According to IRMA (International Recording Media Association), DVD is in 25 percent of U.S. homes, and it has reached this high level of market penetration within just five years, faster than any other consumer electronics product ever. More than 31 million DVD players have been sold, and consumers can now choose from over 125 DVD player models that are marketed under 50 different brand names.

DVD discs have an excellent shelf-life—rated to last at least 100 years if you treat 'em right. Unlike VHS tape, DVD quality doesn't degrade with use, so a movie will look as good the 100th time you view it as it did the first time.

The motion picture industry likes DVD because it's less expensive to manufacture than VHS and has much more robust copy protection. Consumers prefer to buy and rent movies on DVD for the high-quality picture, plus the inclusion of additional bonus features. Extras like "behind the scenes" video clips, deleted scenes, director commentary, or interactive games all add to the perceived value of a DVD disc.

Way Better than CD-ROM

Like CD-ROMs, a DVD can store regular computer data files, but with a capacity up to six times that of a CD data disc. This kind of DVD is called, appropriately enough, **DVD-ROM.** It can come in handy if you want to save the files on your computer's hard drive, but digital file backup wasn't the primary reason DVD was invented.

In the late 1990s, several big-name players in the motion picture industry joined forces to develop a new format for movie distribution. They wanted something that delivered high quality video, but was conveniently-sized like the popular CD format. It needed to be a digital format, not analog like the VHS standard. Most importantly, it needed to have strong copy-protection built in so people couldn't steal . . . er, duplicate and sell their own copies.

Taking all of this into account, the technical wizards came up with the **DVD format.** It's not only a larger capacity disc, but also a robust digital format that allows video to play back consistently on a variety of devices, from TV monitors to computers. If that isn't enough, the DVD format allows for interactivity, multiple video and audio tracks, subtitles, scene selection, and still-image slideshows, among other digital goodies.

Going back a decade or so, proponents of the CD-ROM format had attempted to deliver many of the same interactive and multimedia features that DVD now handles so well. However, they have never achieved the quality, ease-of-use or popularity that DVD has demonstrated. Compatibility has always been a problem. CD-ROM discs can only play back in computers, and are specific to a particular platform (Windows or Mac). Combined with lower-quality video and no standard unifying structure, CD-ROMs have always been a rehearsal for the real deal: DVD.

CD-ROM vs. DVD-ROM

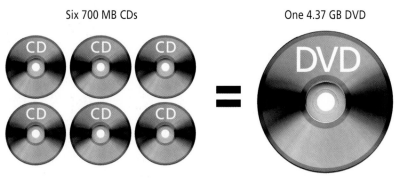

Six 700 MB CDs   One 4.37 GB DVD

DVDs, like CDs, contain digital data files rather than the analog data found on magnetic VHS tape.

Interactivity

Probably the most powerful feature of DVD is **interactivity,** which allows the consumer to control the ways they view a video presentation or other content. Instead of the linear, start-to-finish nature of VHS tape, DVD provides the means to quickly jump to any part of the content they want to view.

Menus

Most DVDs worth watching contain more than just video presentations—they also provide an interactive way for the user to jump to sections or scenes that interest them.

Here's how it works: a DVD will generally display a special video screen soon after it is inserted into a player. This screen presents the choice of several buttons or words. Selecting any one of them will instantly jump you to a particular part of the DVD and play that section of video.

These special selection screens are called **menus.** Like its restaurant counterpart, a DVD menu presents several choices that can be "ordered" upon request. The interactive menu is the one aspect that sets DVD apart. Without it, the overall experience would only be marginally better than VHS tape—the video quality would be superior, but without a way to jump from clip to clip, it would still have that linear thing going on.

Content

Of course, if a menu's main function is to allow a user to jump around to different areas on a DVD, you've got to have a few things on a disc that are worth looking at—in other words, the **content.** The public has embraced the DVD because it adds so much more material beyond the feature attraction. A DVD can contain a lot of different content pieces—including the bonus clips, audio commentary, still images, and the main feature attraction.

A DVD menu provides several destination choices for the viewer. This menu contains four distinct menu items, each of which will take you to a different section of the DVD.

David Blaine
Menu design and animations
©2003 The Pavement
Client: VCI/Channel 4

In the middle of all of this, menus serve as the "glue" that holds everything together and turns the DVD into a cohesive viewing experience. Sure, each piece of DVD content can be interesting on its own merits, but when joined together by a dynamic set of menus, it rises to another level of entertainment or education. And usefulness.

The Designer's Role

Interactive menus are vital to the concept of DVD as a content-delivery medium. As a visual designer, your creative input and menu concepts play a critical role in the DVD experience, both aesthetically and by building a navigation environment that is intuitive and effortless. Filmmakers and videographers do what they do to produce a movie or documentary, but it's the job of the menu designer/DVD author to wrap it up in an attractive package for all to see, admire, and use.

The great part for a designer is that there are so many possible creative directions you can take. Menus can range from the simplest still graphic to the most elaborate full-motion video imaginable.

Print and web designers who venture into the new world of DVD authoring will enjoy breaking out of the constraints of still images and low bandwidth. The ability to deliver full-motion, interactive video in a compact package is a powerful thing. DVD will provide you with new ways to present ideas to your target audience and support your efforts in other media.

But before we get to the possibilities for creative menu design, there are a few technical details you need to know.

Menu design is more than just creating an interface for disc navigation. It encompasses many other creative possibilities.

The Big Squeeze: MPEG-2

You may be wondering why we couldn't just put movies onto the existing CD format, seeing as how it works so well with music. The problem is a matter of file size: digital video takes up many more times the space of CD audio files and there is simply not enough room to store a high-quality, full-length (90+ minute) movie on a 700 MB CD. Heck, there's not even enough room on a 4.37 GB DVD to store a full-length digital movie, unless it's gone through a special squeezing process beforehand called **encoding.** All DVD video must be encoded into either the **MPEG-2** or **MPEG-1** format before being written to a DVD disc. Both MPEG formats allow a digital movie file that was originally very large to be squeezed down to something quite small.

The MPEG-2 video format, while producing a larger file size, provides much better quality than MPEG-1 and is usually the format of choice for movies and any video where quality matters. The important feature of MPEG-2 video is that while the file size may be dramatically smaller than the original, the video image quality remains very high. MPEG-2 video can be compressed a little or a lot depending on what the project requires. It's definitely a balancing act: compress it too much and the image quality suffers, but compress it too little and it won't fit onto a DVD.

If you've ever worked with still photographs for the web, you'll understand the similarities between the web-oriented JPEG format and the video MPEG formats. Both file formats use what the experts call **lossy compression.** This means to yield a smaller file size, bits of digital information are deleted or "lost." The theory is that much of the color and motion information contained in digital images is redundant and therefore not at all necessary to accurately display the image on the screen. So by isolating the bits that are essential and trashing the redundant parts, you end up with an image that looks the same but takes up a lot less space.

You'll need special software or hardware to encode MPEG-2 files—to learn more about this, see Chapter 14.

Authoring

While we may celebrate the creative design possibilities of DVD, we can't overlook the fact that DVD creation can be a very technical undertaking. Doing it right is a specialized craft that you won't learn overnight.

A full-featured DVD disc may contain the handiwork of several different disciplines, including video editing, still and motion graphic design, 3D modeling, audio editing, and more. Knowing how to best fit all the pieces together is the job of the **DVD author.** Part scientist, part visual designer, a DVD author faces several unique challenges when creating a DVD project.

A DVD author's primary goal is to put together a disc that has great-looking video, menus that work correctly, flawless playback in all players, and fits all of the pieces neatly onto a single disc. Accomplishing all of this takes a solid understanding of what can and can't be done within the DVD specification.

It also requires expertise with a **DVD authoring software application.** Authoring software does for DVD what a page-layout program like Adobe InDesign or QuarkXPress does for printed pages: it accepts several different "pieces" and combines them into a single cohesive unit.

Most authors will focus their energies on learning one authoring program that meets their needs, but there are many to choose from. Not all authoring applications are the same and some offer more features and control than others. There are low-cost or even free entry-level DVD applications available, or you can go to the high-end and spend $20,000 or more if you need a little

Spaced Series 1 and 2
Menu design and animations
©2003 The Pavement
Client: VCI/Channel 4

A DVD authoring application interface. This example shows Sonic DVD Producer, but there are many software packages to choose from.

extra kick in your authoring. Fortunately, there are also several powerful mid-range authoring options.

Not so long ago, the late 1990s to be exact, the field of DVD authoring was the exclusive domain of a small number of brilliant, technically oriented types who actually understood the complex programming language that makes a DVD disc work. They were the industry pioneers, the people who laid the groundwork to bring us all the wonder that is DVD. Back then, squeezing high-quality video and audio onto a CD-sized disc was not for the faint of heart or the slight of budget.

These days, DVD technology is no longer the sole domain of the high-end tech geeks. There is a variety of choices now, and the authoring software you choose will ultimately depend upon what you need to accomplish with your DVDs and how much you're willing to spend. See a list of your options in Chapter 15.

DVD Formats Primer

We may talk about DVDs as if they were a single format, but in reality there are several variations on the theme. We won't pretend that it isn't all a tad confusing, but we'll break it down into a few basic categories for you.

Basic format types

All DVDs have their base foundation on the **DVD-ROM** format. This format describes how data is organized and written to high-capacity DVD discs. The type of DVDs we cover in this book are a subset of DVD-ROM called **DVD-Video,** which comes in several different flavors (see the chart on the next page). Also on the market is **DVD-Audio** for high-quality music, but it is a completely different format and not in widespread use.

Despite the abundance of formats, you will probably need to deal with only one or two of them. To help you better understand where your DVD projects fit in, we'll divide the various formats into two groups: **professional** and **consumer.**

DVD-5 single-layer disc   DVD-9 double-layer disc

Data layer 1

Data layer 2

Single data layer

A DVD disc can have either one or two layers of data, depending on the format. The DVD-5 and DVD-R/+R formats are all single layered. DVD-9 discs have two distinct data layers contained in a single disc.

Professional formats

Professional DVDs are manufactured in mass quantities by a special molding process at a specialty facility. They can't be reproduced on your home or office DVD burner.

Probably the most common kind of professional DVD-Video disc is the **DVD-5** (pronounced *DVD five*) format that can hold about 4.37 GBs of data or up to 2 hours of video. This is usually the kind of disc on which your favorite Hollywood movie will be available for purchase or rental.

DVD-5 discs are **single-sided** with a **single-layer.** This means that the DVD data is written to only one side of the disc and all of it is contained on one layer. Even larger capacity DVD formats allow for two layers to be written to the same side of the disc. On a **double-layer disc,** the outer data layer is semi-transparent, so DVD players can read right through it to access the additional information on the second data layer.

A **DVD-9** disc holds nearly double that of DVD-5 because it contains two distinct layers of digital information on a single side.

Some of the less common professional DVD formats include **DVD-10** (double-sided, single layer) and **DVD-18** (double-sided, double layer). There are other formats available, but they are probably not something you would be working with at your home or office workstation.

Consumer formats

Consumer DVDs are created on desktop or laptop hardware devices using lasers to write (burn) data to the surface of a blank disc. They are intended for limited duplication.

The most common disc formats that you can actually create at home from start to finish are **DVD-R** and **DVD+R** (pronounced *dash R* and *plus R*). Both of these are variants of the DVD-5 format (single-sided, single layer), but they compete with each other in the consumer market. Labeled as 4.7 GB discs, you'll really only be able to fit up to **4.37 GB** of data. The difference in the two figures can be attributed to *marketing math*—the manufacturers think a higher number sounds better, so they've measured the capacity at 4.7 *billion bytes*, instead of more familiar *gigabytes*, which computers use. The gigabyte measurement of 4.37 represents the amount of data that can actually fit on a disc.

Hybrid DVD is a common format variation that combines DVD-Video with DVD-ROM on a regular DVD-R or DVD+R disc. A straight DVD-ROM disc contains only computer data files and is readable by a computer, but not a DVD-Video player, since there's no video to play back. However, when you add computer data files to a regular DVD-Video disc you get a Hybrid DVD.

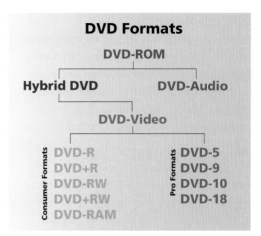

There are a variety of flavors of DVD in both professional and consumer formats. The professional formats are always replicated at manufacturing plants, while the consumer formats can be created with a desktop computer and DVD burner.

Disc burners

DVD-R and +R are write-once formats, meaning you can write to or "burn" data to these discs only one time with a special DVD-writing drive, or **DVD burner** as they're commonly called. This is different from a **DVD-ROM** drive found on some computers, which can only read DVDs but not write to them.

Some computers ship with DVD-R drives and others have DVD+R—it all depends upon which format the manufacturer has chosen to support. Both the -R and +R formats have the same capacity of 4.37 GB and should be compatible with most recent set-top DVD players and computer DVD drives.

Remember, you usually can't use blank DVD-R media in a DVD+R burner nor can blank +R discs be written in a -R burner, although recent models are beginning to allow you to use either kind.

Rewritable discs

You can write data to -R and +R discs only once. But you can buy the pricier **DVD-RW** and **DVD+RW** discs that you can erase and rewrite up to 1000 times. The rewritable formats are great for testing your DVD projects before committing them to a more permanent disc.

You may also come across the **DVD-RAM** format, which is decent for archival purposes, but not DVD authoring. These erasable and rewritable discs are encased in a plastic outer shell and aren't compatible with regular consumer DVD-Video players. DVD-RAM has become less popular since the introduction of DVD-R and +R, and it's unlikely you will ever want to use it for your own projects.

Other Video Discs

You may not be aware of it, but there are other video-on-disc formats available, although none that seriously challenge the quality and storage capacity of DVD. The other kinds rely on an ordinary 700 MB CD-ROM as the storage medium. Blank CD-ROM discs are less expensive than blank writable DVDs, but that may be about the only advantage there is to these non-DVD formats.

VCD (Video CD): This format uses MPEG-1 video compression to allow up to 74 minutes of video to fit on a regular CD-ROM. The image quality is about half that of DVD, roughly comparable to VHS. VCD discs will play on many commercial DVD players but without menus and other essential DVD features. VCDs can be a quick way to store and play back digital video, but the image quality is nothing to brag about. It's a very popular format in China and the Far East.

SVCD (Super Video CD): This is the next step above VCD, but uses the better MPEG-2 video compression instead. The format was created in China as an alternative to DVD and it remains popular there. SVCDs can hold about 35 minutes of high-quality video, and they also have menu capability. Of course it does take several discs to hold a full-length movie. Some DVD authoring programs will allow you to create discs in the VCD and SVCD formats.

Future of DVD Technology

DVD is great now, but it promises to get even better in the future. We're going to see vast leaps in quality and storage capacity. Within a few years we'll see the introduction of higher-capacity discs with the ability to hold more video! This means that we'll be able to create high-definition (HD) DVDs and enjoy **HD-Video,** all on a familiar-sized DVD.

One of the most talked about subjects in the DVD world is something called **Blu-Ray,** a high-capacity technology that uses blue lasers to read a disc instead of the current red laser technology. Blu-Ray promises to increase disc capacity from 4.37 GB to 27 GB, which will open the door for even more creative and practical uses for professional designers and home users.

Opportunities for DVD designers will increase dramatically as both large and small businesses learn the advantages of using DVD for publicity, promotion, public relations, advertising, training, or just archiving vast amounts of data.

DVD's interactive capability not only permits navigation to any area of the disc content, it can provide instant access to web sites by using HTML links on the disc. Professional designers who are already doing print and web design for their clients will start using DVDs as another form of media for content delivery.

Clients who previously didn't have budgets for expensive video production will start realizing the affordable, convenient, and powerful potential of delivering compelling video on DVDs.

Lower prices for digital video cameras and video editing software will enable trainers and educators to utilize DVD's exclusive features of multiple camera angles for selective views of demonstrations. They'll be able to use multiple audio tracks for various video commentaries or multiple language translations.

Great numbers of home users and video enthusiasts have already been lured into the worlds of movie editing and DVD creation by some of the free and low-cost applications that are available for both Macs (iMovie and iDVD) and PCs (Windows Movie Maker, MyDVD). Many of these users will move on to more advanced, (and more expensive) applications to increase their productivity and creative potential. Many others will continue to upgrade their computers, their video and DVD software, and their knowledge just because this stuff is so much fun. And, speaking from personal experience, addictive.

Studies show that DVD technology has been accepted by consumers more quickly than any other consumer electronics product in history. The future of DVD is bright, exciting, and rich with creative potential for both amateur and professional designers. When you combine these factors with DVD's ease-of-use and convenience for end-users, DVD design becomes an essential skill for designers of the future.

Summary

After all that, let's run down the top reasons why DVD is a great video format for consumers and creative professionals.

- ▼ DVD is the most popular consumer format in history and promises to be the format leader for training, education, archiving, and promotional applications, or for any projects that require high-quality video content delivery.

- ▼ DVD delivers high-quality video on portable and durable discs.

- ▼ Consumer DVD players are inexpensive.

- ▼ DVDs have much higher storage capacity than any other consumer media.

- ▼ Consumer DVDs are relatively inexpensive to produce. There are several different variations on the DVD format, but DVD-R and DVD+R are the most common consumer formats and can hold up to 4.37 GB of data.

- ▼ DVD discs play back on a wide variety of consumer devices from TVs to computers to video game consoles.

- ▼ MPEG-2 video compression makes large video files much smaller without losing image quality.

- ▼ DVD can include interactivity. Menus allow for non-linear navigation of video and thematically unify the various parts of a DVD.

- ▼ DVD presents unlimited creative opportunities for menu design.

- ▼ Cost of DVD authoring software and hardware has become affordable for the masses, and prices continue to drop.

- ▼ DVD technology is evolving and will allow more video to fit on a disc with high-definition quality in the future.

DVD: What Can it Do?

Features and functions

DVD is more than just video on a disc. It's also a robust format that allows video, audio, still images, and data files to happily co-exist within a common digital environment. The format permits you, the DVD author, to precisely control the way these different media types are presented to the end user. On discs that implement the full range of DVD features, viewers can customize the presentation to their individual needs or personal tastes. Because of these options, it's not likely that any two people will watch the same DVD in the same way.

Versatility makes the DVD format extremely appealing to consumers, but also makes it a little difficult to wrap your mind around all the possibilities if you're trying to create one yourself. This chapter walks you through the high points, providing an overview of the media types and features at your disposal when creating DVD projects.

DVD Specification

The clever people who created the DVD format were very specific on how DVD discs should function. In fact, they were particular enough to write it all down in a series of documents known as the **DVD Specification** or **Format Books.** The specification was established by the **DVD Forum** (www.DVDforum.org), a group of companies that originally pioneered the DVD format.

Companies that manufacture DVD hardware, blank discs, or decoder software are required to purchase the necessary Format Books and pay a separate licensing fee to use an official DVD logo (based on the type of DVD product they create). They also must have their products tested and verified for compliance. The only source to obtain DVD logo licensing and Format Books is the **DVD Format/Logo Licensing Corporation** (www.DVDfllc.co.jp).

People who create and duplicate their own discs for home or office use won't need to purchase a Format Book or license because

The DVD Logo is a trademark of DVD Format/Logo Licensing Corporation, which is registered in the U.S., Japan and other countries.

The official DVD logo may appear only on licensed DVD hardware, replicated discs, and decoder products. DVDs that you burn on your own equipment aren't allowed to display the logo, nor are they eligible for a license. This is not necessarily a bad thing for you, considering that a license costs $10,000.

consumer-burned projects on DVD-R or DVD+R aren't allowed to use the DVD logo on their labels or packaging. Only licensed DVD manufacturers (called replicators), may affix the DVD logo to their products.

Working without a Format Book isn't a problem for you as a DVD author, since the DVD features you need to know and use are most likely already built into your authoring software. Of course, not all authoring software has the same capabilities—generally, the more it costs, the more DVD features are available. Read more about the features of authoring software in Chapter 15.

If you're a curious, tech-geek kind of person, you *could* pick up a Format Book for $5,000. But assuming you want to hang on to that five grand for the moment, we'll provide a broad overview of what the DVD format will allow you to do. Understand that we are merely scratching the surface and hitting the most important features, but as a starting point, this information will serve you well.

If you need a more detailed technical guide to all things DVD, we recommend Jim Taylor's excellent book: *DVD Demystified*, published by McGraw-Hill. Also, check out his thorough and frequently updated web FAQ at: www.DVDdemystified.com/dvdfaq.html

Media Layers

A DVD-Video disc can contain four basic media types: **video, audio, still frames,** and **subpictures.** In addition, you can also include computer **data files** on the same disc, but these aren't integrated into the video presentation—they're just along for the ride.

The DVD format handles each of the four media types as distinct digital elements to allow for maximum flexibility in playback. Think of each element as a unique layer in a stack. Layers in this digital sandwich can be turned on or off in a variety of combinations depending on how you want the DVD to be viewed. This approach saves precious disc space and allows video tracks to mix and match with alternate audio tracks or subtitles instead of trying to fit several entirely different versions of the same video on a disc.

DVD-Video Format

As we mentioned in Chapter 1, there are a variety of DVD formats, but the kinds of discs you can create and burn yourself are based on the *DVD-Video* format, which includes both DVD-R and DVD+R. You can also make DVD-ROM discs for data storage, but these don't necessarily contain video.

If you're not sure what a DVD-Video disc can do, think of it as nearly any feature you can see or control when watching a DVD movie on your TV set-top player. Computer users can access additional features on a DVD such as data files and web links—we'll cover these later on pages 27 and 29.

Video Tracks

Main feature, bonus material, menu backgrounds/transitions, multi-angles, chapter markers.

Still Frames

Menu backgrounds, slide shows, scene selection menus, information screens, games.

Subpictures

Menu button highlights, subtitles, karaoke.

Audio Tracks

Video soundtracks, menu music, alternate languages, commentary.

DVD-ROM Data

Computer software, HTML and PDF files, digital images, interactive games.

Video

Video and DVD are meant to go together. Like rock and roll or Lewis and Clark, it's hard to imagine one without the other. After all, video delivery and playback is why the format was created in the first place. Not surprisingly, DVD treats video as the star player and allows you to display it in a number of useful ways.

Source files

You can capture the source video material for your DVD from digital video, analog video or film. It doesn't even have to be taken from reality—your video can be a virtual 3D animated sequence. All of these sources can be converted into the required MPEG-2 digital format, although digital video (miniDV, D1, Digital Betacam, etc.) and 3D sequences are easier to convert since they *originated* as digital files.

Tracks

A DVD can contain up to 99 individual separate video tracks, officially called **titles.** Considering that an entire full-length movie could be contained in a single title, this minor "limitation" should give you plenty of options for the other 98 tracks. A DVD disc is capable of holding up to two hours of video, depending on the video's compression rate and how many other elements (menus, still images, audio tracks, data files, etc.) are also on the disc.

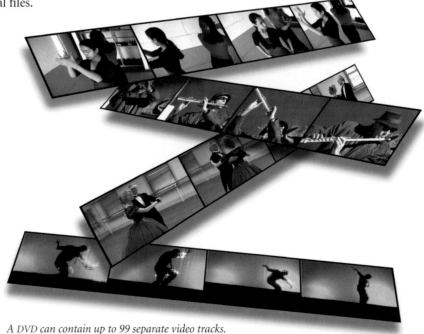

A DVD can contain up to 99 separate video tracks.

Region codes

Most commercial DVDs contain an embedded numeric tag known as a **region code.** The code tells a DVD player in which region of the world the disc is allowed to be played. DVD players sold in each country are usually pre-programmed to only play discs that correspond to their native region, although some players are set to play more than one region. Still, if the disc and the player are mismatched, there won't be anything to watch except an error message. The system was designed to help deter the international video piracy that's been rampant with the VHS format.

There are a total of eight designated regions, with the U.S. and Canada set as "1." If you plan to develop DVDs for overseas distribution, you should know which video format and region number is used in the destination country. If you'd rather not deal with any of this, it's easy to author your project as an **all-region disc** that works in any player.

Video formats

There are two standard video formats used in various parts of the world: the **NTSC** format (dominant in North America and Japan) and the **PAL** format (dominant in Europe and Australia). You can't put both formats on the same disc—your disc must be either NTSC or PAL. A disc should match the DVD player it is used with: NTSC disc with NTSC player, PAL disc with PAL player. The exception is that many PAL players will also play NTSC DVDs. Unfortunately, it doesn't work the other way around—PAL discs don't work in NTSC players. Weird, isn't it?

NTSC and PAL

NTSC and PAL video are different in more than name alone. Each format has a unique frame size and frame rate.

NTSC video has a dimension of 720 x 480 pixels at 29.97 frames per second.

PAL video has a dimension of 720 x 576 pixels at 25 frames per second.

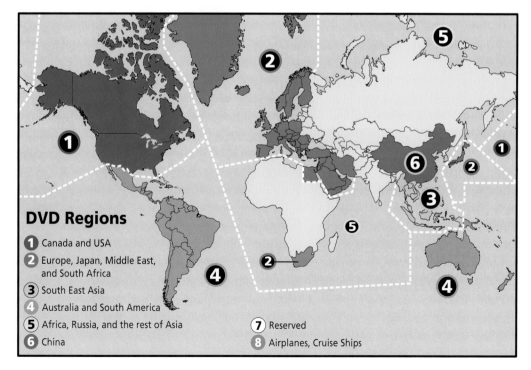

DVD Regions
1. Canada and USA
2. Europe, Japan, Middle East, and South Africa
3. South East Asia
4. Australia and South America
5. Africa, Russia, and the rest of Asia
6. China
7. Reserved
8. Airplanes, Cruise Ships

Each country in the world has been assigned one of six DVD region codes. The remaining two codes are reserved for special uses. DVD players sold in each country are pre-programmed to only play discs that correspond to their native region codes.

Anamorphic widescreen video

A widescreen (NTSC) video image measures 864 x 480 pixels, but the DVD format can only accommodate NTSC video sized at 720 x 480. This size discrepancy makes it necessary to horizontally squeeze the 864 dimension down to 720 so it falls within the allowed limits. A squeezed widescreen movie is known as **anamorphic video.**

DVD players will expand anamorphic video back to its full width during playback.

The examples at the right illustrate the difference between a 16:9 widescreen image and a 4:3 fullscreen video image. Note how the fullscreen image at the far top right is cropped to fill the entire screen. This cropping technique is commonly known as **pan-and-scan.**

There are two types of widescreen video: **anamorphic** *(top left), which is horizontally squeezed during authoring but expanded during playback and* **letterboxed** *(bottom left), which is pre-sized during editing to fit a 4:3 screen with black bars added above and below the image.*

Screen size options

DVD accommodates both **fullscreen (4:3) video,** which fits within a standard television screen, and **widescreen (16:9) video,** which is sized to fit a high-definition, widescreen television. A DVD can contain fullscreen and widescreen video files simultaneously and can easily switch between the two. This switching ability is necessary when the source film (or video) was shot in a widescreen format but the menus are sized for fullscreen. Menus can also be formatted to the widescreen size.

It's no surprise that a widescreen movie looks best on a widescreen television, but you can play it on a regular TV if necessary.

Letterboxed widescreen video is intended for 4:3 TV playback only, and is prepared at a fixed size during editing with black bars above and below the image. **Anamorphic widescreen** video is more flexible and scales to fit either a widescreen or fullscreen television. On a 4:3 TV, both anamorphic and letterboxed widescreen video show black bars above and below the image. If a video editor doesn't want the bars, he can sacrifice some of the image and crop the ends off a 16:9 video to make it fill a 4:3 screen. This cropping technique is called **pan-and-scan.**

Multiple camera angles

Another unique function of DVD is the ability to provide up to eight different camera angles in addition to each primary video track. The viewer can switch between angles with the click of a button on his DVD remote. Alternate angles come in handy for projects like training videos when it's useful to see a task demonstrated from more than one perspective. They can also be used to create interactive movies and present alternate storylines or endings.

The only restriction is that all corresponding angle video segments must be exactly the same length as the primary video stream with which they are associated.

Chapter markers

One of the best things about video on DVD is that you can instantly jump to any scene without the time-consuming rewinds or fast-forwards of videotape. You can embed up to 99 invisible flags, called **chapter markers,** into a single MPEG-2 video stream.

A chapter marker is similar to a bookmark because it flags the beginning of a scene in a DVD video stream. When the viewer activates a menu button, she is immediately transported to the corresponding chapter marker in the video. If you've used the **Scene Selection** feature on a movie DVD, you'll understand how convenient chapter markers are to get you where you want to go.

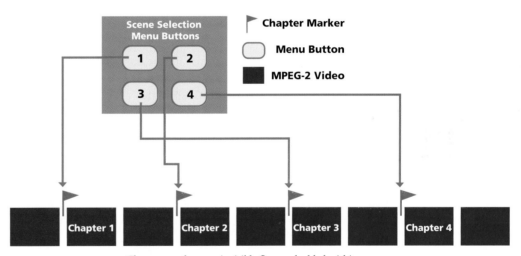

Chapter markers are invisible flags embedded within a DVD video stream that you manually place at the beginning of specific scenes in a video editing or DVD authoring application. When a viewer activates a menu button that's been linked with a chapter marker, she will be instantly transported to that point in the video stream. You can embed up to 99 chapter markers in each video stream.

Looping video menus and seamless transitions

The DVD format allows both motion video tracks and still images to be used as backgrounds for navigational menus. While still menus have their purposes, some of the most interesting, dynamic menus utilize moving imagery to get their point across. A menu that incorporates video is called a **motion menu.** A motion menu can loop indefinitely and keep things interesting for the viewer until she makes her selection. A short video clip can also function as a seamless transition between two menus.

The best menus are designed so the viewer can't detect the point at which the video clip ends and then begins again (the seam is indicated in the graphic above). A menu clip should play for 30 to 60 seconds before looping. This usually provides the viewer plenty of time to make a menu selection before the menu video starts repeating.

The goal for a DVD menu designer is to make the video loop or transition appear to be seamless, with no noticeable difference between the last and first frame of the clip. For more details about motion menus, see Chapter 11.

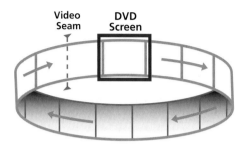

A motion menu loops indefinitely until the viewer makes a button selection.

Audio

If video is the star player on DVD, then audio is certainly the co-star. It's an integral companion to video for the dialogue and ambient soundtrack, but it's also a vital part of the entire DVD experience. Music audio tracks make DVD menus more interesting to use and keep the momentum going between video selections. Supplemental commentary audio tracks overlayed on video provide another level of useful information to the viewer.

Separate from video

For maximum flexibility, the DVD specification calls for audio tracks to be handled separately from video tracks, even when they have been expressly created to synchronize perfectly with the video. Audio is always stripped away from its video track when MPEG-2 encoding takes place, but both are later reunited in the final part of the DVD authoring process called **multiplexing.** Each video track is allowed to associate with up to eight different audio tracks, but they must be exactly the same length in order to sync correctly.

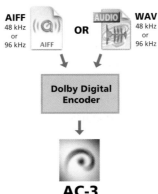

LPCM AUDIO FORMATS

AIFF
48 kHz
or
96 kHz

OR

WAV
48 kHz
or
96 kHz

Dolby Digital Encoder

AC-3
DOLBY DIGITAL FORMAT

You can author a DVD to use an uncompressed PCM audio file, although it will take up more disc space than its compressed counterpart—the Dolby Digital AC3 file. PCM formats like AIFF or WAV are converted into the AC3 format by an audio encoder application such as A.Pack (on the Mac) or Surcode (on a PC).

A Dolby AC3 file can contain up to 5.1 channels, but two-channel stereo (Dolby 2.0) soundtracks are also common on DVDs. To get a 5.1 track, you have to originally record in surround sound—you can't convert a mono or two-channel stereo file and make it sound like a five-channel file.

Audio Formats

More information is available about supported DVD audio formats on the following web sites.

Dolby Digital 5.1
www.Dolby.com

DTS
www.DTStech.com

Most popular audio formats

The DVD format supports a total of five different kinds of digital audio files, but the two most common are **LPCM** and **Dolby Digital.** The first, **LPCM** (Linear Pulse Code Modulation), also known as **PCM,** is an uncompressed audio format. This high-fidelity digital format is the same kind that's used on music CDs. You may be more familiar with **WAV** or **AIFF** audio files, both of which are variants on the basic PCM format.

While PCM is a fine "legal" format for DVD audio, it often fills more disc space than you'd like (being uncompressed and all). That's where Dolby Digital comes to the rescue.

Dolby Digital (or **AC-3**) audio is a compressed, lossy format that delivers great sound, but uses several times less space on a DVD disc than PCM. Dolby Digital files have an average compression ratio of about 8:1. The format supports up to five-channel (five speakers) surround-sound to give your DVDs that theater-style feel. Based on these strengths, Dolby Digital has become the most frequently used audio format on commercial DVDs, with many containing a full 5.1 soundtrack.

The ".1" in 5.1 refers to a sixth channel of low (bass) frequencies that you can play through a specialized speaker commonly known as a **subwoofer.** If a Dolby 5.1 DVD plays on a system with only two speakers, the player downmixes the audio into two channels.

Additional audio formats

Another legal format for DVD audio is **DTS** (Digital Theater Systems). Like Dolby Digital, DTS is a multi-channel, 5.1 Surround Sound format, but is considered by some to deliver even better-quality sound. It doesn't compress audio nearly as much as Dolby encoding does, and it occupies up to three times more disc space. Most DVD authoring applications don't currently support the DTS format (Sonic Scenarist does), but this may change as it becomes more widely adopted.

To complicate matters, a DVD player must have a built-in DTS decoder in order to play a DTS soundtrack, and not all of them do. It's also important to note that a DTS soundtrack on a DVD disc must be accompanied by a PCM or Dolby Digital track.

Encoding software is available to convert PCM audio files into DTS. You should expect to pay at least $2000 for the software.

The two remaining legal audio formats for DVD are **MPEG-2 audio** and **Sony Dynamic Digital Sound** (SDDS). Of these, MPEG-2 audio is rarely used on commercial projects and is not allowed on NTSC DVDs. Only PAL discs will support MPEG-2 audio, so it's not a good choice for most of the DVD market.

Although 7.1 channel SDDS is technically supported in the specification, Sony has never implemented it for DVD and the format is not supported in any existing authoring system.

Surround sound configuration

A DVD surround sound system typically has five distinct speakers and a subwoofer placed around the viewer. A subwoofer is a specialized speaker that delivers a sixth channel, known as Low-Frequency Effects, or LFE, which carries audio in the lower bass ranges.

Both Dolby Digital and DTS support up to 5.1 channel Surround Sound on DVD, although the use of Dolby is much more widespread.

Dolby files don't have to be encoded with the full 5.1 channels. It's common for authors to include a simpler two-channel (Dolby 2.0) mix on their DVDs.

Surround Sound Configuration

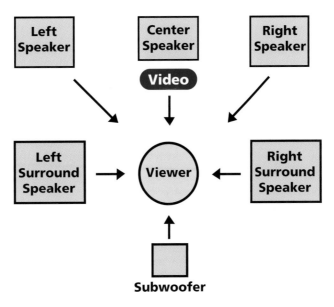

23

Still Frames

Not all the visuals on a DVD have to move. In fact it's kind of nice to see something sitting still once in a while in the midst of all that activity. Although DVD is the realm of motion and video, the static image is still a necessity in several important areas.

Menu graphics

Where would a DVD be without its menus? Menus exist for a practical purpose—they provide choices for navigating the contents of the disc. Still images are well suited for this purpose and often serve as highly creative and useful menu graphics. For some audiences, too much movement can be distracting and make the menu options difficult to comprehend. The lowly still menu provides a welcome bit of calming visual relief and allows the user to focus more clearly on the choices at hand.

Photo slideshows

DVDs are great with video, and they're pretty good in presenting photographs as well. The DVD format allows for **slideshows,** a collection of photographs or still images. You can watch an auto-play slideshow straight through or manually browse the images using the arrow keys on a player's remote.

Each slideshow can contain up to 99 different photographs or other still images. A DVD regards a slideshow as a single video track, so you can put a combination of up to 99 slideshows and video tracks on a disc. If you need more than 99 images in a slideshow presentation, link multiple tracks together for seamless playback.

A slideshow that's authored for auto play-through—displaying each image for a finite period of time, can also be accompanied by a soundtrack. Several authoring programs allow you to synchronize a single soundtrack to a timed series of slideshow images.

Interactive slideshows that depend on the user to manually advance to the next image are not good candidates for a soundtrack because the audio will stop and start over each time the viewer changes a slide.

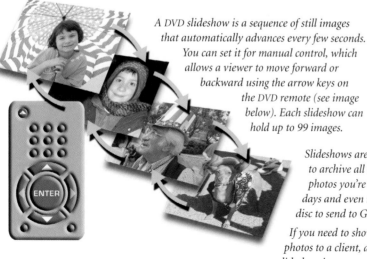

A DVD slideshow is a sequence of still images that automatically advances every few seconds. You can set it for manual control, which allows a viewer to move forward or backward using the arrow keys on the DVD remote (see image below). Each slideshow can hold up to 99 images.

Slideshows are a great way to archive all those digital photos you're taking these days and even make an extra disc to send to Grandma.

If you need to show dozens of photos to a client, a quick DVD slideshow is an easy way to provide previews.

Jacket pictures

When you hear the term **jacket picture,** keep in mind that it has nothing to do with the outer packaging or label on a DVD. A jacket picture is a special still DVD image displayed on a television screen. It has a function similar to that of a book cover—it identifies the title of a DVD and displays a representative still image of the video content. Jacket pictures are not a required DVD element. Some discs don't provide them and some players can't read them either. Still, a jacket picture is a nice touch for any DVD project.

Rarely seen in normal DVD usage, a jacket picture appears when you select the *Stop* (not *Pause*) button on your DVD player in the middle of video playback. This can be useful if you are in the middle of a presentation using a DVD and you need to take a break. Rather than pause the current image and leave it stuck on the screen, a quick press of the *Stop* button summons the more generic jacket picture. Push *Play* to resume the video from the exact point where you stopped it.

Jacket pictures also are helpful when you want to identify a disc placed in a multi-disc DVD player: You can choose the disc you want to play by selecting the representative jacket picture icon.

Information screens

You'll often see **information screens** on a commercial movie disc when you browse the biographical section for the cast. These appear as graphics containing text information about an actor, director, or character from the video content. Information screens can also be useful to present instructions for the viewer on how to use certain features of the disc.

Interactive games

Many kid-friendly movie DVDs include interactive games as part of the bonus material. The DVD format has no official provision for the creation of games, so these interactive challenges are elaborate work-arounds using linked menus.

Menu-based games shouldn't be confused with the more elaborate non-DVD productions that can be built with Macromedia Flash or Director, but they can still be an enjoyable feature for the kids or young-at-heart adults.

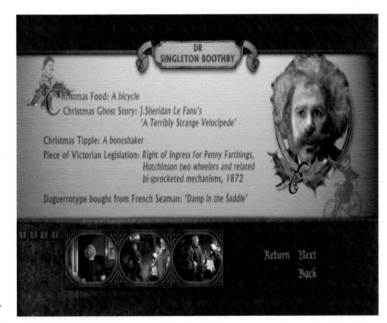

*This **information screen** is a still graphic image that provides information about a particular character in the video. Although its purpose is different from a menu, it functions in the same way. Note the navigation buttons in the lower right.*

The League of Gentlemen Christmas Special
Menu design and animations
©2003 The Pavement
Client: BBC Worldwide Ltd.

Subpictures

Another type of still frame image that can exist on a DVD is a **subpicture** or **subpicture overlay.** Despite a name that suggests that it goes *beneath* an image, a subpicture is a static graphic that instead actually *overlays* a video screen or still frame. Subpictures are not detailed, full-color images—they are simple bitmapped shapes that exist to either accentuate parts of a screen image or superimpose text over a video. A subpicture is only visible in the support of a still graphic or video, never on its own.

Menu highlights

The most common use of a subpicture overlay is to highlight a menu button to indicate that it is selected. A **menu highlight** can appear either within the button's shape, as an outline, or as text characters. Sometimes designers make the highlight an icon or interesting shape near the selected button. The color of a subpicture is assigned within your authoring program. Usually a subpicture displays in only one color, but if necessary it can contain a combination of up to four hues in a single highlight.

Subtitles and karaoke

Subpictures are also used for **subtitles** that appear at the bottom of the video screen. Subtitles are lines of text superimposed over a scene of video that contains dialogue. They're necessary to translate foreign dialogue into the native language of the viewer. A DVD can contain up to 32 different subtitle tracks.

Subpictures are also used for certain DVDs that support **karaoke** sing-a-long videos. The words to the song appear as subpictures over whatever wacky karaoke video images happen to be on the screen.

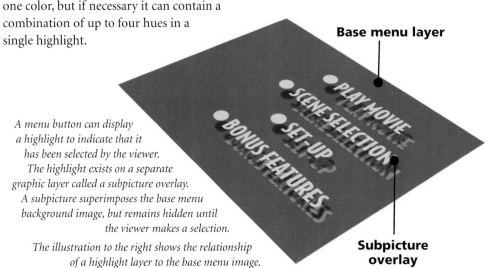

A menu button can display a highlight to indicate that it has been selected by the viewer. The highlight exists on a separate graphic layer called a subpicture overlay. A subpicture superimposes the base menu background image, but remains hidden until the viewer makes a selection.

The illustration to the right shows the relationship of a highlight layer to the base menu image.

Base menu layer

Subpicture overlay

DVD-ROM Data Files

Computer data storage is not part of the DVD-Video specification, but you *can* include data files on your disc in a **DVD-ROM directory.** When you do this, you are technically creating a **Hybrid DVD,** but it's really no big deal. Hybrid DVDs work on any regular set-top DVD player or on a DVD-compatible computer.

Any file that can live on your computer's hard drive can be written to a DVD. Remember that the data files will only be of use when the disc is inserted into a *computer's* DVD drive—your TV set-top player won't know or care that they're there.

Make sure to place your ROM files within their own separate directory folder. If you leave them outside of a folder, it's possible that the DVD player might become confused with the file structure and not play the disc correctly.

Data files on your DVD are quite useful when you need to include additional documentation along with the video presentation. If space allows, you can easily include the authoring source files for the DVD itself or maybe the original digital photographs included in a slideshow. You may want to include other kinds of files such as PDFs, text documents, databases, software installers, HTML files, or Flash and Shockwave animations.

Remember that the more data files you add, the less space you'll have for video and audio.

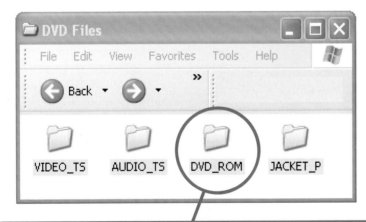

All data files must be placed within a folder like the one shown to the left, although it doesn't have to be named "DVD-ROM."

A DVD-ROM folder is useful when you want to include any type of computer file—from HTML to PDF documents. A user can access the files when the disc is inserted into a DVD drive in a desktop computer. In a set-top player, the user will not see the files.

Captioning Info

More information on Closed Captioning, Line 21 data, and Accessibility can be found at www.JoeClark.org

Additional Features

We've covered most of the outwardly visible functions of a DVD-Video disc, but there are other important features of the DVD specification that you wouldn't readily notice when you view a disc normally on your television.

Closed Captions

Closed Captioning is an accessibility feature that exists for the benefit of people who are deaf or hearing impaired, allowing them to read spoken dialog on a DVD. Like subtitles, Closed Captioned dialogue appears as text at the bottom of a television screen, but it's not a subpicture overlay. Instead, DVD Closed Captions are text instructions embedded in an MPEG-2 video stream. The data is sent from the DVD to the player, and then decoded and displayed by a television itself. Closed Captions will not only display text of the spoken dialogue—it also identifies the speakers and includes sound effect descriptions.

Closed Captioning information is contained as text in line 21 of the video signal. Because of its physical location, Closed Captioning is often called **Line 21** data. The inclusion of Line 21 data is strictly a feature for Region 1 NTSC discs.

Copy protection

Commercial DVDs usually implement some kind of protection system to prevent consumers from illegally copying the contents of the disc. Two of the most widely used systems are **Content Scrambling System** (**CSS**) and **Macrovision.** CSS is only implemented on manufactured discs, not on DVD-R/+R discs you burn yourself. Macrovision is an analog encryption format that you can add to your own locally burned discs, but you will need to obtain a license for this method.

Copy protection may be a deterrent to illegal copying, but like most encryption schemes, CSS was hacked long ago and made public on the Internet, so determined individuals can easily make a copy of almost any DVD-Video disc.

Making or selling copies of a commercial or copyrighted DVD is quite illegal and we strongly discourage you from ever doing that. You wouldn't want people to illegally copy *your* DVD projects, so be an advocate for the respect of digital copyright laws.

Web links

Web links are another useful feature. They allow DVDs to directly launch web pages, provided you play the DVD on a computer connected to the Internet. Sometimes called a **WebDVD,** this type of disc displays web links on a menu screen. When a link is selected, it opens a web browser and displays additional content.

Many Hollywood DVDs are authored to take advantage of the web-savvy **Interactual Player.** These discs include an installer for the Interactual software so users can take advantage of the integrated playback between the video and ROM content on the disc and external content on a web site. Until recently, the Interactual Player was Windows-only, but a Mac OS X version was recently released. You can find the installer software in the ROM section of selected commercial DVD discs (2003 and after).

Authoring a DVD to take full advantage of the Interactual Player's web integration requires the purchase of special programming software tools from Interactual. For developer information, go to Inventor.Interactual.com.

For those who author DVDs with Apple software and want to link to web sites, you also have the option of using **DVD@ccess,** which is built into Apple's DVD Studio Pro and DVD Player software. It doesn't match the features of the Interactual Player, but it does provide simple web linking.

Tying into the Internet means that the fixed content on a DVD can be supplemented with up-to-date information on a related web site. It also opens up other possibilities such as allowing children to play more sophisticated movie-themed games from the web.

Parental controls

You can author DVDs with embedded parental controls designed to prevent underage children from viewing the contents of a disc that's not age appropriate. There are eight numeric levels of control, with "8" being the most restrictive and "1" providing unrestricted access to everything. You can assign the numerical control setting during the authoring process.

Players that support parental controls are configured with a password so when a restricted disc is inserted, authorized adults can correctly enter the code and proceed with the movie. Only high-end professional DVD applications like Sonic Scenarist allow an author to set the parental control levels of a disc.

The Interactual player will display DVD video, web pages, and ROM content all within the same window, making a seamless media experience. A disc must be specially authored to take advantage of the Interactual technology.

End Actions

*A menu is an effective tool for initially getting you where you want to go on a DVD, but it's not able to take you to the next step. There are times when a disc needs to take action without a menu. For example, what happens immediately after a selected video clip finishes playing? Should you be returned to the main menu, or taken to yet another clip? A menu is of no use in this situation, but a pre-set **end action** can automatically perform the next step.*

Your authoring software allows you to assign an end action to each menu or video clip, telling the disc where to go next after that segment plays. Even if you use scripting, you'll still rely on end actions to facilitate navigation.

Behaviors

Most mid-range and high-end DVD authoring programs let you assign special behaviors to the menu navigation. Some applications provide simple behaviors by assigning **end actions** (see sidebar), which control what happens right after a video segment plays.

Others programs go even further with advanced code-based commands called **scripts.** A common script example is one that makes a DVD player remember which menu segments the viewer has already seen and prevents them from replaying again.

Controlling navigational behaviors is not only good for professional projects — your personal DVDs can benefit too. For example, let's say you have a DVD that contains a random collection of home movie clips — all edited together into a single continuous video track. Although each of the clips is a treasured memory, you may not want to sit through all of them every time you use the disc. Maybe you only want to watch little Susie's kindergarten graduation, followed by a clip of brother Kyle's soccer game, which is further into the video.

No problem so far—you can easily add the ability to select and view specific segments with chapter markers and menu buttons, but it's not an entirely perfect solution.

The problem is that once you finish watching the clip of Susie's big day, the video continues playing on through other clips, unless you intervene and press the "menu" button on your remote control to return to the selection menu. Wouldn't it be better if you were automatically returned to the menu after the selected clip finished? Well, it's easily accomplished with the addition of a *script*.

Another interesting behavior made possible by scripting is **story branching,** or **multistory.** This enables video sequences to play back in an order that's different from the original presentation—great for providing side stories or alternate endings to a movie.

There are many other situations like this where DVD scripting makes the user experience much more enjoyable. Scripting is a more advanced authoring feature, but one well worth learning. Your authoring software's capabilities will determine how far you can take scripting to enhance your own projects.

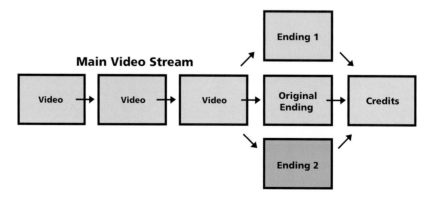

*Some higher-end DVD software allows you to add certain advanced navigational behaviors to enhance the playback experience. In this example of a **multistory** DVD, there are three alternate endings available. The viewer can pre-select the ending he wants to see before he begins to watch the video. Once selected, the new sequence plays back seamlessly.*

Designer's Toolbox

DVD hardware and software overview

DVD authoring is like assembling a digital collage—lots of individual pieces, methodically arranged, emerging as an entirely new creation. The process takes the raw digital materials, or **assets,** from various software applications and combines them all into a single cohesive unit. Unless you're an author working as part of a team, the assets won't just drop into your lap—you have to create them. Each piece needs to be individually crafted with specialized software on a capable computer workstation.

To start the process, you'll need to assemble your DVD tools by deciding what software you need and the kind of computer it will best run on. That may sound relatively simple, but there are a lot of choices to be made. Your selections will be based partly on the scope of your first project, partly on your own preferences, and the rest on the depth of your pocketbook.

In this chapter, we'll review the hardware and software categories necessary, or at least helpful, for you to produce your own assets and assemble them onto a finished DVD.

Hardware Overview

If you want to create your own DVDs, you've got to have the right equipment. The basic price of admission into the world of DVD creation is the investment in a capable computer system, a few key peripheral devices, and authoring software.

Because consumer DVD authoring is a relatively new phenomenon, your equipment should be as up-to-date as possible. Parts of the DVD process can be processor intensive, particularly video encoding, so the faster your system is, the sooner you'll complete your projects. Let's review the many options in DVD development hardware, starting with the computer.

Windows or Mac?

You can create great-looking DVDs on either Windows PCs or on Apple Macintosh computers. A full range of authoring and content-creation software is available for both platforms. Each has its specific strengths, but both can achieve professional results.

There are many Windows-based DVD authoring packages on the market, providing a good choice of prices and features. Although the selection is more limited on the Mac, the available DVD software is top-notch and is arguably among the best of the bunch.

Our recommendation is to stay on whichever platform you're comfortable with and buy the best DVD software you can afford.

Hardware in the DVD Authoring Workflow

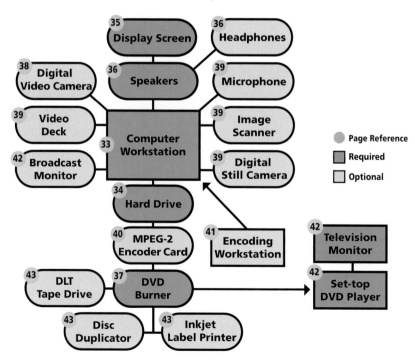

This diagram displays the range of hardware typically used in the DVD authoring process.

You may require some, or all of these devices depending upon the types of DVD projects you develop.

For the benefit of entry-level authors, the pieces of hardware you'll absolutely need to start out with are color-coded in the darker green, while the optional accessories are coded in the pale green.

For mid-range to professional projects, many of the items designated as "optional" will actually be essential.

Numbers in the yellow circles are page references where you'll find an explanation for that piece of hardware.

Software decides

Regardless of your chosen platform, you're probably in one of two camps: Either you already have a computer and want to find out if it can handle the demands of DVD software, or you're in the market for a brand-new computer and want to buy something that's tailor-made for authoring. In the end, the requirements of your chosen DVD software will always determine what kind of hardware you'll need. It's safe to assume that a new top-of-the-line computer will handle anything you throw at it, but if you can't afford the top, you'll want to know what you can get by with and still end up with acceptable results.

Windows hardware

A cross-comparison of the requirements of several DVD software applications suggests that you really shouldn't use *anything less than* a PC with an Intel Pentium III 500 MHz processor, 128 MB of RAM, running Windows 2000 or ME. While this is the *bare minimum*, most software will benefit from a faster machine and a snappier operating system.

Our recommendation for Windows users is an expandable tower computer with an Intel P4, 2 GHz (or better) processor, 512 MB of RAM running Windows XP (Home or Pro).

With this set-up or something better, you can easily run any kind of DVD software on the market today.

Macintosh hardware

Macintosh DVD software needs to run on Macs with at least a 500 MHz G4 processor, 256 MB of RAM (or better), and using the latest version of the OS X operating system. A dual-processor G4 or G5 Mac would be sweet, if you can spring for it.

G3 Macs generally aren't fast enough to crunch the video for a DVD, and current Apple DVD software won't even install on them. Some users have been able to hack this software into running on a G3 machine, but we don't think it's worth the time and trouble.

While there *are* some non-Apple entry-level DVD applications that will run on a G3 Mac, *our recommendation* is to get a G4 or G5 and enjoy the experience, instead of frustrating yourself with a too-slow computer.

Why not both?

People in many homes and offices use both Macs and PCs in their everyday setup. Even if you prefer one over the other, having access to both platforms can come in pretty handy. It means you can run any available software application you want.

Sometimes the DVD authoring process is shared between Macs and PCs. Often, the Macs will be used for menu design and motion graphics while the PC handles the authoring. In other situations, the PC will serve as an MPEG-2 video encoding station, while the Mac does the authoring duties.

Of course you don't *have* to do it this way, but by using both, you can let each platform play to its strengths or your personal preferences.

Recommended Windows PC Hardware

Desktop tower CPU

Intel P4 (2 GHz) processor or better

512 MB RAM or better

120 GB hard drive or better

1 or 2 Firewire ports; USB 2.0 optional

DVD writer that supports DVD-R/RW, DVD+R/RW

17-inch monitor or better

Windows XP Home or later

Recommended Macintosh Hardware

Desktop Tower CPU

G4 (1 GHz) processor or better. G5 preferable.

512 MG RAM or better

120 GB hard drive or better

1 or 2 Firewire ports; USB 2.0 optional

DVD writer that supports DVD-R/RW, DVD+R/RW

17-inch monitor or better

Mac OS X version 10.2 or later

Required Hardware

Once you've chosen your computer platform and processor speed, make sure your system is fitted with the following *must-have* components. We consider these essential to be features of a DVD authoring workstation. Some systems will ship with these features included, and others will require you to add-on.

Connectivity

FireWire: The **IEEE 1394** standard and Sony's **i.Link** brand are both better known as **FireWire,** a high-speed data transfer protocol developed by Apple Computer. With a throughput of 400 Mbps (megabits per second), it has become a standard for connecting peripheral devices like DV cameras, hard drives, and scanners to Macs and PCs. A newer version, **FireWire 800,** can transfer data at an amazing 800 Mbps.

Most new computers come with standard FireWire connectivity built right in. If your computer is FireWire-deprived, you can easily remedy that by installing an inexpensive (around $49) FireWire PCI expansion card with 2 or 3 connector ports.

USB 2.0: Another high-speed data transfer protocol, **USB 2.0** connections can move files at a speedy 480 Mbps. Many newer computers, hard drives, and scanners are equipped with both USB 2.0 and FireWire connectors.

The original USB 1.1 is not a high-speed protocol (only 12 Mbps) and is not particularly useful in DVD authoring and video. It is, however, fine for connecting keyboards, scanners, and digital still cameras.

Storage

Hard Drives: DVD and video files will quickly fill your available hard drive space. You'll want to have enough elbow room to work on several projects at the same time, so try to get a large capacity internal or external hard drive that holds at least **80** to **120 GB.** If you can afford it, you might want to get something even larger. You can never have too much drive space (or RAM).

Drive speed matters too. When you work with video and DVD, be sure your drive is rated at **7200 rpm** for optimal video performance.

DVD authoring and video editing files occupy large amounts of hard drive storage space. Be sure to use a drive that has at least 80 GB, but larger capacity is even better.

For best results, get a drive that runs at 7200 rpm.

Display

A 32-bit color monitor with at least 1280 x 768 pixel resolution is optimal to effectively preview your work. At a minimum, you'll want to have a 17-inch monitor, but don't turn down a super-large 23-inch flat panel if one just happens to come along. Extra screen space is mighty helpful in video work.

LCD flat-panel: Flat-panel screens have begun to outsell the bulky CRT monitors, and for good reason. They take up less room, and the LCD display doesn't refresh and flicker like a regular CRT, therefore reducing eyestrain.

If you're in the market for a new monitor to do video and DVD work, by all means, get a flat-panel. Your eyes will thank you and your desk will have more open space.

CRT: The old reliable CRT monitor has been with us for a long time now and still does a fine job as a computer display. For color accuracy, many print designers still swear by 'em. The downside is that they take up more deskspace compared to a flat-panel monitor and can be more difficult to stare at for extended periods of time.

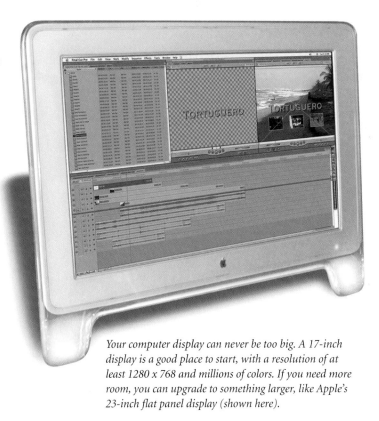

Your computer display can never be too big. A 17-inch display is a good place to start, with a resolution of at least 1280 x 768 and millions of colors. If you need more room, you can upgrade to something larger, like Apple's 23-inch flat panel display (shown here).

Audio output and speakers

Built-in audio: Some computers, including Macs, come with built-in audio output. This means they will have at least one jack for connecting external speakers and will often have a small internal speaker.

Audio card: Computers lacking built-in audio can be upgraded by adding a **sound card** in one of the PCI expansion slots. The card provides a connector jack to plug in your external speakers. A basic card costs around $20 to $30.

External speakers: Audio is a huge part of video and DVD, so you'll need to have some decent external computer speakers connected to your authoring workstation. Some models already ship with speakers, while others don't. Speakers do differ in audio quality and you can spend $20 to $200 depending on how particular your ears are.

Headphones: You also may want to have a set of headphones handy in case you're editing or authoring in an open office space with co-workers to consider. Listening to a video soundtrack with headphones also allows you to discover any unwanted pops or audio artifacts that you'll need to edit out of the final cut.

Headphones are helpful if you work in a shared office space. They deliver better quality sound than built-in computer speakers.

Your DVD authoring workstation should include a set of good speakers to accurately test the sound quality of your DVD projects.

DVD burner

No authoring system would be complete without a writable DVD disc drive on hand. An **internal writable DVD drive,** or **burner,** will allow you to test your DVDs during authoring and then produce the final disc when your work is finished. DVD drives are currently sold with write speeds of **1x, 2x,** and **4x.** The faster 4x is clearly your best choice, since you won't wait nearly as long for your disc to burn.

Most burners also double as DVD players, so you can proof your own discs or watch Hollywood movies right on your computer.

DVD writable drives are essential for authoring. The most versatile models support both DVD-R and DVD+R media.

When buying a new computer, don't confuse a playback-only DVD-ROM drive with a DVD-R or DVD+R writable drive. A DVD-ROM drive will *play* a DVD just fine, but it doesn't know the first thing about burning a disc. If you have a choice, try to get a **hybrid DVD drive** that writes to all consumer disc formats, including DVD-R/RW, DVD+R/RW and CD-R/RW. No need to be locked in to a single format when you can easily have all.

External DVD burners are also available if your system doesn't ship with one already built-in. These will typically connect via a FireWire cable and are just as good as an internal burner. They have the added advantage of mobility and can be used on multiple computers. External DVD drives can cost from $200 to $400, depending on the brand, write speed, and formats supported.

DVD Recorders:

If you're new to DVD, you may not know the difference between a **DVD burner** *and a* **DVD recorder.**

A DVD burner requires a computer workstation to process and write the finished video files to a blank disc.

By contrast, a DVD recorder has no need for a computer. It connects directly to a video camera or VCR, encodes the data internally, and records it to a blank DVD disc.

For quick video transfers to disc, a DVD recorder can be a big timesaver, especially if you don't care about creating a professional DVD with custom menus. A recorder is great for archiving old home movies from tape or saving your favorite TV show on DVD, but using one really can't be considered true DVD authoring.

Professional, creative DVD jobs still require the use of an authoring computer and a disc burner.

Vintage home movies on DVD?

A good first practice project may involve transferring your family's vintage home movies from 8mm film to DVD.

The first step is to migrate the films to a more recent format, preferably something digital, like miniDV, but VHS will work too. You can do this by setting up your old 8mm projector and using your video camera to shoot a video of the movie on the screen.

If you no longer have a projector, you can have the film professionally transferred to tape by a local video service provider.

When the movie has been moved to the new format, you can use your DV camera or analog converter to import it into your computer's video editing program, and then onto DVD from there.

Optional Hardware

There are the things you can't live without, and then there are the *nice-to-haves*. Our DVD *nice-to-have* hardware items may not be 100 percent essential for every project, but they sure can make your job a lot easier and allow you to create a better-quality end product. Depending on the kind of project you're developing, some of these items may, in fact, turn out to be indispensible, especially if you are doing it all yourself.

Input devices

DVD authoring requires you to collect digital asset—everything from video files to still graphics will be incorporated into your project. Here are a few devices that will help you capture the necessary source assets and bring them into your authoring system.

DV camera: A **digital video camera** will allow you to import **miniDV** (or pro DV formats) into your computer for editing. Most DV cameras use a FireWire connection to import the video stream into a computer. This is a handy device for capturing short clips for use in menu designs. See Chapter 4 for more information about digital video cameras.

Analog converter: Even if you don't own a *digital* video camera, you can still use footage from your **analog video camera** (8mm, Hi-8 or VHS) by using a *converter box*. The analog converter acts as a bridge between your camera and the computer, digitizing your video on the fly. Analog converters usually cost around $200.

If you already own a DV camera and an analog camera, you may not need a converter box. Some DV cameras will also convert analog video via an **AV cable** connected between an analog camera and the DV camera. Check your DV camera's specifications to find out if it has analog conversion ability.

Remember that analog video has roughly half the resolution of digital video and will never look quite as sharp, even after the conversion to DV format.

A digital video camera is necessary if you plan to shoot and edit your own video clips. It can also be helpful in the creation of short video clips for use in DVD menus.

Video deck: Instead of capturing video directly from your DV camera, you might consider a video deck. This specialized device is kind of like a VCR for miniDV tape (or other formats)—its sole functions are playback and recording. It connects directly to your computer via FireWire or other high-speed interface.

A video deck is definitely professional-level hardware, but it's useful for extensive video editing sessions and saves your DV camera from the wear and tear of frequent rewinds and fast-forwards that occur during the *batch-capture* process.

Digital still camera: DVD slideshows and menus require source photographs, and a digital still camera is the perfect gadget to capture them with. For the best clarity, make sure your camera is capable of capturing images at 3-megapixels or higher.

Image scanner: Not every graphic you want to use can be captured with a digital camera, so it's helpful to have a desktop image scanner available. Whether you want to digitize old photographs or import an interesting texture, a scanner is a valuable item for menu design.

Microphone: There will be times when you need to capture narration or sound effects for a DVD menu or video edit. You could do this with a DV camera, but if you don't have one, you can record directly into your computer using a simple USB microphone. Prices range from $30 to $50 for units that work on either PCs or Macs.

Digital still cameras and image scanners are handy devices for capturing images and graphics that you intend to use in your menu designs.

MPEG-2 encoder card: You should seriously consider buying an MPEG-2 encoder card if you plan to create DVDs for a living or if you have massive amounts of video to encode. The professionals call this **hardware encoding,** and it's a tremendous timesaver for long video encodes where speed and quality matter. An encoder card fits into one of your computer's PCI expansion slots and has connection ports for your video deck or DV camera. The process is simple: just connect your deck into a port at the back of the card and adjust a few settings in the controller software. Your video will be converted into a DVD-ready MPEG-2 file in *realtime*, or something pretty close to it. Some cards can simultaneously convert the video soundtrack into the Dolby AC-3 format. **Realtime encoding** means that if your video is an hour long, it will take an hour to encode.

Several hardware MPEG-2 encoder cards are on the market. Sonic (www.Sonic.com) offers a line of encoder cards for Windows, including the **SD-500, SD-1000,** and the **SD-2000.** On the Mac side, the **MediaPress X** encoder card and software from Wired, Inc. (www.Wiredinc.com), is compatible with the current OS X systems.

These encoders can produce outstanding results, but they're not exactly cheap—entry-level prices start at around $500, and the pro models start at around $4000. Of course a good hardware encoder will pay for itself quickly in time savings alone.

It's also possible you won't need to use a hardware encoder card. For infrequent encoding jobs, the alternative is **software encoding,** which doesn't involve any special equipment. All you need is an encoding application that takes your source video files and compresses them into the MPEG-2 format.

A hardware encoder card fits into one of your computer's PCI slots and does realtime video conversion to the MPEG-2 format. A quality encoder card can cost $4000 or more.

There's nothing wrong with using a software solution, but these applications generally won't do realtime encoding, and could take several times longer than with the hardware method. The duration of encoding time depends on the length of your video and the quality level you want—high-quality MPEG-2 encodes could take hours to produce.

If you have time to wait, software encoding is your most economical solution. A software encoder will cost a fraction of what a decent hardware encoding card does, while still providing excellent quality MPEG-2 files for your DVD.

Encoding workstation: Often DVD authors dedicate a separate computer workstation for the sole purpose of encoding video. In professional authoring houses, projects are deadline-driven and need to progress quickly, so dividing up the workload and processing time makes a lot of sense. While one workstation is doing the actual DVD authoring, other computers across the room are cranking out MPEG-2 files. This arrangement is probably unnecessary for the casual DVD author who moves at a more leisurely pace.

A dedicated MPEG-2 encoding workstation is a great idea if your DVDs are long and your available time is short. A second computer can take care of the time-consuming encoding work while you're busy with menu design or the finer details of authoring.

Quality control and testing

While DVDs are created on computers, they are often played and viewed on non-computer devices. There's almost always a difference between the way a DVD looks on a computer screen and how it displays on a television. A DVD author should know what to expect when her disc crosses from the computer realm over to "the other side." The following equipment will help ease the transition and allow you to make informed adjustments along the way.

Television: An ordinary, cheap television set for proofing is a very good way to judge how your DVD will look to the rest of the world. A low-quality set is best so you can accurately see how your disc appears in the least-optimized viewing situation. If you can make it look good there, it will absolutely shine on high-end equipment.

Broadcast monitor: A computer screen displays images in **progressive scan,** but a regular television set uses **interlaced scan,** which can look quite different. A professional **broadcast monitor** also displays interlaced video, but it can be connected directly to your video editing computer. It allows you to see how your video looks in interlaced scan *while*

you're editing, instead of waiting until a test DVD is made. A broadcast monitor is helpful for color proofing to make sure that your video and menus appear as you intended. Broadcast monitors don't need to be large— a 14-inch model will do just fine. Expect to pay around $700 or more to add this pro item to your set-up.

See Chapter 10 for more information about interlaced and progressive video.

Set-top DVD player: The real measure of success for any DVD is how well it works in an ordinary set-top DVD player. You'll want to have a player available and use it religiously in the disc testing phase to weed out any glitches in your authoring. Make sure you purchase a recent model, something made after 2001, to ensure compatibility with DVD-R or DVD+R discs. Check to see if the model is compatible with DVD-RW or DVD+RW discs too, since you'll also want to use those for testing purposes.

You can't beat a consumer DVD set-top player and a TV for testing the image quality and playback capabilities of your freshly burned DVDs.

Output devices

When the authoring and testing is complete, there are still a few more steps to get your disc out into the world on the right foot.

Disc duplicator: Duplicating a short run of 10 to 25 discs with a regular DVD burner can be a real chore. You could babysit your computer's DVD burner, swapping disc after disc, hour after hour, until they're all finished, but frankly, that doesn't sound like too much fun to us.

A better alternative is to load a stack of blank discs into a **disc duplicator,** press a button, walk away, and let it burn! When you come back a while later, your finished discs will be stacked and waiting for you. In addition to this convenience, some duplicators can print a fancy, color inkjet label onto each disc.

The **Primera Bravo** (www.PrimeraTechnology.com) is a good entry-level duplicator that also prints labels onto the discs. It costs under $2000. **Disc Makers** (www.DiscMakers.com) also offers a range of full-featured duplicators in their **Elite System** product line.

Label printer: What about inkjet labels for individual discs? A DVD with a color label imprint is perceived as having more value than one without. But you don't want to use adhesive labels because the extra weight could throw the DVD off-balance in a player, or the label could peel off and render the disc unreadable.

To work correctly, a DVD label should be printed directly on the surface of the disc. Fortunately, you don't need an expensive disc duplicator to imprint on a single disc.

Epson (www.Epson.com) has recently begun to sell low-cost ($200) inkjet printers that can print right onto a DVD or CD, and other vendors will likely follow suit. For label printing, the duplicators and inkjet printers require a special non-branded disc that has a blank white surface designed to accept the ink. Blank discs are sold in bulk packs from the printer and duplicator manufacturers and most disc vendors.

DLT tape drive: Some DVD projects exceed the capabilities of a burner or duplicator. A project might be destined for the higher-capacity DVD-9 format, or it could require CSS copy protection. In these cases, your authored files need to be saved to DLT.

DLT stands for **Digital Linear Tape,** a preferred professional medium to transport your finished DVD files to a replication facility. While many replicators now accept DVD-R discs for pre-mastering, DLT is still required if the DVD has CSS protection or is authored in the double-layered DVD-9 format.

A good DLT drive costs at least $1000 to $2000, but you may be able to find a less-expensive used model on eBay. Blank DLT tapes are available for around $50 each, but you'll get a better deal if you buy in bulk.

DLT drives require a SCSI connection to the host computer (sorry, no FireWire for this one). If your computer doesn't already have a built-in SCSI port, you can add one inexpensively with a PCI expansion card. Chapter 17 explains more about DLT.

Duplication vs. Replication

There are two methods to reproduce the DVDs you create. The first and least expensive for short runs is **duplication.** *A duplicated disc is burned on your home computer with a DVD-R/+R writable drive.*

For large quantities, you'll need to take your project to a company that does DVD **replication,** *an injected molding process. See more about each of these methods in Chapter 17.*

The Primera Bravo Disc Publisher is one of several DVD disc duplicators on the market. This particular model burns short runs of DVD discs and also imprints a color label on each one. It's great.

Software Overview

You may need some key hardware to get going with DVD, but software is the real brain of the operation. A collection of custom software is necessary to first create the individual pieces, and then later to bind them together to form a DVD.

To the end user, a DVD appears to be a seamless presentation, and no one is likely to suspect that it's a mixture of several distinctive parts. But behind the curtain, the DVD author not only understands each piece and how to create it—he also understands how to make all the parts work together and *appear* seamless to the end user.

Each piece of the DVD puzzle is created with its own unique software application that was programmed for the task. By our count, there's a total of nine distinct software categories that contribute a unique asset to the end product (see the chart below). Depending on the price, some software packages have more than one digital trick up their sleeves and you may not need to use every application listed here.

We'll remind you that each software category represents a specialized discipline that can't be mastered overnight. Take your time and don't expect to learn it all at once.

Software in the DVD Authoring Workflow

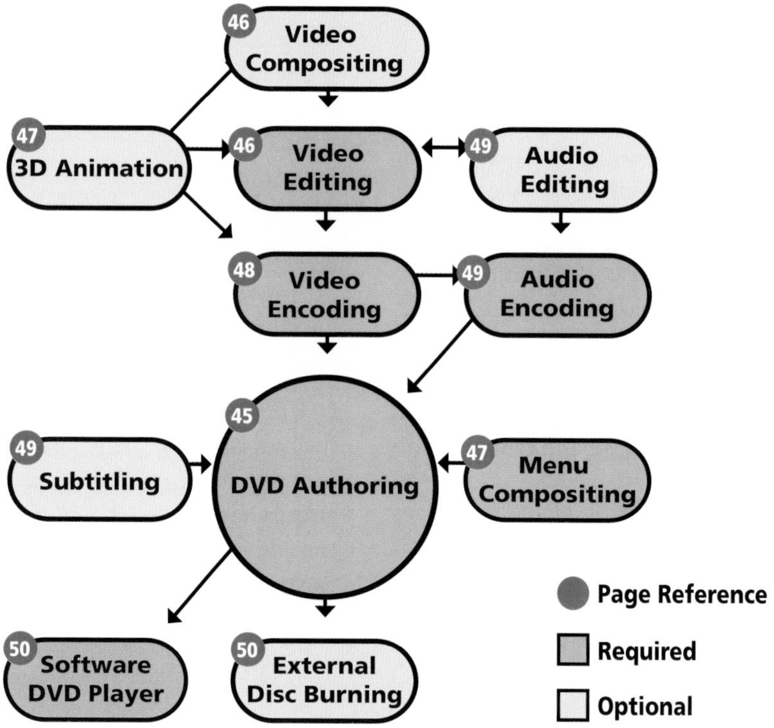

This diagram displays the range of software applications typically used in the DVD authoring process.

You may require some, or all, of these applications depending upon the types of DVD projects you develop.

For the benefit of entry-level authors, the software categories you'll absolutely need to start out with are color-coded in the bright yellow, while optional programs appear in light yellow.

Numbers in the red circles are page references where you'll find an explanation for that category

For mid-range and pro-level projects, many of the "optional" applications will be necessary.

46 Video Compositing
47 3D Animation
46 Video Editing
49 Audio Editing
48 Video Encoding
49 Audio Encoding
49 Subtitling
45 DVD Authoring
47 Menu Compositing
50 Software DVD Player
50 External Disc Burning

● Page Reference
▨ Required
☐ Optional

All-in-one DVD authoring

The following pages cover the main categories of software applications you'll need to author a full-featured DVD, but for entry-level authoring, you may not need them all. Some entry and mid-level authoring packages integrate many key features right into their interface. Functions like video capture, encoding, compositing, menu creation and disc burning may all be contained within one convenient package.

If it sounds too good to be true, it is . . . and it isn't. No integrated authoring software can deliver the kind of control available with the individual external applications, but it *can* create a simple, good-looking DVD.

The all-in-ones may be a good place to dip your toe into the DVD authoring pool, but if you have aspirations for projects on a grander scale, you'll quickly decide to jump in head first with more advanced software.

All-in-one authoring software includes **myDVD, Roxio CD & DVD Creator, NeoDVD, Sony Click to DVD** for Windows, and **iDVD** (with iMovie) for Mac.

DVD authoring software (required)

The hub of any DVD project is the authoring application. This is the software that rolls all the individual assets together into a single DVD disc. Think of it as a kind of smart glue that binds the project together and controls how the assets will be viewed.

There's a wide variety of authoring programs available, ranging from inexpensive entry-level to pricey high-end. Some of the newer applications are the most innovative and intuitive, positioned in the affordable mid-level range.

A cross-section of popular authoring software includes **Adobe Encore DVD, Ulead DVD Workshop, Pinnacle Impression, Sonic DVD Producer,** and **Sonic Scenarist** for Windows, and **Apple DVD Studio Pro** and **Sonic Creator** for Mac.

Chapter 15 provides an overview of authoring software in each price range and describes their capabilities and differences.

DVD Studio Pro 2 is one of many options for a robust and affordable DVD authoring software package.

Video editing software (required)

Next to DVD authoring software, a video editing application is probably the most important software choice you'll make. Called a **non-linear editing application** or **NLE,** you use it to import raw video **(DV)** footage from your camera and edit vacation videos, documentaries, or even a polished feature movie. You can add transitions, titles, soundtracks, or special effects to give your project that professional look. The video you produce and edit here will ultimately end up as the main attraction in your DVD, so you'll want to use an application that gives you the best quality and all the features necessary for your production.

As with authoring applications, there's a wide selection of NLE software on the market, ranging from free to thousands of dollars.

Some examples of popular NLE video software include **Windows Movie Maker, Pinnacle Edition, Adobe Premiere Pro, Avid Xpress DV** for Windows, and **iMovie, Final Cut Express, Final Cut Pro, Avid Xpress DV** for Mac.

Chapter 4 covers some of the most popular video editing programs.

Video compositing software (optional)

A video compositing application does for video what **Adobe Photoshop** does for still images. It allows you to manipulate a video clip in every way. For example, you can create animations, adjust colors, add type, apply image masks, or add special video effects.

It's known as **compositing** software because it allows you to layer parts of different video clips and graphic images, melding them into a single *composite* video. If you've heard the term **motion graphics** when discussing video, it was probably referring to something created with compositing software.

Compositing is an essential process for creating **looping DVD menus** that include motion video. Some video editing applications have a few compositing features built in, so you may not need to buy a stand-alone compositing package unless you've just got to have more features.

Well-known compositing software examples include **Adobe After Effects** and **Discreet Combustion,** available on both the Windows and Mac platforms. See Chapter 11 for more about video compositing.

Adobe After Effects is a very popular and affordable compositing application. It provides a wealth of possibilities for special effects, animation, and video layering.

Menu compositing software (required)

Still-image compositing software is essential for creating DVD menu graphics. Similar to a video compositing application, this software will allow you to layer and manipulate still graphics and photographs. This category is dominated by a single product: **Adobe Photoshop.** Photoshop is the standard for bitmap image manipulation and is used extensively in print, web, and now video graphics.

Photoshop is extremely versatile and can be used to stylize a photo, design a menu, enhance slideshow images, design a jacket picture—the list is endless. Photoshop files can be layered, which also comes in handy to create and align *subpicture overlays* (see page 26).

The application has its roots in print, which means it includes features for high-quality printing. If these features aren't important to you, consider **Adobe Photoshop Elements,** a $99 sibling to Photoshop. For creating DVD menus, it's nearly as good as Photoshop and has most of the same features.

See Chapter 10 for more about using Photoshop to create DVD menus.

Adobe Photoshop, or its lower-priced sibling Photoshop Elements, is your best bet for designing DVD menus, subpicture overlays, and informational screens.

3D animation software (optional)

Some DVD menus are designed as complete virtual three-dimensional environments, rendered entirely with 3D animation software. You may not want to use 3D menus on your first time out, but you should keep the idea in mind as a possibility for future advanced projects.

Most 3D software can export a rendered scene to a video file format, which will be necessary if you want to incorporate it into a DVD. 3D software is typically difficult to learn and can take a long time to master, but there are entry-level programs available to get you started. Some *compositing* applications have limited 3D capabilities built in, which may be enough to suit your needs.

Noted 3D animation software includes **3ds max, Maya, SoftImage 3D, LightWave 3D, Electric Image Universe 5** for Windows, and **Maya, LightWave 3D, Electric Image Universe 5** for Macs.

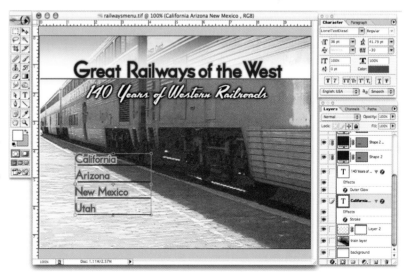

Transcoding?

Transcoding *refers to the process of converting a video file already saved in one format into a different format. An example would be a QuickTime .mov video file converted to the MPEG-2 format. Some software encoder applications can also perform transcoding, but not all.*

Transcoding video files for DVD should be done only when the original uncompressed source files are unavailable for encoding.

Audio editing software (optional)

Your video editing software will have some built-in audio features, but if you need to go beyond that level, you'll need a separate audio editing program. Audio editing becomes necessary if you need to "clean up" or enhance a poorly recorded vocal track or produce a **music soundtrack** to accompany your video. Some applications will allow you to perform sophisticated layering of audio tracks, known as **mixing.** The process of enhancing an audio track to sound better than the original recording is called *sweetening.*

You can import edited audio clips into your video editing software or export them directly as PCM formatted WAVs or AIFFs.

Audio software examples include **ProTools** and **Adobe Audition** for Windows, and **ProTools, BIAS Peak,** and **Apple Soundtrack** for Macs.

Software encoding applications convert source video streams into DVD-ready MPEG-2 files. You don't have to pay high prices to get great quality. An encoding package like TMPGEnc Plus (shown here) is priced at $48.

Video encoding software (required)

All video destined for DVD must be converted into the MPEG-2 (or MPEG-1) format through a process called **encoding.** Encoding squeezes out the redundant bits and makes a video track file small enough to fit on a DVD disc.

Files that have been encoded into MPEG-2 format usually have the extension **.m2v,** which identifies it to the authoring software as an allowable video asset. A software encoder will also strip the audio track from the video, saving it as a separate PCM file (WAV or AIFF), ready for Dolby compression, or direct import into an authoring application.

We mentioned earlier that *hardware encoding* is a much faster process, but for many DVD authors, **software encoding** is the best choice. The output quality of a software MPEG-2 encoder can be on par with a hardware encoder, but the process is usually slower.

Some entry-level authoring applications provide built-in encoding functions, but many authors prefer to have more control over their MPEG-2 files with a separate piece of software. There are a number of stand-alone MPEG-2 video encoders available, priced from $60 to several hundred. They don't all produce the same results — some provide better quality encodes than others.

Examples of software encoders include **TMPGEnc Plus, CinemaCraft Basic, Canopus ProCoder** for Windows, and **Innobits BitVice,** and **Apple Compressor** for Macs.

See Chapter 14 for more about encoding.

Audio encoding software (required)

Audio files, although much smaller than their video counterparts, can still benefit from compression. The most common compressed audio format for DVD is **Dolby Digital,** often referred to by its extension name: **AC-3.**

An audio encoder will import either a WAV or AIFF file and convert it to the AC-3 format. AC-3 files can contain up to five-channel surround sound, which makes this format extra appealing to quality-conscious authors.

The other five-channel compressed format is **DTS,** a competitor to Dolby Digital. DTS files require their own separate encoding software such as that provided by **Surcode** (www.Surcode.com).

Dolby Digital audio encoding functions are included with some DVD authoring programs such as **Sonic Producer** (www.Sonic.com), **Adobe Encore DVD** (www.Adobe.com), **Ulead DVD Workshop AC-3** for Windows (www.Ulead.com), and **A.Pack** for Mac (included with DVD Studio Pro).

Stand-alone Dolby encoding applications include **BeSweet** (DSPguru.NoTrace.dk), and **Surcode** for Windows (www.Surcode.com), and **Nuendo AC-3 encoder** (www.NuendoUK.com) for Windows and Mac.

Subtitling software (optional)

Most authoring packages in the mid-range to high-end can import subtitles and will either bundle external software or have integrated subtitling features. Regardless of where the subtitling feature is found, you will still be working with an interface that allows you to synchronize a subtitle with an underlying video image. The files generated are bitmap graphics, a type of *subpicture overlay.* There are a variety of subtitle formats, so make sure that your subtitling software will export into a format that your authoring program will understand.

Subtitling can be a lengthy and exacting process, and many companies specialize in this service if you can't do it yourself.

Authoring applications that support the import of subtitles include: **Adobe Encore DVD, Sonic ReelDVD, DVD Producer,** and **Scenarist** for Windows and **Apple DVD Studio Pro** for Mac. Some of the subtitling software titles include: **FAB Subtitler** (www.Fab-Online.com), **Subtitle Workshop** (www.Urusoft.cjb.net), and **Stream SubText** for Windows (hem.Passagen.se/jmorones/inicio.htm), and **Eva** for Mac (www.Instrumentality.org/eva.html).

Subtitling Tip:

Adding subtitles in the DVD authoring environment is not the same as adding captions or subtitles to a movie in your video editing software. Read more about DVD subtitling in Chapter 2.

Subtitle Workshop is one of several applications available for creating DVD subtitles. Like other software in this category, it allows you to preview your subtitles superimposed over the corresponding video segment.

Software Tip

The free **VideoLAN VLC** *is Open Source software that plays the .VOB (video) files within a DVD's VIDEO_TS directory. It's not a regular DVD player, but it remains a good option for previewing DVD video streams.*

It's available for all platforms, including Windows, Mac and Linux.

www.VideoLAN.org

Software DVD player (required)

You'll want to test your authored DVD files before you write them to a disc. It's important to determine that the data was written correctly and that it all looks the way you expected. To do this, you'll need a **software DVD player.**

Provided that you purchased a computer with a built-in DVD-ROM or DVD-R/+R drive, there's probably a software player already installed. Your authoring software also may be bundled with a player. If you don't have any of these options, you can always buy a software DVD player for $30 to $70, depending on the features included. They all mimic the remote functions of a set-top player and are a good first indication of how a disc will perform on a hardware player.

Software DVD players include **WinDVD 5, Sonic Cineplayer,** and **Cyberlink Power DVD** for Windows, and the **Apple DVD Player** for Mac.

External disc burning software

(optional)

Most DVD authoring software has a built-in "burn disc" command that will let you write your work to a DVD-R or +R disc without leaving the program. That's fine, but in most cases, we prefer to use an external application to burn our DVD files because we can first test them with a software DVD player (see below) before committing everything to a disc.

To generate the proper DVD files, you must prompt your authoring software to *build* **VIDEO_TS** and **AUDIO_TS** directories and save them to your hard drive. Once the files have been created, you are free to use your disc burning software to write them to a DVD.

Examples of popular DVD burning software include **Roxio CD & DVD Creator, Ahead Nero, Sonic RecordNow Max** for Windows, and **Roxio Toast** for Mac.

See Chapter 17 for more about disc burning.

A software DVD player provides controls that simulate the functions of a hardware set-top DVD player.

Kansas Device Voice Drum
® 2002 Song and Dance, Too, Inc.
Artwork by Animusic (www.animusic.com).

Video & Audio Overview

Essential hardware and software

DVD projects require **content,** and unless you're working on a big-budget project with an entire team, *you* are probably the person who will create that content. This chapter tells you what kind of hardware and software you'll need to create audio and video content for your DVD projects.

If you've just recently started your trek into the worlds of audio and video editing, there are two things you should know: First, thanks to the amazing computer hardware, digital camcorders, and software now available, you can create incredible movie projects without being an expert in the fields of audio, video, or editing. Second, you could spend your entire career studying audio, video, or editing. So be patient and learn as you go.

The software solutions presented in this chapter are entry-level and mid-range—popular, mainstream applications that are easy to learn and reasonably affordable. And they all create files suitable for use in a DVD project. The software applications featured here are among the most popular, but they represent only a fraction of the options that are available.

Since most of these products have manuals that are around 500 pages long, we can only try to give you a sense of what the programs do, what they look like, and why you care. We hope to also give you an idea of how user-friendly and technically accessible these applications are, even though they're incredibly powerful, versatile, and provide capabilities previously available only to full-time professionals.

Hardware You'll Need

The most essential hardware item you need so you can *create* content is a digital video camera. Beyond that, you need a fast computer and plenty of hard disk space to store the digital video files that you import from the camera. The number of capable computers and cameras you have to choose from is overwhelming, but there are certain features you should look for as you make your hardware decisions.

A fast computer

Because digital editing and rendering requires intensive computer processing, you'll be pretty miserable if you're not using a reasonably fast and powerful computer. We've used a range of computers for video editing and have decided that processor speeds slower than 450 MHz require too much patience and time. Because video editing demands processing power, some editing applications may recommend that you use a system with at least an 800 MHz processor. Also, be aware that video editing applications may require a certain operating system. Make sure the software you plan to use is compatible with your computer's operating system.

Your computer should have a high-speed communication card called IEEE 1394 to which you can connect your digital video camera. Some computers and cameras use brand names for the IEEE 1394 connection, such as "FireWire" (Apple and some PCs) or "i.Link" (Sony). Many current computers have at least one IEEE 1394 connection, but if your computer doesn't have one already built-in, you can buy an IEEE 1394 card and install it in an available expansion slot on your computer.

Additional hard drives

Digital audio and video files on your computer require lots of hard disk space. Even with the huge storage capacity that most computers have today, you'll need more. One minute of uncompressed video takes more than 200 MB of disk space; audio files add up to over 10 MB per minute.

Fortunately, hard drives are coming down in price and going up in capacity. If you have an extra bay available in your computer, consider installing an extra hard drive for video projects. Or you can easily add one or more external FireWire (IEEE 1394) or USB 2.0 drives. Hard drives vary in rotational speeds (5,400 rpm and 7,200 rpm). For video work, get the fastest drive possible (7,200 rpm).

In addition to increasing storage capacity, a second hard drive can make some aspects of video editing more efficient. For instance, when the computer has to render certain video effects or transitions, the process of reading from and writing to the same disk will be slower and less efficient than if your editing software is on one hard drive and your project on another. This enables the computer to read one drive while writing to another.

While there are many good external hard drives on the market, we prefer LaCie d2 FireWire hard drives because their "fan-less" design makes them virtually silent.

A digital video camera

When buying a video camera, choose one that will be easy to connect to your computer. For convenience, choose a digital video camera that has an IEEE 1394 (also called FireWire or i.Link) connection. Most of the current digital video cameras have connectors that can be plugged straight into your computer's IEEE 1394 port. If your camera doesn't have a FireWire or i.Link connection, you can buy a *converter* that will bridge the gap between a camcorder and computer.

Another consideration in choosing a video camera is the quality of the video it can capture. Even less expensive video cameras have surprisingly good quality, especially if you limit your choices to popular brands such as Sony, Canon, JVC, or Sharp. The main quality difference is determined by how many "CCD imagers" are built into the camera. CCD (Charge–Coupled Device) is a technology used to build light-sensitive devices: A three-CCD camera (also called a "three-chip" camera) captures sharper images and colors than a single-CCD ("one-chip") camera.

Three-chip cameras are more expensive, but provide better video quality, most noticeably in dimly lit scenes. If you're creating personal video projects, you may be quite satisfied with a more affordable single-CCD camera.

What if your video camera isn't digital?

Our discussion of hardware and software assumes you're using a digital video camera with a FireWire or i.Link connector, which makes it easy to capture digital video footage to a computer.

The most popular mid-range video cameras use MiniDV tapes. Digital video captured on MiniDV tape has a higher resolution than analog video formats such as 8mm, Super 8mm, or Hi-8, and produces better quality video for DVD projects.

If you have an analog camcorder and analog video tapes, or if you have VCR tapes that you want to import into your computer, there are several ways you can convert the analog video to a digital video format (DV):

▼ Connect a FireWire analog-to-digital converter between your video source and your computer. A few affordable converters are Hollywood DV Bridge from Dazzle (www.Dazzle.com), Studio from Formac (www.Formac.com), and Director's Cut from Miglia Technology Ltd. (www.Miglia.com).

▼ Connect your analog video camera to a digital video camera, record your analog video onto the tape in the digital camera, then import the video into a computer from the digital video camera. Some digital camcorders allow you to pass video straight through to the computer.

▼ Connect your VCR to your digital camcorder (most digital camcorders have an analog, or A/V, in/out connector), and record the VCR video onto a tape in the digital camcorder.

There may be some loss of quality in the conversion from an analog source, and the quality of the converter itself may affect the conversion results.

File Formats, Transcoding, and Other Tidbits

As a DVD designer/producer, your ultimate goal is to create content that is in a DVD-compatible format.

Video format for DVD

The official DVD specification requires **video** to be in the **MPEG-2** format. MPEG (Motion Picture Experts Group) is a digital video compression standard that dramatically reduces the size of digital video files while retaining very high quality.

DVDs will accept MPEG-1 formated video, but MPEG-1 is much lower quality and optimized for smaller picture sizes rather than full-size movies.

Transcoding and encoding

Most nonlinear editing applications (often referred to as NLE applications) that you'll use to edit digital video and audio can export video as MPEG-2 files, ready to use in a DVD authoring application.

NLEs that do not export video in the MPEG-2 format can *export* or *save* in other formats that you can then **transcode** (change from one format to another) to the MPEG-2 format;

you'll use **encoding** hardware or software to do this. Many entry-level DVD authoring programs, such as DVDit! and iDVD, do this automatically when you import files.

There are many encoders available. Software encoders, although not as fast as hardware encoders, offer a very attractive combination of affordability, convenience, and quality. Technology leaders such as Apple, Discreet, Media 100, and Sonic Solutions offer popular encoders that can either work as plug-ins you can access from your favorite editing program or use as stand-alone applications.

Even when video editing software *can* export projects in the MPEG-2 format, some DVD designers prefer to use a favorite third-party encoder rather than the one built into the software. Experienced professionals may use certain encoders for different types of video, since some encoding software may favor speed over quality, or may be better at compressing certain kinds of scenes, such as video that contains a lot of fast motion. Software encoders all use their own algorithms to define the encoding procedure, so results may vary dramatically if you encode the same video with different encoders.

Note

Since all NLE (Nonlinear Editor) applications need to perform the same kinds of editing tasks, they all provide many of the same features and tools, but packaged and organized in their own ways.

A partial list of features you should expect to find in a robust NLE can be found on page 64.

Entry-level NLE vendors omit many of these features so they can provide a less complex and more affordable version of their products.

QuickTime Pro is a versatile software encoder that can open different kinds of audio and video files, then transcode them to a large variety of other formats.

Apple's **QuickTime** application is best known as a free, cross-platform player for multimedia files, but it's also a very powerful *transcoder* when you upgrade to the QuickTime Pro version (about $30). Many NLEs can export or save projects in the QuickTime format. The example on the previous page shows a video sequence that we edited in an NLE, then opened in QuickTime to export and transcode to the DVD-compatible MPEG-2 format.

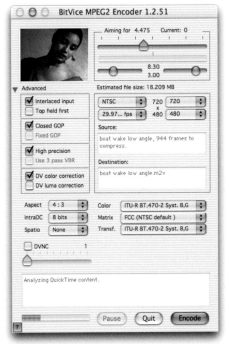

BitVice, shown above, is a stand-alone encoder with which you encode DV files into the MPEG-2 format. Software such as this lets you encode video efficiently with a technology known as VBR (Variable Bit Rate). VBR compares data information between frames and makes compression decisions that vary from frame to frame. The small preview window in the upper-left corner will show the video stepping forward and back as the software compares frames.

Digital video format

When you import video from a camcorder into your computer, it's saved in a **DV** (Digital Video) format.

On a Macintosh, the DV format is handled by QuickTime and the imported video clips are QuickTime files.

On a PC, imported video files are saved as Windows Media Files or AVI files. Some Windows-based NLEs prefer to use a file format called AVI (Audio Video Interleaved), a Microsoft sound and motion picture file format. Any number of encoders, including QuickTime, can transcode AVI-formatted files into the MPEG-2 format.

Audio formats

DVD specifications also have specific requirements for **audio files.** Audio must be either Dolby AC-3 format or a Linear PCM format, which includes both WAV and AIFF files. WAV is a standard PC audio format developed by Microsoft, and AIFF (Audio Interchange File Format) is a Macintosh format. Your NLE software (Adobe Premiere, Final Cut Pro, etc.) can export audio in the required formats.

Video standards

When you create a new project in a digital video editing application, you must choose a **video standard** for the project. There are three different video standards used around the world: **NTSC, PAL,** and **SECAM.** NTSC is the video standard in North America and Japan; PAL is the standard in Europe and Australia; and SECAM is the standard in France, countries of the former Soviet Union, and certain other countries.

Note

MPEG-2 is a video-only format. When you encode a movie as MPEG-2, the audio part of the movie is extracted and saved as a separate audio file. The two files are synced back together when you import them into your DVD authoring software.

Video Editing Software

The possibility of digital video editing on personal computers has opened a floodgate of incredibly powerful software applications that make movie creation easy, fun, and addictive.

Digital video editing applications are referred to as **NLE (Non-Linear Editing) systems.** Non-linear editing allows you to work with clips and sequences of video in a non-sequential order. If your background doesn't include traditional editing of film or video tape, you probably won't ever fully appreciate the advantages and convenience of non-linear editing.

Digital video editing also offers an advantage even the most inexperienced editor can appreciate: it's non-destructive. You can do anything to your video (shorten it, speed it up, slow it down, apply a special effect, or distort it) and the original clip is always there, untouched and ready to use. This non-destructive feature opens the door to creativity and experimentation and virtually eliminates the intimidation and fear of working with video, knowing that you can't really harm any of that irreplaceable footage.

There are an amazing number of video editing products available. Shop around to find the one that suits you best. The ones we've chosen for this chapter are mainstream, popular options whose price tags range from free to moderately expensive. We've organized the applications into two categories: **entry-level** and **mid-range.**

There are also professional, **high-end** NLE systems (such as Scenarist and some Avid products) that are technically inaccessible or too expensive for most users, such as freelancers, consumers, small businesses, and us. While this may cause us to experience just a little technology-envy, the software we *can* afford is capable of doing everything we need—and more.

Entry-level video editing applications

This category of software is defined by affordable prices and some limitation of professional video editing features. Although the term **entry-level** implies the software is best suited for small, personal projects rather than professional ones, many entry-level applications offer professional-level quality and features. The limitations include things such as a small number of audio and video tracks available for editing, exclusion of some special edit tools (ripple, roll, slip, and slide), and the absence of certain professional project-management features.

When applying effects and filters or when editing audio, entry-level applications do not provide the high degree of control over the effects that mid-range and high-end applications offer.

The following pages show popular entry-level applications that combine short learning curves with professional-looking results.

If you upgrade from an entry-level application to a mid-range one or if you switch to a competitive editing product, you'll notice many similarities in the way various applications work—the transition will be fairly easy.

Roxio VideoWave *(Windows)*

Roxio VideoWave (about $100) is an entry-level video editing application that captures video from a digital video camera to a PC in the AVI file format. AVI (Audio Video Interleaved) is a Microsoft file format for sound and motion pictures. Movies can be exported to a DVD format (MPEG-2).

When you select one of the tool icons in the Mode selector (the left vertical edge), the interface changes to include tools for that edit mode. For instance, select the Cutting Room icon and the Viewscreen on the right can be used to set In and Out Markers and trim the current video clip.

The Library is where captured clips are stored. Drag clips from the Library into the StoryLine to compose a movie.

To add transitions, click between two clips, then click the Transition icon in the Mode selector.

The StoryLine is where you drag clips in the order you want them to play.

The Cutting Room Viewscreen.

To trim unwanted video from a clip: Use the player controls or the playhead slider to advance the video to the point you want the clip to start, then click the "Mark In" button (bottom-left corner of the Viewscreen). Next, use the controls or slider to advance the video to the point you want the clip to end, then click the "Mark Out" button (bottom-right corner of the Viewscreen).

Click the "Apply" button to make the changes.

When you select one of the Edit tool icons in the Mode selector, the interface changes to provide tools for that edit mode. When the Capture icon is selected (shown right), the Viewscreen shows the video in the camera. Click the "Video-Audio" button to start the video capture.

The Capture Viewscreen.

Video-Audio capture button.

Export your movie.

iMovie (Macintosh)

iMovie is FREE and comes bundled with newer Macs. You can also download it from Apple's web site at www.Apple.com/software. Current versions of iMovie require Mac OS X. The iMovie interface is shown below.

When a digital video camera is connected to your computer, iMovie detects it and puts itself in "Camera mode" (as opposed to "Edit mode"). Use the controller buttons located below the Monitor window (shown below)

to scroll to a point in the video you want to capture, then click the "Import" button to start and stop the import when you choose. The captured clips appear in the Clips pane. Or click the "Import" button and capture *all* the video on your tape.

iMovie detects scene breaks and creates new clips each time the video camera was turned on and recording (in iMovie Preferences, you can turn off this option and capture multiple scenes as a large, single clip).

The Monitor.

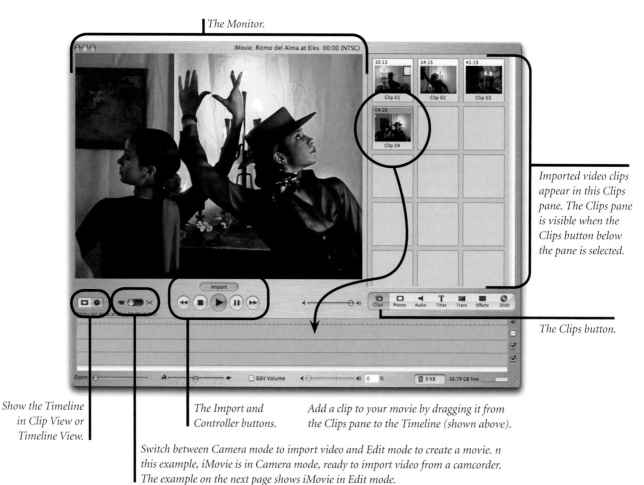

Imported video clips appear in this Clips pane. The Clips pane is visible when the Clips button below the pane is selected.

The Clips button.

Show the Timeline in Clip View or Timeline View.

The Import and Controller buttons.

Add a clip to your movie by dragging it from the Clips pane to the Timeline (shown above).

Switch between Camera mode to import video and Edit mode to create a movie. n this example, iMovie is in Camera mode, ready to import video from a camcorder. The example on the next page shows iMovie in Edit mode.

iMovie cannot *log* video clips (create a list) with exact timecode information from the video tape as you capture them, which makes large-project management and long-term storage more difficult (this may not be a big concern for smaller projects). One of the advantages of a *log-and-capture* feature is that,

when you finish a project, you can throw away the huge digital video clips that use so much storage space on your hard drive. If you ever need to work on the project again, software with a log-and-capture feature can recapture the same video clips from the original tape and rebuild the entire project for you.

The Monitor shows a preview of the video. Click on a single video clip in the Clips pane (right) or on a single clip in the Timeline (below) to preview just that clip.

*Click anywhere in the Timeline **except** on a clip to preview **all** clips in the Timeline.*

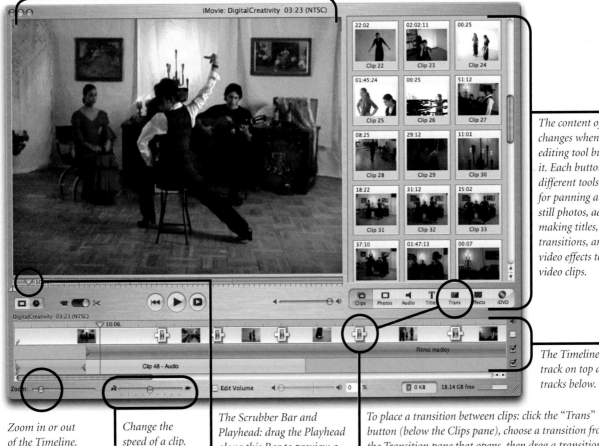

The content of this pane changes when you click the editing tool buttons below it. Each button reveals different tools in the pane for panning and zooming still photos, adding audio, making titles, choosing transitions, and applying video effects to individual video clips.

The Timeline has one video track on top and two audio tracks below.

Zoom in or out of the Timeline.

Change the speed of a clip.

The Scrubber Bar and Playhead: drag the Playhead along this Bar to preview a clip in the Monitor.

To place a transition between clips: click the "Trans" button (below the Clips pane), choose a transition from the Transition pane that opens, then drag a transition icon and drop it between two clips in the Timeline.

ArcSoft ShowBiz *(Windows)*

ShowBiz (about $80; also comes bundled with MyDVD software by Sonic) provides one video track and two audio tracks, a large collection of animated intros, transitions, sound effects, and some nice video effects. You can view the Timeline in "Storyboard mode," which shows only large graphics and transitions (shown below), or in a traditional "Timeline mode" (as shown on the next page).

When you export in DVD format, ShowBiz looks for MyDVD to create a DVD project.

To capture video from a camcorder, click the "Capture" button (shown to the right) to open the "Capture" window (below). Use the Camcorder controls to play the tape and see a preview in the top of the Capture window. When you're ready to capture video, click the Record button (the red dot).

ShowBiz automatically detects scene changes and saves each scene as a separate clip in the Media window.

The Media palette. To see available titles, effects, or transitions in this palette, click the Text, Effects, or Transitions tab.

The Player previews a single clip or an entire movie.

Camcorder controls.

Choose to show the Timeline in either Storyboard or Timeline view.

To place a video clip in the Timeline: drag a clip from the Media palette (shown above) into one of the media placeholder boxes in the Timeline.

Use these buttons to create, open, or save projects, capture video, export a movie in various formats, adjust certain default settings, and access the ArcSoft web site.

These tabs determine which tools are visible in the palette window below.

Use the Trim tools to select just the portion of a clip that you want to use.

To create a transition between two clips, click the Transitions tab, then choose a transition style from the pop-up menu. Drag the chosen transition from the Transitions palette to a transition icon located between two clips.

Undo and Redo buttons.

This is an empty media box into which you can drag video clips, stills, titles, or animation.

The Player preview window shows the video effect applied.

To add effect filters to a video clip, click the Effects tab, then choose an effect category from the pop-up menu. Drag the chosen effect from the Effects palette and drop it on top of a clip in the Timeline.

Click the Expand or Contract button to change the size of elements in the Timeline.

Pinnacle Studio *(Windows)*

Pinnacle Studio (from Pinnacle Systems, about $130) is a versatile entry-level editing application that includes a surprising number of features. Studio has a variety of advanced timeline editing techniques such as split edits, J-cuts, and L-cuts, a SmartSound music generator, and some Hollywood FX transitions and effects. Studio can output your movie as an AVI or MPEG file.

The Album contains video clips imported from the camcorder. The tabs on the left side of the Album give access to the Video Scenes section (shown here), Transitions, Titles, Frame Grabs (still images and graphics), Sound Effects, and Disc Menus (DVD templates).

The Edit tab shows all the editing materials and tools. Drag video clips from the Album to the Timeline.

The Player previews single video clips or entire movies.

Undo, Redo, and Help buttons.

Use the Transport controls to play a preview.

The Toolbox buttons open toolboxes in which you can alter audio and video clips, add titles, create background music using SmartSound's music generator, record a voice-over, add visual effects, and more.

The Jog buttons let you step the movie forward or back one frame at a time.

The Timeline contains one video track (with audio), a title track, a second audio track, and a background music track.

Click the Capture tab to capture video from an attached camcorder. Captured clips are placed on the Album pages. Automatic Scene Detection creates separate clips when scene changes are detected.

Use the Camcorder controller to control the video playback of the attached camcorder.

The Player previews the video in the camcorder.

The Diskometer displays the amount of space available on your capture drive and the approximate amount of video that can be stored on your drive.

Click the green "Start Capture" button to capture video and automatically place video clips on the Album pages.

Windows Movie Maker *(Windows)*

Windows Movie Maker is a FREE video editor from Microsoft and is compatible with Windows Me and Windows XP operating systems. You can download it from the Microsoft web site.

Windows Movie Maker has many features: a wizard to guide you step-by-step through capturing and editing your movie, 30 video effects, 60 video transitions, dozens of title styles, fast rendering, one video and two audio tracks, an AutoMovie feature, ability to capture and output wide-screen format (16:9), and more.

Movie Maker's default file capture format is Windows Media Video Series 9, but you can choose to capture using other formats, including the more useful DV-AVI format.

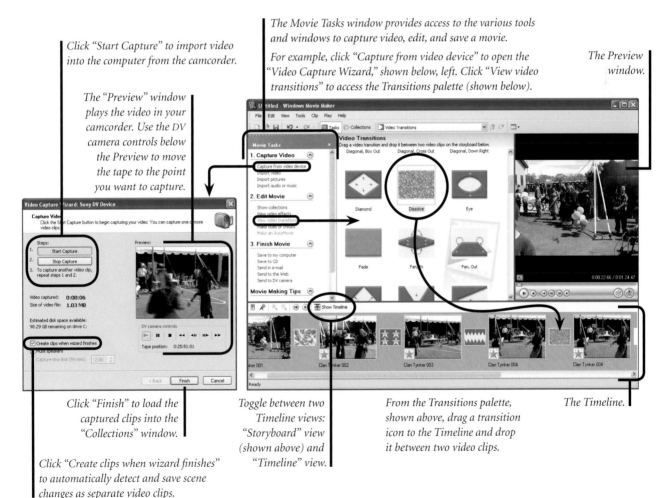

Click "Start Capture" to import video into the computer from the camcorder.

The "Preview" window plays the video in your camcorder. Use the DV camera controls below the Preview to move the tape to the point you want to capture.

The Movie Tasks window provides access to the various tools and windows to capture video, edit, and save a movie.

For example, click "Capture from video device" to open the "Video Capture Wizard," shown below, left. Click "View video transitions" to access the Transitions palette (shown below).

The Preview window.

Click "Finish" to load the captured clips into the "Collections" window.

Click "Create clips when wizard finishes" to automatically detect and save scene changes as separate video clips.

Toggle between two Timeline views: "Storyboard" view (shown above) and "Timeline" view.

From the Transitions palette, shown above, drag a transition icon to the Timeline and drop it between two video clips.

The Timeline.

Striping Tip

*When you shoot video, your camcorder puts a **timecode** on the tape. If you stop and restart the camera or if you rewind the tape to preview footage, it's easy to accidentally create a break in the timecode when you advance the tape to start recording again. Whenever a timecode break occurs on the tape, the timecode starts at zero again, which makes the "logging" feature of editing software useless.*

*To avoid this problem, **stripe** your tapes: put a blank tape in your camcorder, put the lens cap on, then press the record button and record over the entire tape. This puts an unbroken timecode on the tape. Rewind the tape and you're ready to shoot without the possibility of any timecode breaks.*

If you don't have time to stripe your tape, *make sure to do this: before you start taping your next scene, rewind the tape to a point where the new recording will overwrite the last several seconds of the previous scene.*

Mid-range video editing applications

The **mid-range** category includes very powerful, professional applications that can be used for commercial or personal projects. These software programs could easily fall into the *high-end* category except that they're affordable and easy to use.

The difference between mid-range and entry-level editing programs is dramatic. In addition to the convenience of non-linear and non-destructive editing, mid-range programs provide an **impressive array of features** meant to attract the attention of professionals. Some of the feature highlights include:

- ▼ *Log and capture:* You can create a list of exact timecodes for the clips you want to capture, then automatically batch-capture all the designated clips from the camcorder. The log enables the software to easily reconstruct projects and recapture the same video clips from the original tape if you've deleted the previously captured clips from your hard drive. In professional environments this feature saves many gigabytes of storage space.

- ▼ *Offline editing:* You can capture low-resolution video files for quick work on rough cuts or for working on a computer with limited storage space, then recapture the video clips at a high resolution.

- ▼ *Customizable work spaces:* Choose from preset window configurations or create a custom window and palette layout that you save as a preset.

- ▼ *Up to 99 audio tracks and 99 video tracks for editing:* Apply a variety of compositing modes to different video tracks.

- ▼ *Timeline keyframing* for effects and animation.

- ▼ *Advanced* audio editing and mixing features.

- ▼ *Customizable organization* of project assets: Create bins (folders) in which to keep your project files.

- ▼ *Project-management features:* Find and delete unneccesary files or reconstruct projects from original tapes.

- ▼ Easy access to *professional-level edits:* Ripple, roll, slip, and slide edits.

- ▼ *Automation* of moving clips to the Timeline with transitions included.

- ▼ *Timeline markers* to help position elements precisely in the Timeline.

- ▼ *A storyboard feature* for rough visualization of a project.

- ▼ *Batch-processing features:* Export multiple files in various formats, plus adjust the settings for testing or preparing for different types of media.

The applications shown on the following pages represent just a few of the choices available for digital video editing, but they're among the most popular.

Final Cut Pro and Final Cut Express *(Macintosh)*

Final Cut Pro (from Apple, $999) is a popular professional application on the Mac platform. It is compatible with other indispensible industry-standard programs such as Adobe Photoshop and Adobe After Effects.

Beyond editing capabilities, Final Cut Pro 4 includes LiveFonts, which are customizable animated fonts for titles; Soundtrack, an intuitive tool for creating original musical scores; a MultiTrack Audio Mixer; Compressor, state-of-the-art MPEG-2 encoding (the format required for DVD) with split-screen preview of source and output; and more.

The Viewer window previews individual video clips. Tabs give access to controls for altering size, opacity, rotation, motion, creating titles, and other effects. The white area of the scrub bar below the clip indicates the selected part of the clip that will be placed in the movie by dragging it to a position in the Timeline.

The Canvas window previews the entire timeline. Tabs show various sequences that you create. Organizing a large project into sequences makes it easier to manage. You can make a copy of a sequence to experiment with editing variations.

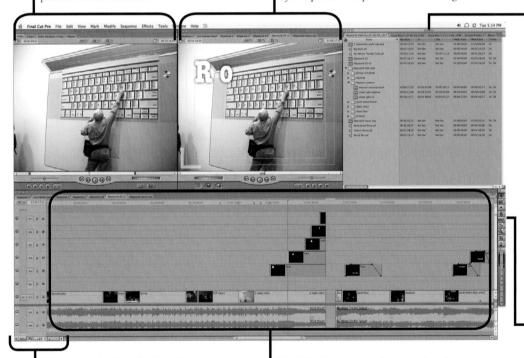

The Browser window shows all the assets for your project: sound files, video clips, graphics, and sequences. You can create bins (folders) to organize your project, and you can change the view of the Browser window to a large-icon graphical view in which you arrange the clips in a storyboard style.

Video clips with a diagonal red line are offline: they've been logged, but have not been captured from the camera to the hard drive.

These controls affect the Timeline view and the visibility of certain timeline controls such as keyframes, video clip opacity, and audio clip volume controls.

The Timeline window shows a selected sequence that contains video clips and audio tracks. You have the option of using up to 99 video tracks and 99 audio tracks. This example shows seven video tracks and two audio tracks. The tabs at the top-left of the Timeline represent other sequences in the project.

Tools for selecting, editing, viewing, and altering clips. Here you'll find the ripple, roll, slip, and slide edit tools, plus other essential tools.

Logging Tip

*Always **label your cassette tapes** with unique names so later you can easily recover clips that may no longer exist on your hard drive.*

*When you **log your clips** in the video editing software, you can enter a name for the video source that matches the unique name on the cassette. This way you can easily find the correct tape when the software later instructs you to insert that tape in the camcorder so it can recapture the logged video clips.*

In Final Cut Pro (shown to the right) type the cassette tape name in the text field labeled "Reel."

The Log and Capture procedure in Final Cut Pro

Final Cut Pro's "Log and Capture" window, shown below, will *log* (make a list of) clips of video that you need to capture and store on your hard drive while working on a project. From the "File" menu choose "Log and Capture…." The "Log and Capture" window displays a preview of the video tape in your camera. Navigate forward or back through the video tape using the controller buttons below the preview. You can set *In* and *Out* markers that determine exactly what points in the timecode will be used to define the start and finish of a segment of video.

To log a clip using In and Out markers:

1. Pause the video at the point where you want the captured clip to start, then click the "Mark In" button in the lower-left corner of the Preview pane.

2. Advance the tape to the point where you want to end the clip, then click the "Mark Out" button in the lower-right corner of the Preview pane.

3. In the Logging pane (below, right), type a name for the "Reel" (the same name you used to label the current video cassette tape).

4. Click the "Log Clip" button to open the "Log Clip" window (shown on the next page).

5. Type a name for the clip (and a descriptive log note if you want), then click OK.

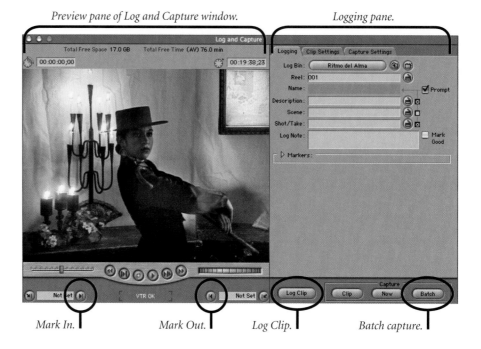

Preview pane of Log and Capture window.   *Logging pane.*

Mark In.   *Mark Out.*   *Log Clip.*   *Batch capture.*

The "Log Clip" window opens when you click the "Log Clip" button., shown on the previous page.

The "Mark Good" checkmark lets you mark the best clips in case you want to capture just those, leaving the other clips to be captured later, if you decide you need them.

Final Cut Express is similar to Final Cut Pro, but lacks many of the professional and project-management features found in Final Cut Pro. It does not include LiveType, Soundtrack, or some of Final Cut Pro's other advanced features. However, the price tag of $299 makes it an excellent choice to start video editing, then upgrade to the power of Final Cut Pro when you feel the need.

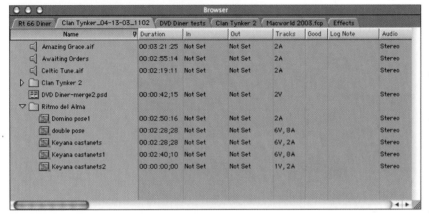

As you log clips that are to be captured, they appear in the Browser window. The red line indicates that the clips are "offline" and have not yet been captured to your hard drive.

The **clip** that you just named appears in the Browser window, above, with other project assets. After logging all the clips you want from the tape in your camera, you can capture them all to your hard drive using "Batch" capture: click the "Batch" capture button in the lower-right corner of the "Logging" pane (shown on the previous page).

Logging all your clips creates a list of the exact timecode location of all your source video files. Instead of using expensive hard drive space for permanent storage, you can delete digital video files when you've finished a project and automatically recover them from the original tapes when necessary.

If you need to give an unfinished large project to another editor, it can be very difficult finding a way to deliver 30 or 40 gigabytes (or more) of digital video files. If you used log-and-capture for your project, you can email the tiny project files and have a courier deliver the source video tape. When the editor on the other end opens the project, the editing software will ask for the tape and recapture the exact clips that you originally logged.

Adobe Premiere *(Macintosh and Windows)*

Adobe Premiere (about $550) is one of the most popular non-linear editing systems, especially on the PC platform. Its integration with other Adobe products such as Photoshop, Illustrator, After Effects, LiveMotion, and GoLive make it an easy choice for many editors. Premiere also includes a History palette so you can return to any point in your editing session, collapsible Timeline elements to show or hide editing details, and many options for viewing video clips and the appearance of palettes and windows. In the Windows version of Premiere you can export directly to MPEG-2 format.

The Project window is where you store and organize the audio and video clips for a project. Choose from three different views: List, Icon, or Thumbnail. Icon view is the current choice. In Thumbnail view you can drag the clips around to create a storyboard layout.

The Monitor window can show a preview of an individual clip (Source view) or of the entire Timeline (Program view).

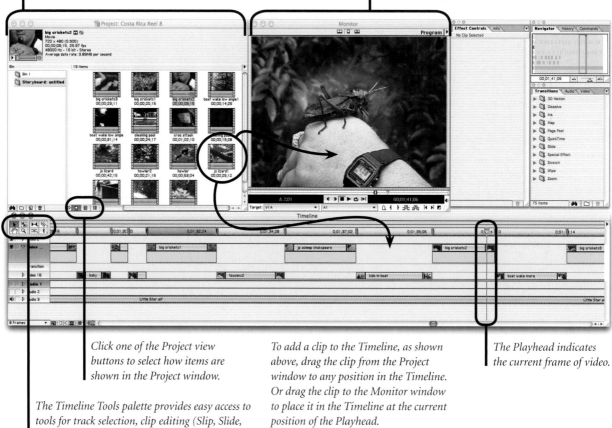

Click one of the Project view buttons to select how items are shown in the Project window.

The Timeline Tools palette provides easy access to tools for track selection, clip editing (Slip, Slide, Ripple, and Roll edits), Fade and Link tools, and tools for marking In and Out Points of clips.

To add a clip to the Timeline, as shown above, drag the clip from the Project window to any position in the Timeline. Or drag the clip to the Monitor window to place it in the Timeline at the current position of the Playhead.

The Playhead indicates the current frame of video.

The log-and-capture procedure in Premiere

Premiere's log-and-capture window is called *Movie Capture*, shown below. When your camera is attached, the Movie Capture window previews the video that's in the camera.

To log and capture video clips in Premiere:

1. From the "File" menu choose "Capture," then from the submenu choose "Movie Capture."

2. Click the "Logging" tab in the Movie Capture window to show the Logging pane.

3. Use the player controls located beneath the preview pane to pause the tape at the point you want a clip to start (the "In" point), then click the "Set In" button (shown at right).

4. Use the player controls to advance the tape to a point where you want the clip to end (the "Out" point, then click the "Set Out" button (shown at right).

5. Type a name for the source tape in the "Reel Name" text box, a name for the clip you're about to log in the "File Name" box, and any descriptive text you want in the "Comment" box.

6. Click the "Log In/Out" button to open the "File Name" window (shown at right, middle), which contains the File Name and Log Comment you just entered. Click OK.

As you log clips, they're added to a list in the "Batch Capture" window, shown at the bottom of the page. The diamond shape next to each log entry indicates that the clip will be captured when you click the "Capture" button (the red circle shown below in the Movie Capture window). If you decide you don't want to capture a particular clip, click the diamond next to the clip to turn it off. When a clip has been captured, the diamond changes to a checkmark.

Set In and Set Out buttons.

Log In/Out button.

Player controls.

Capture button.

The "File Name" window opens when you click the Log In/Out button in the Logging pane of the "Movie Capture" window (left).

Video Tip

*When taping with your video camera, **don't record anything important** on the first thirty seconds or the last thirty seconds of the tape. The batch capture process sometimes has problems with the timecode of clips that are too close to the beginning or end of a tape.*

The Batch Capture window shows clips that have been logged or captured.

Vegas *(Windows)*

Sonic Foundry's **Vegas** (about $500) offers a lot of features, including high-level color correction; professional media-management tools with search and sort features; software tools for professional editors such as a waveform monitor, histogram, and vectorscope; sophisticated audio tools; unlimited audio and video tracks; and more. A "split screen bypass" feature lets you see what a clip looks like with or without an effect or color-correction applied. You can also use the split screen to compare a video clip with a Photoshop graphic. If you have a scrollwheel on your mouse, you can use it to zoom in or out of the Timeline. "Scripts" enable you to complete repetitive tasks automatically. Vegas is also available as **Vegas+DVD** and includes **DVD Architect,** Sonic Foundry's DVD authoring application (about $700).

The Video Capture window.

Click the "Capture" tab to show the "Video Capture" window.

Use the Player controls to operate the camcorder and position the tape for capture, then click "Capture Video."

The Explorer window shows all your project files. Use this window to create, name, or delete files and folders. Drag or double-click a file to place it in the Timeline (shown on the next page).

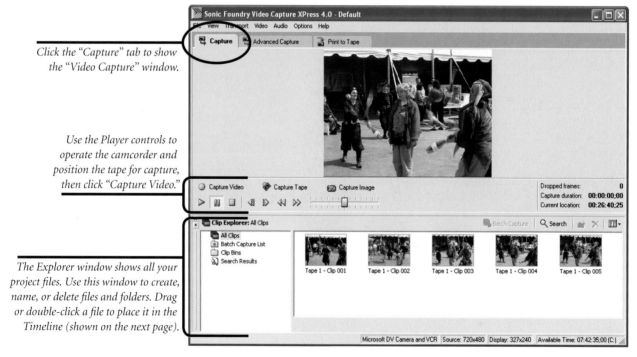

The Vegas interface and tools differ dramatically from most of the other popular nonlinear editors, but the differences, once you get used to them, are powerful and efficient. Sonic Foundry's reputation for excellent audio technology shows in Vegas' audio-editing capabilities. Innovative tools (such as "track envelopes" that use "rubber bands" for controlling all sorts of clip attributes) make this relative newcomer a serious contender. **Vegas LE** (Light Edition) is also available; it provides two video and four audio tracks.

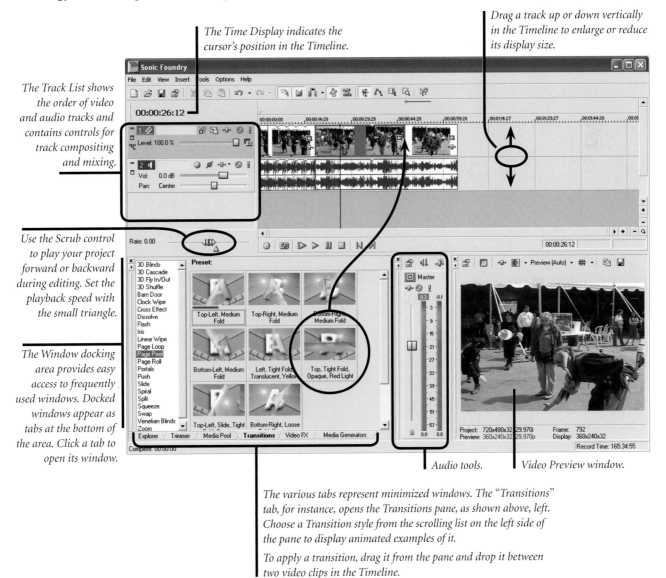

The Time Display indicates the cursor's position in the Timeline.

Drag a track up or down vertically in the Timeline to enlarge or reduce its display size.

The Track List shows the order of video and audio tracks and contains controls for track compositing and mixing.

Use the Scrub control to play your project forward or backward during editing. Set the playback speed with the small triangle.

The Window docking area provides easy access to frequently used windows. Docked windows appear as tabs at the bottom of the area. Click a tab to open its window.

Audio tools.

Video Preview window.

The various tabs represent minimized windows. The "Transitions" tab, for instance, opens the Transitions pane, as shown above, left. Choose a Transition style from the scrolling list on the left side of the pane to display animated examples of it.

To apply a transition, drag it from the pane and drop it between two video clips in the Timeline.

Avid Xpress DV *(Macintosh and Windows)*

Avid develops hardware and software solutions for professional editors, broadcasters, and production studios; their products are designed to work with many different formats, from film to DV. **Avid Express DV** is an affordable (close to $1,000) DV-only version of their industry-standard software, and it includes the DVD authoring program, DVDit.

Among its many features are more than 100 realtime effects, great titling effects, and unparalleled color-correction tools. Other features include a three-window view (next page) that shows previous, current, and next scenes, a split-screen monitor to show clips with or without an effect applied, sophisticated audio tools, and more.

Avid Xpress DV's video log and capture procedure is very easy: The "Record" Tool (circled below) also serves as a "Mark In," "Mark Out," and "Log" button. Click once to mark the begining of a capture (Mark In) and click again when you want to mark the end of a clip (Mark Out). The tape pauses and the button changes to a "Log" button. Enter a name for the clip in the "Name" field, then click the "Log" button to add the logged clip to the list in the Log window (top-left corner). After you've logged all the clips you want from the source tape, you can batch-capture them using the "Batch Record" command in the "Bin" menu.

Note

Avid Xpress DV has a limit of eight video and eight audio tracks, but the ability to "nest" multiple effect layers within a single video layer actually translates to unlimited layers for effects.

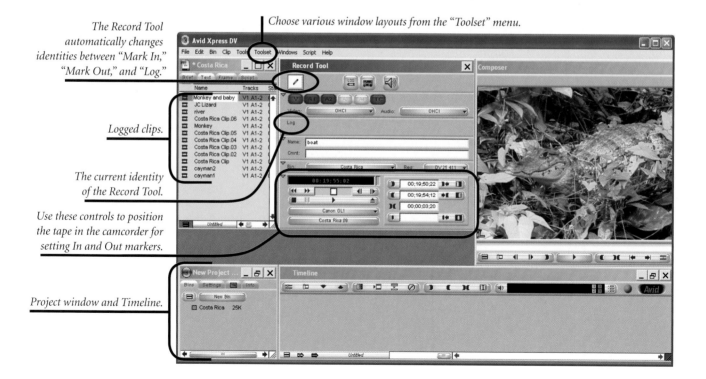

Choose various window layouts from the "Toolset" menu.

The Record Tool automatically changes identities between "Mark In," "Mark Out," and "Log."

Logged clips.

The current identity of the Record Tool.

Use these controls to position the tape in the camcorder for setting In and Out markers.

Project window and Timeline.

The "Color Correction" Toolset features powerful color-correction tools and a three-window setup to compare color balance between scenes. In the example below, the "Next" monitor (far right) shows a split screen to compare the clip with and without a correction applied.

The **Avid Xpress DV PowerPack** version (just under $1,300) adds even more functionality, with extras such as the Avid DV FilmMaker's Toolkit (advanced tools for editing and managing projects), the Avid Illusion FX Pack (plug-in effects such as Lightning, Melt, and Kaleidoscope), an Image Stabilization AVX Plug-in (to eliminate camera movement from video clips), and Boris title animation software (Boris FX and Boris GRAFFITI).

HSL (Hue, Saturation, Lightness) and Curves color-correction tools are provided.

To add a split screen effect to a monitor (as shown to the right), click the "Dual Split" button.

Remove effect.

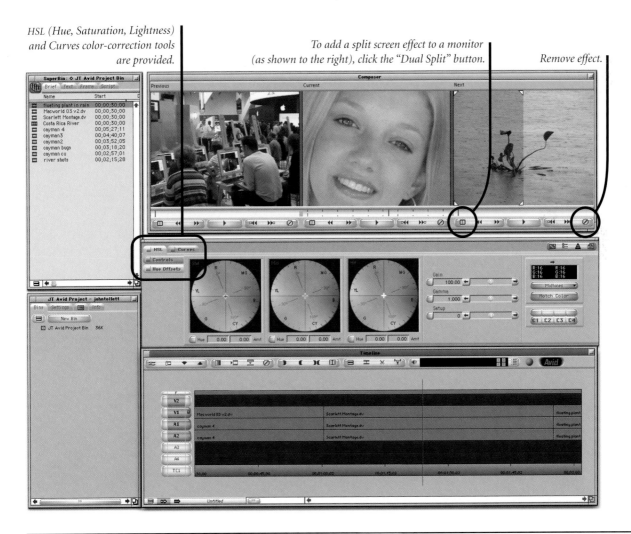

Pan-and-Zoom Software

One of the most powerful video effects you can add to a project is a technique in which you zoom in or out, and pan across still photos. For instance, if you're producing a documentary-style movie for a client about the history of his business, there are probably old photographs that would add a lot of visual interest to the video. A smooth pan or a slow zoom creates a more interesting visual than using static shots of the photos.

This technique, popularized by the documentary filmmaker Ken Burns, is even named the "Ken Burns Effect" in iMovie. While most of the popular, mainstream editing software programs let you create this effect, software that specializes in creating pans, zooms and rotation of stills may give you an extra measure of control and allow you to use larger images so you can zoom in closer without image quality deterioration.

MovingPicture *(Macintosh and Windows)*

StageTools MovingPicture (shown below) makes smooth pans and zooms of still images. It's available both as a plug-in called MovingPicture (about $200) for most of the popular NLEs (nonlinear editors) and as a stand-alone application called MovingPicture

Producer (about $200). A "Rotation" option can be added to either version for an extra $69. MovingPicture allows you to use extreme-zooms on images up to 8,000 x 8,000 pixels without the pixelation that you usually see when you enlarge an image so much.

Use the player controls in the bottom-left corner of the Viewer to preview the animation.

The Stage shows the loaded image.

The yellow box shows the Camera view. Position and size this box to frame the view you want for each keyframe.

The Viewer shows a preview of your pan and zoom moves.

Click the Keyframe icon to set a keyframe in the Timeline.

The Timeline.

Click one of the Stage Size Controls to change the view size of the image on the Stage.

To create a pan-and-zoom effect:

1. Load an image into MovingPicture.

2. Drag the yellow box (the camera view) to a position where you want to start the movie. Make the box larger or smaller by dragging its bottom-right corner.

3. Click the "Keyframe" icon beneath the "Viewer" window to create the starting point.

4. Click on a point in the Timeline where you would like to create the next keyframe (the next significant move in the animation), then size and position the yellow box over the image to create the desired camera view at the current keyframe position.

5. To set the keyframe, click the "Keyframe" icon beneath the "Viewer" window. Add more keyframes if needed.

6. Use the player controls beneath the "Viewer" to preview the results of your settings.

The composite example below shows how the camera view changed in the Viewer when the bottom-right corner of the yellow box was dragged to resize it for three different keyframes.

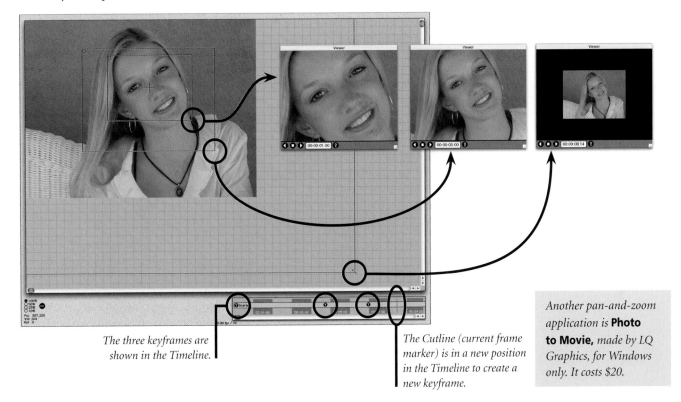

The three keyframes are shown in the Timeline.

The Cutline (current frame marker) is in a new position in the Timeline to create a new keyframe.

Audio Editing Software

Audio editing is a completely new world for most designers, but it's critically important. If you're a designer from the graphics world, you may be surprised to realize how many digital audio editing solutions are available and how powerful and sophisticated even the entry-level products are.

Digital audio editing, like digital video editing, is non-linear and non-destructive. With these tools you can work magic on audio files: modify the volume level of an audio selection, change the duration of a selection without changing the pitch, change the pitch of a selection without changing the duration, change the sample rate, convolve a sound (apply the characteristics of one sound onto another), fade sound in or out, convert sound between mono and stereo, layer sounds, and much more.

Digital audio software uses terminology you may not be familiar with:

Sample rate is the number of times per second that a digital sample is taken from an analog audio file during conversion to a digital format. Audio on a CD, for instance, is recorded at 44,100 samples each second, referred to as 44.1 kHz (kiloherz). *DVD specifications require that audio be 48 kHz, or 48,000 samples per second.*

Bit resolution refers to the number of *bits* (pieces of information) in each audio sample. Audio can be 8-bit, 16-bit, 24-bit, or 32-bit, although many of the more affordable software applications do not support more than 8-bit resolution. Larger bit numbers mean higher fidelity and better quality.

The bit resolution determines the audio's **dynamic range,** the number of steps to describe audio level from quiet to loud. To calculate the dynamic range in decibels, multiply the bit rate by 6: an 8-bit recording has a dynamic range of 48 decibels.

Although the subject of audio is very complex and technical, there are great audio software solutions that make it possible to jump in over your head and do amazing things while you learn all about it.

Dedicated audio-editing applications provide a great many features, effects, and controls. But keep in mind that the most popular *video* editing systems also have *sound* editing built in and will do more than you'll ever need for most projects; in fact, most of the built-in sound-editing features surpass the capabilities of traditional analog audio production tools.

We mention several popular applications here, but there are many others available ranging in price from free to very expensive. No matter which package you choose, you'll be amazed at the emotional, psychological, and entertainment power that edited audio adds to your video projects.

Note: Be sure to check for license information or usage limitations of any library audio files you use or buy. Some music collections have restrictions that limit their legal use to educational or non-commercial projects.

Audio Tip

Audio software can save sound files in a variety of formats, sample rates, and resolutions. Higher sound quality settings mean larger files that require more storage space and will increase the final size of your DVD project.

Stereo files are twice the size of mono files; 16-bit files are larger than 8-bit files; and files that use a 48 kHz sample rate are larger than files with a 44.1 kHz sample rate.

Peak DV *(Macintosh)*

Peak DV by Berkley Integrated Audio Software, Inc. (BIAS) is a nonlinear, non-destructive application for audio editing. Beautifully designed, it provides advanced professional tools for processing and editing audio, supports many popular MIDI sampling keyboards, and provides advanced sampler support. It's compatible with video editing applications such as iMovie, iDVD, Final Cut Pro, Final Cut Express, DVD Studio Pro, and Premiere. You can add third-party plug-ins for digital filtering, noise reduction, reverb, equalization, and other effects. A QuickTime Movie preview window is available so you can edit audio to synchronize with a QuickTime movie version of your video file.

The File Overview shows a waveform for the entire file. A white rectangle indicates the section of audio that is currently shown in the Waveform Display below.

Customize the Toolbar to contain the tools you use most often.

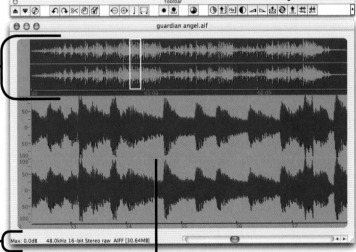

The Transport window shows elapsed time and provides Transport controls for both playback and recording.

The Cursor palette contains special tools:
Blending Tool *(far-left icon) smooths edited sections of audio.*
Hand Tool *lets you grab and move a waveform around its window.*
Magnifying Glass *zooms in or out.*
Pencil Tool *lets you draw on the waveform to erase unwanted noise in the audio or create your own effects.*

The Audio File Info Bar shows the sample rate, bit resolution, file format and file size. The Max Level Indicator in the lower-left corner shows the highest amplitude level in the audio file.

The Waveform Display is a large graphic representation of the current audio file. The two waveforms indicate that the file is stereo. Drag across the waveform to select a portion of the file, then perform any number of editing operations: copy a selection and paste it into a new position, trim away everything except your selection, adjust the volume of a selection, or apply sound effects. The possibilities are limitless.

Sonicfire Pro *(Macintosh and Windows)*

Sonicfire Pro from Sonic Desktop Software is a professional tool for creating customized soundtracks using SmartSound's royalty-free music collections. The software enables you to preview, buy, and download any cut (music selection) in the SmartSound Library for a price that's affordable and reasonable, or you can buy entire collections of music on CD.

A SmartSound music score consists of **Smart Blocks** of music that you can copy, paste, delete, and rearrange to create your own score. When you drag the right edge of a Smart Block to lengthen it, SmartSound recomposes the music to fit the new duration. Smart Blocks contain variations that make your options as a composer virtually unlimited.

The **Movie Window** (below, left) allows you to import a movie and create a score for any scene or for the entire movie by dragging Smart Blocks to the Timeline. You can even import your own music that's not from SmartSound's library and have SmartSound automatically recompose it to fit longer or shorter durations.

The "SmartSound Assistant" guides you through steps of making a musical selection.

The "SmartSound Maestro" button opens the SmartSound Maestro window (shown on the next page), where you search for available music selections on your computer or on the SmartSound web site.

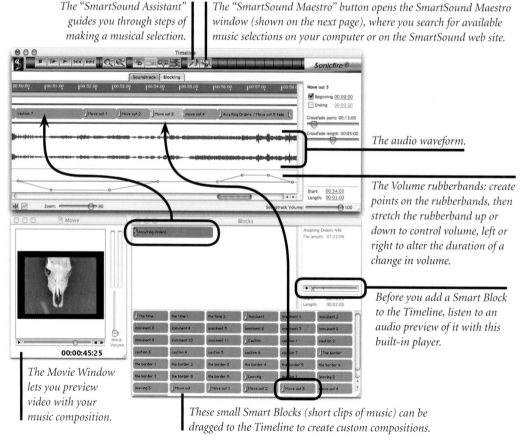

Drag a musical selection from the upper area of the "Blocks" window to the Timeline; then drag the right edge of the selected Block left or right to change its duration. SmartSound will automatically recompose the selection to match the new duration.

Or drag different Smart Blocks from the Smart Blocks window (lower-right) to the Timeline above to create your own musical arrangement.

The audio waveform.

The Volume rubberbands: create points on the rubberbands, then stretch the rubberband up or down to control volume, left or right to alter the duration of a change in volume.

Before you add a Smart Block to the Timeline, listen to an audio preview of it with this built-in player.

The Movie Window lets you preview video with your music composition.

These small Smart Blocks (short clips of music) can be dragged to the Timeline to create custom compositions.

Volume "rubber bands," similar to the volume controls found in video-editing software, give you complete control of your audio volume. The "SmartSound Maestro" button in the Toolbar (shown on the previous page) helps you find SmartSound music that may be on your computer, a CD, or the SmartSound web site. The Maestro window (shown below) lets you search for a style and intensity of music. If the music you choose is on the SmartSound site, you can click the "Purchase" button and download the file immediately.

The SmartSound Maestro shows a list of music found based on the criteria in the top three panes.

*A **CD icon** next to a selection means the selection is on a CD that has been catalogued to your computer.*

*An **Internet orb icon** means the selection is available on the SmartSound web site.*

*A **hard drive icon** means the selection is on your computer.*

Information about the current selection.

A description of the current selection.

Listen to an audio preview of your selection. If the selection is on the SmartSound web site, click the "Purchase" button to download the file.

Add the selected music to the soundtrack at a specific location in the timeline.

Click the Open button (here it's gray because the selection is online and needs to be purchased) to place the selected file into the Blocks window (shown on the previous page) where it can be composed into a completely new arrangement.

SmartSound Movie Maestro *(Macintosh and Windows)*

Movie Maestro, another product from Sonic Desktop Software, is similar to Sonicfire Pro but intended for home movies rather than professional projects. The price has been scaled back accordingly. The interface is simpler and most of the advanced features are missing, such as volume rubberband controls and the ability to compose your own arrangements using the component blocks of a music selection.

Movie Maestro music collections are recorded at 22.1 kHz, which is CD-ROM/multimedia quality. For audio that will be used on DVD projects, audio files must be 48 kHz. If you choose Movie Maestro for its attractive price (about $50), buy SmartSound's "Pro" music collections that are recorded at higher sample rates (44.1 kHz).

SoundSoap *(Macintosh and Windows)*

SoundSoap ($99, from BIAS) is an application for professional-quality noise reduction that's also easy to use for those of us without a professional audio-editing background.

In addition to saving audio files that can be imported into a movie project, SoundSoap can open an entire movie project and *clean* the soundtrack (that's why it's called Sound*Soap*). It's available as a stand-alone application or as a plug-in for other host audio applications, such as Peak, Adobe Premiere, Pinnacle Studio, or Wavlab.

SoundSoap can salvage an unusable audio file or can change the sound of your project from amateurish to professional. In the example below, the plug-in version of SoundSoap is shown in front and Peak DV is in the background. The "Wash Window" shows the digital file before (left side) and after (right side) SoundSoap cleaned it up.

Noise Tip

Old analog tape recordings that have been digitized and copied to a computer are notorious for hissing, scratchy sound that's barely usable or totally unusable. Even the worst of these kinds of files can usually be dramatically improved with SoundSoap.

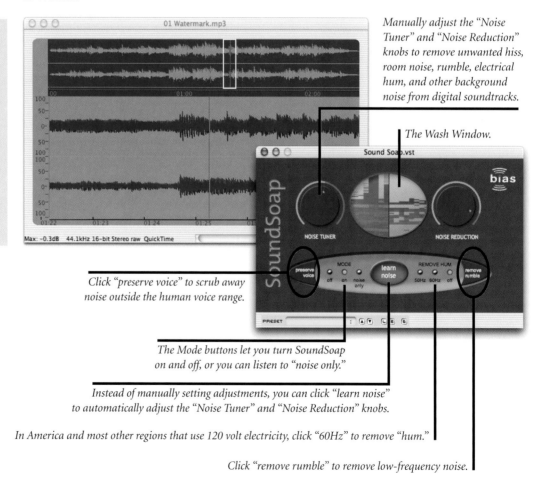

Manually adjust the "Noise Tuner" and "Noise Reduction" knobs to remove unwanted hiss, room noise, rumble, electrical hum, and other background noise from digital soundtracks.

The Wash Window.

Click "preserve voice" to scrub away noise outside the human voice range.

The Mode buttons let you turn SoundSoap on and off, or you can listen to "noise only."

Instead of manually setting adjustments, you can click "learn noise" to automatically adjust the "Noise Tuner" and "Noise Reduction" knobs.

In America and most other regions that use 120 volt electricity, click "60Hz" to remove "hum."

Click "remove rumble" to remove low-frequency noise.

Amazing Slow Downer *(Macintosh)*

Even if your video projects are small, personal projects without the need for sophisticated audio editing, the inexpensive **Amazing Slow Downer** (less than $40, by Roni Music) can be very useful. Amazing Slow Downer focuses on just a couple of the features found in more expensive audio-editing applications: *duration* and *pitch*. Change the duration of a music soundtrack without changing its pitch, or change its pitch without affecting the duration of the soundtrack.

When you edit a movie and the video sequence is just a few seconds too short or long for a particular audio track, you can change the speed of the audio track with the slider (shown below) so that it plays slightly faster or slower to match the length of the video without any detectable difference in the sound (if you avoid extreme adjustments of the speed).

Or you may have adjacent audio clips in your movie that would sound better if you raise or lower the pitch of one of the clips. A "Karaoke" function (the "KA" checkmark in the bottom-left corner) lets you reduce or remove vocals or certain instruments from a song. The results will vary, depending on how the stereo material was recorded.

Other Applications

ProTools is another popular audio editing application for Windows and Mac OS X; see www.DigiDesign.com.

You might also want to look at Cakewalk for the PC, www.Cakewalk.com.

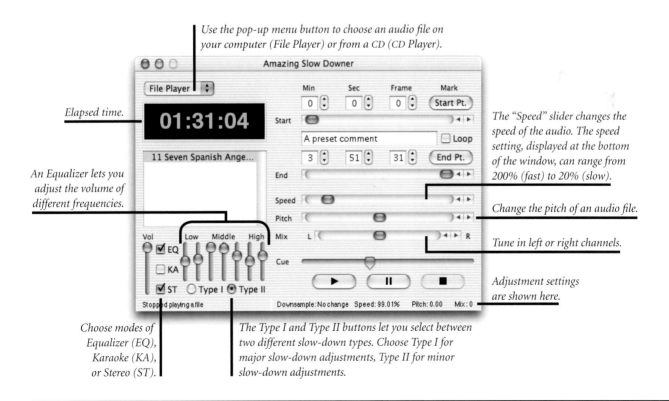

Use the pop-up menu button to choose an audio file on your computer (File Player) or from a CD (CD Player).

Elapsed time.

An Equalizer lets you adjust the volume of different frequencies.

The "Speed" slider changes the speed of the audio. The speed setting, displayed at the bottom of the window, can range from 200% (fast) to 20% (slow).

Change the pitch of an audio file.

Tune in left or right channels.

Adjustment settings are shown here.

Choose modes of Equalizer (EQ), Karaoke (KA), or Stereo (ST).

The Type I and Type II buttons let you select between two different slow-down types. Choose Type I for major slow-down adjustments, Type II for minor slow-down adjustments.

SPARK *(Macintosh)*

SPARK, by TC Works, is available in several versions: SPARK ME is free; SPARK LE is low-priced (about $50), and sometimes bundled with video-editing software such as Adobe Premiere; SPARK XL is a robust version (about $500) that includes many high-end features designed for full-time audio professionals.

The main WorkSheet window contains the Data Base view, where all your audio files are organized; the Play List view to organize files for CD-burning; and the Edit view, where the audio waveform is seen as both Overview and Detail views, and where you can select segments of the waveform to modify and edit.

The Master View window contains master controls and four slots for "FX Machine" plug-ins, power tools for creating real-time sound manipulation, sound design, and master processing. Several FX Machine plug-ins come with SPARK, and you can buy others.

FX Machine plug-ins add extra power and creative control.

The Transport Bar provides player controls and shows the timecode.

The Master View window provides audio level controls on the left. The right side provides space for up to four FX Machine plug-ins. Click the "Add" button to place plug-ins in the window, then double-click a plug-in icon to open its controls, such as the MaxIT Master window below.

The WorkSheet window contains the Data Base view (upper-left corner), the Play List view (upper-right corner) and the Edit view (bottom section).

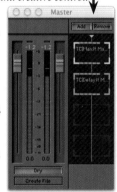

The MaxIT Master plug-in, an audio mixer for creating audio effects.

The Edit view includes an Overview (above) and Detail view (below) of the waveform.

Section Two

DVD menu design: structure, style, design and production guidelines, usability, and video compositing

Domino (above) and Keyana (below), from the Ritmo del Alma DVD

You might be a DVD designer if . . .

▼ you know Amaray from Jewel.

▼ you max out your credit card for a SCSI card and a DLT.

▼ you care that a DVD holds just 4.3 gigabytes
instead of 4.7 like the packaging says.

▼ you sometimes buy plain white cardboard discs.

▼ you care if pixels are square or not.

▼ you spend time squeezing Photoshop files
to 480 pixels tall.

Sample DVD Projects

A gallery of project ideas and menu designs for personal and commercial projects

The DVD menus featured in this chapter reflect just a few of the many types of personal projects you can create for yourself and professional projects you can create for others. These projects are smaller and less complex than most of the professional titles showcased in Chapter 12 because they were produced for local clients and friends with limited budgets. In other words, they're probably similar to the types of projects you'll design to start your own DVD design career (or hobby).

In addition to the examples shown here, there are many other types of presentations that can benefit from the multimedia and interactive capabilities of DVD. If you're a professional designer, your existing clients are a great starting place for developing project ideas. The documentation and presentation of special events, from weddings to annual sales meetings, are more entertaining and effective when presented with the multimedia and interactive features of DVD.

We've organized our samples into the categories of *entertainment, business, self-promotion, event, documentary,* and *personal.* Some of the design comments refer to "bitmapped subpicture highlights"; see Chapter 6 for details on what these are and how to create them.

Entertainment

Entertainment DVDs, in the form of Hollywood movies, are familiar to all of us. But now the Hollywood moguls have some serious competition—everyone else. Where we lack star power and budgets we can substitute creative freedom, originality, and unknown actors (aren't you tired of seeing the same actors in every movie?).

Whether you're a serious movie-maker or just experimenting, independent movies are now a real possibility for many people. If you're connected with a school drama department or a theater group, you can video performances and offer DVDs to parents and patrons, or use the DVD for critiques and teaching.

Independent movie

From home to Hollywood and from churches to motorcycle clubs, movies are being made in record numbers. Tired of predictable "Hollywood formula" movies? Make your own and enter a film festival. Better yet, start a film festival for yourself and your movie-making friends. Small movie theaters will often rent their space for a reasonable fee and can project from a DVD player. You can stage either an "invitation-only" event or run an ad in the local newspaper.

This simple menu offers two options: play the movie by selecting the "Play" button (above, right) or proceed to a "Scene Selection" menu (below, right) by selecting the "Scenes" button. The graphical button shapes, created in Photoshop, are overlayed with "subpicture" hotspots that fill with a tint of yellow color when selected. A hotspot's fill color is affected by whatever color is beneath it, so take care when choosing a highlight color for hotspots.

The stronger the tint of color assigned, the more opaque it is and less influenced by colors beneath. But opaque colors also obliterate graphical details and contrast that define buttons and text. It's best to use very light tints.

In this example, the tint of yellow over the light purple button color creates an acceptable tan color. You can test the effect of color tint overlays in your DVD authoring software or in Photoshop. In Photoshop, create a new layer, fill a rectangular shape on the layer with a highlight color similar to those found in authoring software, then adjust the opacity of the layer to similate a DVD highlight.

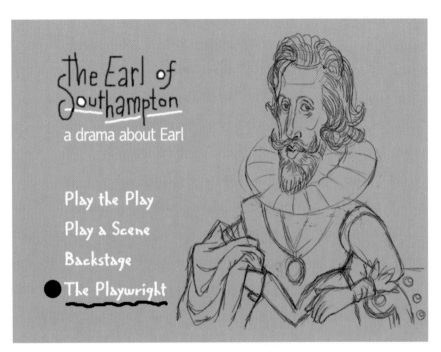

Drama

A menu doesn't have to be made up of photographic or video images. Illustrations or even crude scribblings can create original and unique looking menus. This menu for a school play features a rough sketch as the main visual element, with a handlettered title drawn in Photoshop.

Other than the parchment-colored background, the colors are limited to black and white to create a sketchbook look and to avoid having colorful items distract from the main visual.

The clunky highlights that indicate *selected* menu items (the aliased black dot and the crooked black line) are meant to fit in with the playful theme of the play.

Recital

It's not always a good idea to abandon the use of descriptive text as menu items, but for personal projects or extremely simple menus structures, an alternative way of identifying menu items can add interest and be graphically appealing.

This DVD contains four performances by Scarlett. Each numbered video automatically returns to this menu, so no submenus are needed.

The invisible highlight *hotspots* of the menu are large rectangles on the outside edge of each image that fill with a tint of white when *selected*. The hotspot appears as a gray shape when selected (a white tint over the black backgound) and adds to the checkerboard pattern of the design.

Business

When educated about the potential benefits, accessibility, and affordability of customized DVD presentations, the response of most businesses and organizations is enthusiastic and positive.

Professional designers have a new, viable marketing solution to offer their clients. Advertising agencies and design studios can blow away the competition by adding an exciting, compelling DVD presentation to their old-fashioned portfolio presentation. Businesses also have the option of training their own staff to create DVD projects.

The potential for using creativity and multimedia to accomplish marketing and public relations goals is greater than ever because DVDs can deliver information in a number of exciting ways.

For instance, private or public schools can create a year-long DVD project for students that becomes both a memento and a tool for recruitment and fundraising. Restaurants could offer a DVD for sale that features the chef and his featured recipes. A large business, such as a medical center, has dozens of departments that can benefit from DVD's ability to present information or training in an accessible fashion.

The opportunities are many, for both designers and businesses.

Hands On Community Art

Non-profit organizations such as Hands On Community Art can use DVD presentations for public relations, fundraising, and community outreach efforts. The Hands On fundraising strategy includes creating an annual DVD to send to previous donors that showcases the success of existing outreach programs. The DVD presentation creates more interest, conveys the benefits of the programs, and expresses the enjoyment of the participants more effectively than an expensive color brochure.

The first screen to play is a split-screen introduction by the organization's founder and director. The introduction can be skipped by selecting the menu item.

The consistent elements that tie these menus together are the logo, the highlight style and color used to indicate selected menu items, and the showcase of art created at the organization's facility.

Use of the Hands On logo as the real-life banner displayed around the community gives a unique look to each menu and presents an image that's compatible with community involvement, volunteer workers, and mobility.

To avoid visual competition with the logo, the typography for other menu items is kept plain and simple.

The art gallery menu links to video presentations of original art created at Hands On Community Art. The background is dark and plain so the art images dominate the screen. The swatch of a colorful collage in the upper-right corner adds some visual interest and provides a thematic connection to other menus that show the same decorative corner style.

Bonanza Creek Ranch

Bonanza Creek Ranch is a working ranch that includes an old western town movie set that's used for Hollywood movies, parties, and all sorts of special events. The DVD serves as a live motion brochure, showing off the town's authenticity and western atmosphere much more effectively than a printed brochure. Copies of the DVD are made as needed and given to movie producers and event planners.

The *first play* (the content that plays when you first insert a disc into a DVD player) shows a stagecoach arrive and stop in front of the dance hall, banjo music playing in the background. The last frame of the scene dissolves into a menu still frame of the scene (shown below).

The highlight technique used for selected menu items is a rectangular shape stroked with yellow. Font style and color decisions are based on western style and legibility. All submenus use still shots taken from the video. We retouched and enhanced some of the still frame captures we used as menus to ensure menu legibility. The foreground of the main menu (right) has been darkened with Photoshop's "Burn" tool to increase the contrast of the white type against the light color of the street.

While submenus vary in design somewhat to ensure legibility of the typography, a unified design approach is always present: we used town scenes for menu backgrounds and created consistent typography and color schemes.

The submenu image on the left uses a sepia-tone image to help convey the late 19th century atmosphere of the town.

The yellow, rectangular highlight shape that indicates a selected menu item has the simple, added touch of decorative extensions on each end of the shape to simulate a decorative style typical of the era. Bitmapped highlight shapes that are made up of perfectly horizontal and vertical shapes are ideal for indicating selected items.

The Bonanza Creek Ranch DVD contains video shot during events, video of the interior of buildings, bands and entertainment groups that are available for events, night shots for atmosphere, and PDF versions of floor plans, photographs, and contact information, plus a résumé of films that have been shot on the property.

Self-Promotion

DVD is an ideal medium for self-promotion. Non-profit organizations, bands, performance artists, or any business that wants to present themselves in a compelling way should consider developing a DVD. Digital versions of traditional promotional materials, such as brochures and technical documents, can also be included in the ROM section of the disc.

The close-up menu detail on the left shows the bitmapped highlight element (the subpicture) as it appears in Photoshop.

Lead Veins rock-and-roll band

The Lead Veins, a Portland, Oregon rock group, has a DVD that features live performance videos shot in nightclubs during their summer tour across America. Practice sessions, interviews, and home movies add interest and humor to the content. The DVD-ROM section of the disc contains text documents of the songs' lyrics.

The design attempts to reflect the pounding energy and aural chaos of the music. The typography reflects the band's edgy, alternative style, while the animated Lead Veins title shakes and pulsates relentlessly. The four tilted, overlapping images at the top are motion video clips that add to the menu's nervous energy.

Menu highlights (subpictures) must go on top of a menu, but you can create the illusion that the highlight is behind other menu elements. In these menus, the yellow, bitmapped highlights appear to fall behind the menu text. We created this illusion in Photoshop by erasing the yellow line wherever it overlayed a letter of text. The bitmapped highlight word is aliased (jaggy), but in this case, the design style justifies the use of "jaggy" and "grungy" elements.

We composited the inset video clips and the animated band name in video editing software, exported as an MPEG-2 file, then placed them in DVD authoring software. The bitmapped highlights (the yellow items) are included in the Photoshop menu design file that was imported into the DVD authoring software. Authoring software lets you create a rectangular "hotspot" on top of a menu that displays a bitmapped image when a viewer selects that hotspot. The bitmapped highlight image is always *black* in the Photoshop file (see the close-up menu detail above-left), but with DVD authoring software you assign the highlight color that the highlighted subpicture displays.

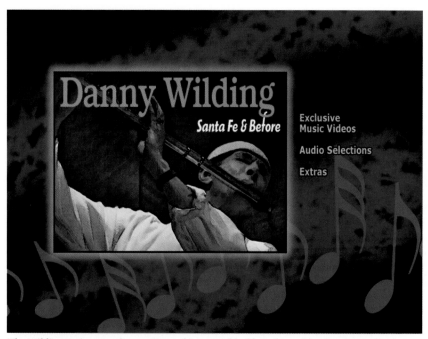

The Wilding main menu is a static graphic created in Photoshop with a looping audio soundtrack featuring Danny's alto flute music.

Danny Wilding flute music

The Danny Wilding DVD showcases Danny's beautiful and haunting alto flute music. Soundtracks from previous albums, a conversation with the artist, and several performances taped exclusively for the DVD are also included.

Danny uses the DVD for self-promotion and as part of a press kit. Instead of keeping an inventory of discs, he burns a new one whenever necessary.

We used a simple overlay technique to create a highlight over menu items. DVD authoring software lets you draw rectangular shapes (hotspots) on top of menu graphics. From a menu in the software you can assign a color to fill the shape when it is selected (or moused-over). In this menu design, when a viewer selects a hotspot, the shape fills with a rose color at 26 percent.

The "simple overlay" technique for creating highlights can be surprisingly versatile. With a little experimentation you can create color highlights that look very nice. And because they're subpictures, they're lightning-fast. (See Chapter 6 for details about highlights and subpicture overlays.)

Submenus follow the same graphic theme with different images of the artist to add visual interest. A small inset motion clip with flute audio loops against the large, static background image.

We stroked the text with black to enhance its legibility.

Clan Tynker

Clan Tynker is a multi-talented group of performers who provide dazzling entertainment at all types of festive events including parties, grand openings, dinners, renaissance festivals, films, and fundraisers. Their act is a mixture of juggling, magic, acrobatics, clowning, and even (gasp!) fire-eating. Since Clan Tynker possesses so many diverse skills, it can be difficult to describe just how good they are to potential clients. For this reason, a DVD that contains selected video clips from their act provides the perfect means to showcase their talents.

In this main menu screen, video from the *fire show* provides a dramatic backdrop to introduce the members of Clan Tynker.

Because the Clan Tynker's performances are so visually interesting, it was a natural choice to incorporate imagery from the act into the DVD menus.

As with the fire-eating scene shown above, this submenu uses an image of the crystal balls that Elijah so skillfully glides through his hands. Each translucent orb provides the perfect visual container to display motion vignettes of each member.

In another submenu, Marygold and Rebekah hold the Clan Tynker banner, which also doubles as navigation. This menu has been designed to allow the performers to "break out" of the act itself and present the menu selections directly to the viewer.

This design not only provides an opportunity to reinforce the name and identity of the group, it also allows members of Clan Tynker to "interact" with the viewer, making for a friendly, more personal connection.

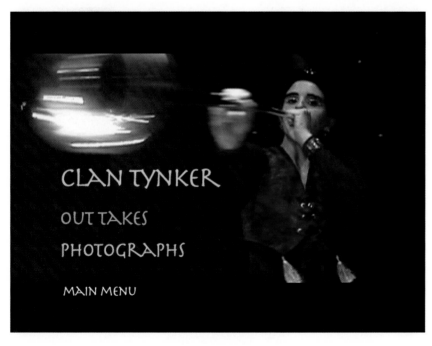

This still submenu has a simple layout, but presents an interesting image of Marygold trumpeting the start of the show. Other menus on the DVD feature similarly styled individual photographs of each of the members of Clan Tynker.

While a potential client will get their best demonstration of the act by watching the video, the DVD menus serve as a visual shorthand, allowing the viewer to quickly understand who Clan Tynker is and catch a glimpse of their collective charm and ability.

Ritmo del Alma Flamenco

The Ritmo del Alma (Rhythm of the Soul) DVD features young and inspiring flamenco dancers. Performance videos, interviews with the dancers, and rehearsal footage shot in their mentor's dance studio are included on the disc. Ritmo del Alma can use the disc in place of auditions, for public relations purposes, and as a priceless archive of this stage of their dance careers. Also, having performances on DVD enables them to critique performances from an audience perspective.

The main menu provides buttons to five main areas of content. The three most important buttons include small motion videos that show a preview of the content. The "selected" button state is indicated by a red underline highlight, as shown on the selected "Gallery" button.

Enchanted by the young dancers' beauty and talent, we created a series of fine art prints, made from single frames of video, then used the prints as a design theme for the entire menu system. The "Gallery" submenu provides a link to the art prints as a slideshow. The "Limited Edition Prints" menu links to an information screen (a graphic) containing information about ordering prints. Other menu buttons link to video clips related to the art prints.

The submenu designs continue the highlight technique used in the main menu, a red underline to indicate that a button is *selected*.

To create a strong visual connection between menus, the submenus for the three main areas of content (Domino, Keyana, and Performances) include the small motion video clips that are found on the main menu. Every submenu uses the same highlighting technique of red underlines to indicate a selected button. The red lines are "subpictures," bitmapped graphics which are created in Photoshop and whose behavior and color are assigned in DVD-authoring software.

The vertical alignment of menu items makes navigation with a remote control easy and intuitive.

Extra space separates the "Main Menu" button from the other menu buttons to place *related* items in close proximity, visually organizing the information in the menu.

All submenus show some variations in design, but the main design elements of typography, highlight style, and color scheme are consistent.

Event

At most social events, major or minor, you'll usually find someone taking video of the proceedings. This is all well and good for the person behind the camera, but the majority of the attendees will probably never see a single frame of that video. Why? It's not because the videographer doesn't want to share—it's just that until the advent of DVD, there wasn't an efficient way to distribute a video presentation to the people who would be interested.

Now with DVD, any event video can be quickly packaged and inexpensively sent to the participants in a format they'll actually want to watch.

Biking Across Kansas

The best event DVDs contain video that will be worth watching in the future. They usually involve groups of people actively doing something interesting or unusual. Video of people just standing around doesn't often make for a compelling DVD experience. Seriously, when was the last time you sat down to watch a video of people making idle conversation?

Biking Across Kansas (BAK) is anything but idle—it's a gigantic group of cyclists who pedal their bikes across the state of Kansas within a single week. It's a real physical and mental challenge for most participants and by the time they cross the finish line, they all have a profound sense of accomplishment.

Since the BAK experience means so much to those who have participated, a DVD is the ideal way to encapsulate the memories of that week.

The DVD includes video and photographs that chronicle each day of the tour, plus interviews with participants, organizers, and support staff.

The menu artwork is designed to evoke memories of the road and rural scenery of Kansas. The main menu uses the visual metaphor of road signage to provide navigational links to the content.

The scene selection menu background is another familiar landscape—this one depicting a lone cyclist standing triumphantly in the middle of a wheat field.

This example and the other BAK DVD menus use a mix of video clips and still photographs to get the messages across.

As a people-oriented event, it's fitting that the menus are inhabited by images of cyclists immersed in the landscape itself.

Burns Supper

This DVD documents a *Burns Supper* event, one of thousands of such annual events that celebrate the birthday and life of the revered Scottish poet Robert Burns. The disc can be made available to participants and attendees and also to promote similar future events.

Since Burns Suppers follow a set format, the disc can also be used as a training tool for other people who want to organize their own Burns Supper.

The content of the Burns Supper DVD is organized into the three menu buttons: Toasts, Entertainment, and Music. Stills from the video represent each category and are repeated on submenus.

The button highlighting technique we used in this menu system is a variation of the *simple overlay* technique (in which you draw a "hotspot" rectangle on top of the menu and instruct it to fill with a tint of color when "selected").

Instead, we drew a rectangular hotspot and set the "normal" (unselected) button state to fill with a 33 percent tint of black, and the "selected" button state to have a 0 (zero) percent fill.

As shown here, the result is that unselected areas of the screen are dark, and the selected hotspot area appears to glow, although it's actually no brighter than the original menu graphic.

The menu system's limited color scheme is based on the colors that dominate the video—warm colors of brown oak, gold trimmings, and brass candelabras. The subdued colors echo the elegant formality of the evening.

The menu is accompanied with a looping bagpipe soundtrack. Some of the menu items launch straight into a video. Other menu items, such as the "Songs" button, open third-level menus that offer additional content choices.

The "Return to the main menu" button on all submenus makes navigating to any section of the disc from any menu quick and easy.

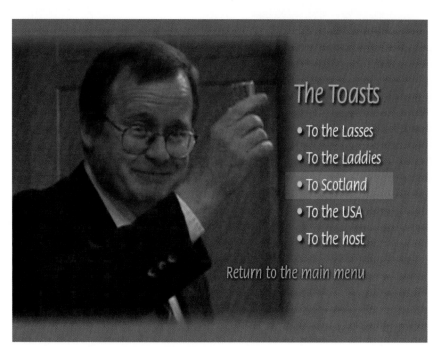

All the toasts listed on this submenu are traditional toasts offered at a Burns Supper. In addition to the bulleted items, the menu *title* ("The Toasts") is also a button. When selected, all the "toast" scenes, represented by the bulleted menu items, play as one movie.

Or you can view individual toasts (short individual scenes that make up the longer "toasts" movie) by selecting one of the bulleted menu items. In the DVD authoring software, you can place *chapter markers* at selected points within movies. You can link menu items to markers, which let a user jump to specific scenes within a movie.

Documentary

You don't have to be Ken Burns or Michael Moore to create your own documentary videos on DVD. If you're equipped with a video camera, any topic that interests you is fair game for the documentary treatment. Your topic doesn't have to be monumental, just as long as you can make it interesting to your intended audience. DVD is a great medium for documentary videos because it allows the viewer to either watch the entire presentation or simply select specific scenes of interest. You'll want to design your documentary menus with the viewer in mind and be sure to include chapter markers that allow people to easily locate major sections.

Ozark Folk Music

The menus for the *Ozark Folk Music* documentary DVD are designed to evoke a feeling of times gone by, just as the music itself is representative of an earlier era.

The main menu is dominated by an image of a single musician, presented in muted tones against a background of weathered boards. The menu layout and typeface are kept intentionally simple to reinforce the basic down-to-earth nature of Ozark folk music.

This submenu retains the visual themes of rustic boards and a lone guitar player, but the colors are more intense to reflect the contemporary nature of the linked interview video. The colorful clarity of the menu underscores the fact that Ozark folk music is not necessarily a thing of the past, but still survives in the present through the efforts of contemporary musicians.

This menu for "The Songs" section focuses on the hand-crafted traditional instruments that play such a vital part in the authentic sound of contemporary Ozark music. Imagery of the guitar and piano keys visually ties this submenu to the topic.

School yearbook

Some schools now plan and produce DVD versions of a school yearbook. In some cases the teacher in charge of technology classes organizes teams of students to video school activities throughout the school year, then the class produces a school DVD at the end of the year. Some schools may have the yearbook staff include a DVD yearbook project with their traditional yearbook work. Or why not document a school year yourself, without involving the school. Loan the video camera to the teenagers now and then to tape themselves having fun. You can attend the sporting events and grab shots of them in the stands, the team on the field, and other parents freezing in the bleachers.

The DVD yearbook shown here is a project shared by several high school friends. The main menu features a large still image with an inset looping slideshow of the student-producers' portraits. The photos slowly dissolve from one to another.

To show menu highlights, menu items are overlayed with a bitmapped color version of the text. The highlighted word is jaggy, but that's the nature of bitmapped subpicture overlays. The bitmapped subpicture in the main menu doesn't completely cover the anti-aliased text below it, leaving some gray pixels visible (below, left). We used the pencil tool in Photoshop to retouch the bitmapped text and hide the gray pixels (below, right).

Layout simplicity and unusual photos make the menus interesting and easy to use. The most recognizable architectural features of the campus are incorporated into the menu designs, but not as the usual campus beauty shot.

Each menu plays a looping soundtrack clip of a song from a local band (used with permission, of course).

The "memories" button on the main menu (previous page) links to school-related slideshows that play soundtracks of the students' favorite music.

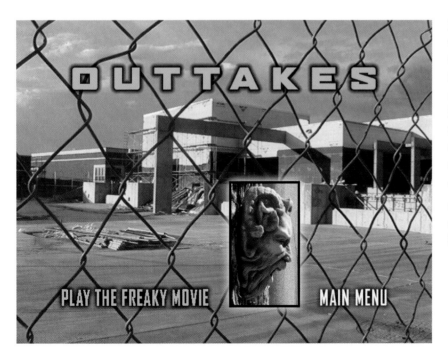

Features that are always popular with viewers are outtakes and bloopers. Outtakes are not only fun to watch, they're fun to edit and add soundtracks. This outtake menu features a composited, small inset movie just for fun. The gargoyle head rotates around and dissolves into close-up shots of students imitating the expression on the gargoyle's face.

To create effects such as an inset movie over a still photo, you must use video compositing software. See Chapter 11 for an overview of video compositing.

Looking for Mary

The "Looking for Mary" DVD documents Robin's trip to England to research a Shakespeare authorship project. The menu design is planned around subdued, conservative colors and unique typography. The black horizontal bar serves as a device to visually organize the menu elements and creates a feeling of widescreen spaciousness.

Selected menu items are indicated by the small swan icon. In the DVD authoring software, the swan is a bitmapped, subpicture overlay (see Chapter 6). The swan is present on the left side of every menu item, but it's invisible until a viewer selects the button hotspot.

In each of the four menus shown here, the swan icon shows which menu item has been selected.

The swan icon, shown below, is jaggy-looking, but that's the nature of subpicture overlays, and it's an acceptable compromise for the speed with which it shows an item has been selected.

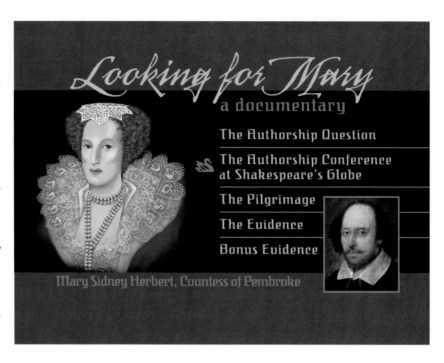

The use of the black horizontal bar also serves a couple of other design functions: it creates separation between the content items and the "Main Menu" button at the bottom of the screen, and it provides a strong visual similarity between all submenus.

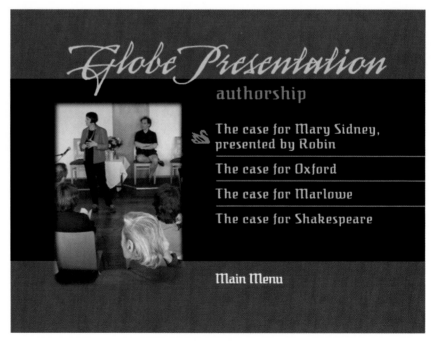

When you design a menu to include a large area of flat color, burn a test disc early in the design process, even if the design is not finished, to make sure the color you picked works well on a TV screen. Some colors may experience unusual and unexpected color shifts between the computer's screen display and a TV monitor's display.

Submenus that contain more than one image retain a strong visual organization and hierarchy by showing the primary image in full-color (for more emphasis) and the secondary image in a colorized blue hue (less visually dominant).

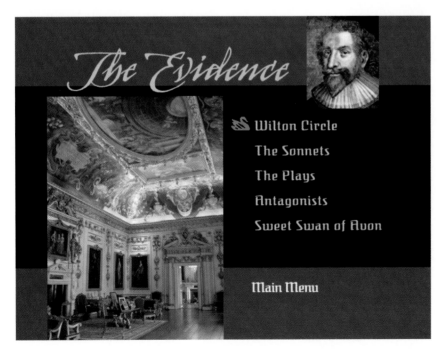

The small inset portrait in this submenu dissolves to still images of other portraits, scenes from Shakespeare plays, and pictures of Wilton House. Such an effect is created with video compositing techniques, described in Chapter 11.

All of the "Looking for Mary" menus have a low-volume soundtrack of 17th century lute and harpsichord music.

Personal Projects

Personal DVD projects can be anything from an independent feature movie to an archive of home movies. Personal projects are often most enjoyable because they allow you to experiment and have fun without worrying about getting approvals from clients. Personal projects are the perfect place to sharpen your DVD authoring skills, experiment with menu designs, and try various techniques for menu highlighting and menu transitions. They can include home movies, old-movie and digital photo archives, weddings, reunions, birthdays, anniversaries, family histories, video greeting cards, and more.

Home movies

Menu design doesn't have to be complex and time consuming. The *clean and simple approach* works well for almost any project. This example is a straightforward text approach listing the five movies included on the disc. The simple color scheme and textured background make the menu pleasant to look at and add a small degree of design awareness.

The highlight technique is the same as explained on page 122, in which the *unselected* area of the screen is shaded with a tint of color (black in this example), and the *selected* button is a brighter color because the invisible *hotspot* rectangular area that defines the button is assigned a *fill color* of *None*.

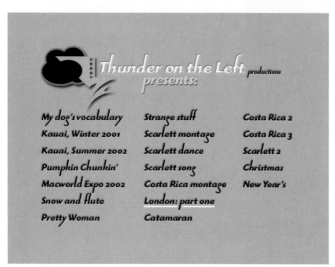

This example is a menu for a collection of nineteen different home movies. A text menu is a good solution for such menus since there's not a single theme to represent them all. When you design a text-heavy menu like this one, be extra careful to choose a font that is bold enough and not too small to be legible on a TV screen.

Each of these movies returns to this main menu when it has finished playing. A simplistic menu design approach such as this is ideal when you have many items to include and not much time to develop a menu system.

A menu with so many items listed needs strong alignment of the items to prevent confusion when navigating with a remote control. It's not ground-breaking design, but it's organized and easy to use—important considerations.

Vacation movies

Vacation movies are in grave danger of losing their reputation for being hideously boring. Edit long, boring scenes down to a minute or two, put transitions between the scenes, add a memorable music soundtrack, and suddenly home movies become works of art. DVD's ability to jump instantly to a scene of choice makes watching home movies a joy instead of a chore. And what better way to practice video editing, menu design, and DVD authoring.

The Nepal menu design conveys a feeling of fun with large oversized type and a whimsical typeface (Whimsy). The playful interaction of contrasting font sizes in the headline adds visual interest. When you use an unusual font such as Whimsy, remember that *contrast* makes a design interesting. If *all* the text in the menu were set in Whimsy, the design wouldn't be as appealing.

The background texture provides a touch of "old-world" flavor, and it adds some visual interest to what would otherwise be a large area of flat color.

Selected menu items are highlighted with a tint of yellow, designated in the DVD authoring software.

The "Main Menu" button is designed to stand out from the others, making it easy to see among so many buttons.

Old movie archives

Many families have reels of old 8mm home movies just lying around in a closet or attic gathering dust and rapidly deteriorating. The best way to preserve these fond memories forever is to get them digitized and burned onto a reliable, long-lasting DVD disc.

While you're at it, these new DVDs will be a lot more fun to watch if you create custom menus and place chapter markers at the beginnings of each new scene. This way, you can go back later and pick the segments you want to see, rather than sitting through the entire video or attempting to fast-forward. This menu allows the viewer to select specific scenes from a ninety-minute video.

One of the most effective menu design styles for a home movie is to use extracted still or motion images from the video itself. Look for special moments in the video that can be used in menus to visually summarize the feeling of a past event. This could be a short clip of you taking your first steps, wrestling with your dad, or opening gifts at a long-ago holiday celebration. In some cases, your decision to focus on a specific past event in the menu design can provide one of the most poignant moments on the DVD.

Birthdays and anniversaries

A special birthday or anniversary DVD can be a special and memorable gift for a friend or loved one.

This example shows the main menu for a DVD commemorating Roni's 40th birthday. A six-minute video retrospective is featured, combining a mix of old photographs and home movies to present a year-by-year look at the milestones and people in her life.

Also included on the birthday disc is a collection of over forty short video and audio greetings from friends or family members who couldn't make it to the celebration or just wanted to be included in the record.

Rounding out the DVD is a slideshow of still images featuring selected photos from her childhood.

The DVD format is uniquely suited to combine this collection of video and audio clips into a single presentation, making it a gift that will only become more precious over time.

Video greetings and digital postcards

Some people make DVDs of their vacations *after* they return home, but we say, "Why wait?" Now that DVD burners are an affordable feature in laptop computers, you can easily carry a complete video solution along with you wherever you go. With very little effort, you can take video clips from your DV camcorder, import them into your computer, and author a quick DVD from the road. The resulting disc is a high-quality video postcard that can be easily mailed to anyone who might be wondering just how much fun you're really having. A DVD postcard will let your friends get a glimpse of what they're missing while you're *still* on vacation.

Digital photo archives

The old family slideshow projector may be a thing of the past, but you can still put together a collection of photographs on DVD to entertain your friends, relatives, and any captive audience available.

DVD slideshows are much better than the projected versions of the past because you can play them nearly anywhere and never have to lug around a screen, slidetray, or projector. You can also get fancy and add a musical soundtrack to accompany your slideshow as it advances.

When designing a menu that leads to a slideshow, it's helpful to indicate the duration of the show so if you give the disc to someone else, they will have some idea of what they're in for.

DVD Menu Structure

Integrating content and navigation

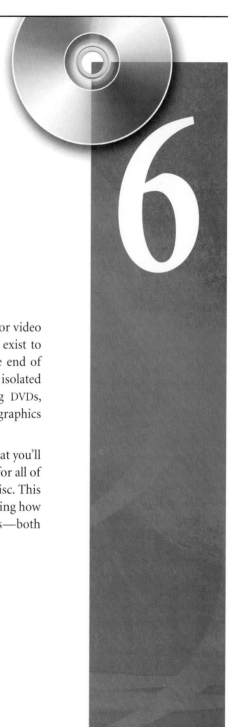

When you hear the term *DVD menu*, you may automatically think of a still image or video clip that displays navigation buttons. You're basically correct in that menus *do* exist to provide disc-wide navigation. On a simple, no-nonsense DVD, that may be the end of the explanation. But as a DVD author, you'll want to think past the notion of isolated navigation screens and consider the bigger picture. On the most interesting DVDs, navigational menus are but one part of an integrated series of video clips and graphics that collectively support the main video presentation.

If you plan to create visuals for DVD, you first need to understand the scope of what you'll be designing. As a menu designer, it will be your mission to create a unified look for all of the visual elements and ensure that they relate well to the video portion of the disc. This chapter will walk you through the structure of content, menus and buttons, showing how they integrate on a DVD. In addition, Chapters 7 to 11 also discuss various aspects—both aesthetic and technical—of menu design.

DVD Titles

*An individual video segment, such as a movie, is technically known as a **title**.*

*A group of titles is commonly known as a **VTS** or **Video Title Set**. A DVD can contain up to 99 different title sets.*

Content

There are two distinct kinds of visual information on a DVD disc: **content** and **menus.** Simply put, the *content* is the part that you want to watch, and the *menu* allows you to get there. This description might seem oversimplified a bit, but for the purposes of DVD design, it's important to understand the distinction.

Looking more closely, DVD content can be broken down into two types. The **main content** consists of the featured motion picture or video—the core material that compelled someone to create the disc in the first place. This is sometimes called the *title*.

Additional video segments, audio tracks, or still images are often called **bonus content** because they exist to support and provide illumination to the *main content*. Bonus content is one of the main reasons the DVD format is so popular with consumers.

*DVDs contain two kinds of visual information: **content** and **menus**. The content may be the main attraction, but menus play a vital role, providing structure and a way to navigate the content.*

DVD Content ⬤

DVD Menus ▢

Links ▪ ▪ ▪ ▪ ▪

Menu System

While *content* may be the main attraction of a DVD, **menus** play a vital supporting role by providing cohesion and structure to the entire production. A menu adds **interactivity** to the disc, a virtual tool that allows the viewer to explore and control the digital environment.

The visual element known as a *menu* is the central piece of the larger whole called a **menu system.** It's a network of video clips and still screens interspersed between the content segments. Think of a menu system as everything on a DVD that is *not* part of the main or bonus content. The menu system not only provides a means to get to the featured content, but also makes the journey entertaining. A lone *menu screen* is a functional necessity, but a well-designed *menu system* provides much more than interactivity—it infuses the disc with excitement and character.

Conceptualizing and building a menu system is no simple task. A complex system will contain still images, video clips, and audio tracks. It's the job of a **visual designer** to create each part of a menu system, making sure these elements work together seamlessly to support the video content on the disc.

A DVD might also contain informational screens that have more content than navigation. They are still considered part of the menu system.

Elements of a Menu System

We consider the following visual elements to be the building blocks of a DVD menu system. Not all discs will necessarily contain the full range shown here, but you'll probably recognize at least a few of these from watching commercial DVDs.

Navigation

The first and most obvious piece of the system is the **navigational menu,** or just plain **menu** itself. This is the cornerstone, the screen that contains buttons and text that link to video content or other menus.

From a visual standpoint, there are two kinds of navigational menus: those that move and those that don't. The moving kind is known as a **motion menu,** a short video loop that repeats in the background with navigation buttons superimposed in the foreground. A **still menu** also provides navigation, but there's no video involved—it's simply a static graphic background image.

Navigational menus can be divided into two groups, based on their role in the system. The **main menu** provides the primary navigation for a DVD—it's the central hub or control center for all the elements on the disc.

You can have only one *main menu* on a DVD, but there can be many lower-level **submenus,** each providing navigation and control to a particular sub-section of content. Every submenu links directly, or indirectly, back to the main menu.

The most interesting navigational menus are those that serve a dual purpose: Their primary function is to provide clear navigational choices, while reinforcing and expanding on the unique themes in the content portions.

This diagram illustrates one possible hierarchy of elements in a DVD menu system. Not every DVD needs to contain the full array shown here.

*The two base components are the **main video content** and the **main menu,** but both are integrated into the overall network of supporting elements. Other parts of the menu system are described on the following pages.*

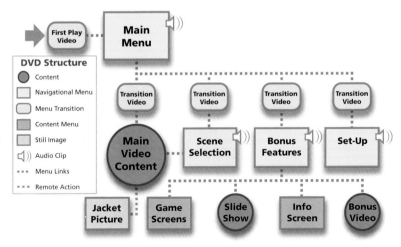

Menu Terms

*Terminology listed in the official DVD specification is often vague and at times downright confusing. For instance, a main menu is specified as the **title menu** or **system menu** (not to be confused with "menu system"). A submenu is curiously known as a **root menu.***

*It's helpful to recognize the official DVD naming conventions in case you happen to encounter them, but we still prefer to use more straight-forward terms such as **main menu** or **submenu** that more accurately describe common DVD functions.*

Transitions

Short video clips that support and enhance the navigational menu are called **menu transitions.** They act as buffers between segments to keep things flowing smoothly and provide visual integration between dissimilar elements. Menu transitions keep things lively, creating the illusion of forward movement throughout the content on the disc.

Most menu transitions are placed between *navigational menus* to avoid an abrupt change from one screen to another. These short video clips gracefully transport the viewer from the end of one menu to the start of another. In addition, they might also be used to smoothly transition between a menu and the beginning of a video content section. A transition can be an elaborately designed production, or it may appear as a simple cross-fade from one menu into another—it all depends upon the theme of the main video content.

A **seamless menu transition** creates the illusion that you're watching a continuous video stream from a menu to a content section (or menu to menu). Seamless transitions begin with the *last frame* of a still or motion menu, display a short (one to two second) video sequence, and end with the *first frame* of the selected content (or another menu).

Transitions are most effective when they are very brief, bridging the gap in two to three seconds. Any longer and they wear out their welcome and might be perceived as unnecessary obstacles to the selected content.

Another type of menu transition is an introductory video segment that appears as the first visual after the viewer puts a DVD in the player. This initial video, or **first play,** as it's called in authoring terms, eases the viewer into the *main menu*. It can also be a useful visual device to set the tone for both the menus and content on the disc, or to display a legal warning about copyrights. A DVD isn't required to begin with a video clip—the first play is often the *main menu*.

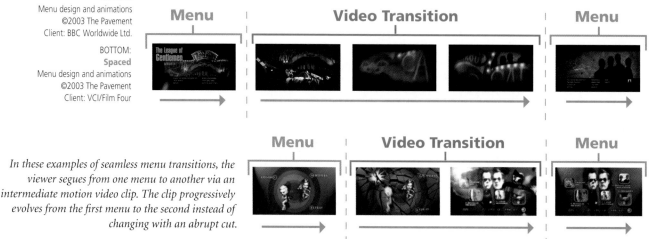

In these examples of seamless menu transitions, the viewer segues from one menu to another via an intermediate motion video clip. The clip progressively evolves from the first menu to the second instead of changing with an abrupt cut.

Content menus

Depending on their intended role, some elements in a menu system can be called **content menus** because they provide supplemental information—additional *content* that supports the feature video. These hybrid screens are regarded as *menus* since they contain navigation buttons that allow the viewer to move from one screen to another or return to the main menu.

Text screen: One popular type of content menu presents biographical text information about a movie's cast members, or instructions on how to use a particular function on the DVD. Although these screens could technically have a motion video in the background, it's best for text-heavy screens to appear as still graphics. A distracting background video makes the text less legible and can challenge a viewer's reading skills.

Jacket picture: You reach most screens in a menu system by selecting buttons on the main menu or a submenu. The exception is the **jacket picture,** which is only seen when you interrupt playback of a video track. If a disc has been authored to include this feature, press the "Stop" button on your player's remote to reveal the jacket picture. Press "Play" to make the jacket picture go away and resume the video from where you stopped it. Jacket pictures are always still images without a soundtrack or a hint of navigation. See pages 25 and 255 for more about jacket pictures.

Interactive games: You can also use *content menus* to create simple **interactive games** on a DVD. Most often these take the form of multiple choice challenges intended to entertain children. These games work just like regular menus, complete with buttons that link to other screens. Behind the curtain, it's all an elaborate collection of still images with an occasional video clip inserted to add a bit of movement.

Fatboy Slim, Big Beach Boutique 2
Menu design and animations
©2003 The Pavement
Client: Eagle Vision

Menus can be configured to present interactive games on a DVD, as shown in this example. Menu-based games are simple exercises in multiple choice, as compared to the more sophisticated Flash or Director-created challenges sometimes included in a DVD-ROM directory.

Content Menus and Audio

It's possible to associate audio with a series of still content menus, but we don't recommend it. A still content menu usually appears among a series of still screens which the viewer actively navigates with their remote arrow buttons.

A single audio track can only be assigned to a specific still menu—it can't span a series of separate screens. So if you associate an audio track with each menu in a series, it plays only as long as a menu is being viewed. When the viewer advances to the next menu, the current audio track stops and the next menu's audio begins to play from the beginning.

This isn't the kind of experience you want to impose upon your viewer. We think audio tracks should play seamlessly or not be included at all. Better to have an unobtrusive and silent series of menus than one with erratic and annoying audio playback.

Audio

The only non-visual component of a menu system is the **menu audio track,** but it greatly enhances the entire DVD experience. Navigation menus, transitions, still text screens, and games can all be accompanied by a soundtrack. This musical or vocal track provides added excitement to the experience, helping to keep the viewer engaged while making their button selection.

Most often the menu audio track is an instrumental music piece, either extracted from the main video content or carefully selected from an external source to blend with the overall personality of the menu system.

Audio tracks need to match the duration of the *motion menu* they support and loop in sync with the video. By contrast, a *still menu* is a single frame and will display indefinitely until a button is selected, so its associated audio track can be of any duration. Clips longer than 60 seconds are probably a waste of disc space since most viewers aren't going to linger long enough at a menu to listen to an entire full-length song.

By the same token, make sure your audio track is at a minimum of 30 to 60 seconds long so that it won't loop too often and annoy the viewer. A snappy ditty that sounds great the first time will quickly wear thin if it's looped one too many times.

Be aware of the volume settings for the audio track that accompanies your menu. Set it low enough so the viewer can tolerate the audio during their time spent with the menus. Blasting the viewer with a loud music track is just plain annoying and can be an obstacle to usability.

Just as you strive to maintain continuity between all of the visual elements in the menu system, make sure your audio tracks follow the same rule. Similar musical themes, seamless looping tracks, smooth transitions between clips, and consistent volume levels will help keep the audio integrated into the overall experience.

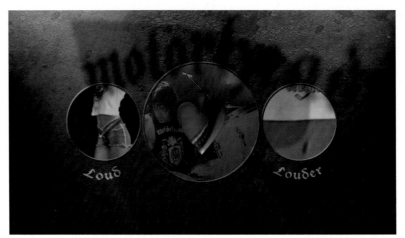

Motörhead 25 & Alive Boneshaker
Menu design and animations
©2003 The Pavement
Client: SPV

A DVD menu system should include an associated audio track to engage and entertain viewers while they make their button selections.

Menu Buttons

A navigational menu presents several options, letting viewers decide which parts of the DVD content they want to see. These options might be displayed in the form of words or as graphic elements, but in authoring lingo they're all known as **buttons.** Buttons might occupy a small area of the menu image or they may dominate the entire screen. A single DVD menu can contain up to 36 buttons, although most of the time that's way more than you'll need.

Under the hood, a DVD button exists as an invisible rectangular area, or **hotspot,** over the button artwork on the background menu. A hotspot contains information that defines what will happen when the button is activated, most often a link to another menu or content area. Hotspot areas must be square or rectangular—circles and polygons are not allowed within the DVD specification.

Standard button labels

A DVD button is meant to be selected, so it's important that the viewer recognizes a button as a navigational option. You can create that recognition in several ways, but buttons are most commonly identifiable if you use familiar terms to label them. Some of the **button labels** used on commercial DVDs have become standard terms associated with specific functions. The following is a list of the most common DVD button labels.

Play: When a viewer selects the "Play" button, he understands that a video segment will begin to play. If this button is located on the *main menu*, it indicates playback of the *main content* video, but if the term appears on a *submenu*, it indicates playback of a video clip relative to that menu.

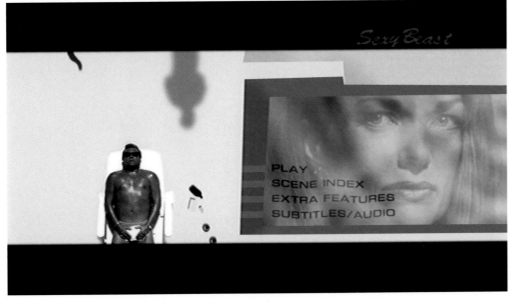

Sexy Beast
Menu design and animations
©2003 The Pavement
Client: VCI/Film Four

This main menu from the movie "Sexy Beast" presents a set of standard button label terms that are familiar to most DVD viewers. These four buttons link to all of the content areas contained on the disc.

Scene Selection: The *Scene Selection* button is most often found on the main menu. It takes the viewer to a submenu that presents options (buttons) to select a certain scene from within the main video.

Set-Up: If a viewer selects the *Set-Up* button, a submenu appears that contains options for customizing the playback of the DVD. This is usually where a viewer can activate subtitles, commentary, or soundtrack options before or during movie playback.

Resume: A *Resume* button is often placed on the set-up menu. This button allows a viewer to return to his original place in the video after he has interrupted video playback.

Bonus Features: Many DVDs have buttons called *Extras* or *Bonus Features* (or some combination of the two), indicating there is additional content to view beyond the main video. When a viewer selects this button, it takes her to a submenu containing links to the supplemental materials.

Main Menu: A standard part of most submenus, this button always returns the viewer to the main navigational menu screen. It's the DVD equivalent of the "Home" button found on web sites. It lets a viewer return to the starting point if they "get lost."

Previous Menu: On a disc with multiple menu levels, the *Previous Menu* button takes viewers up a level from the current submenu.

Back and Next: A series of still text screens or a photo slideshow requires *Back* and *Next* buttons to allow the viewer to navigate between the screens. These options are also recognizable in the form of an arrow icon— a left-pointing arrow for *Back* and a right-pointing arrow for *Next*.

Sexy Beast
Menu design and animations
©2003 The Pavement
Client: VCI/Film Four

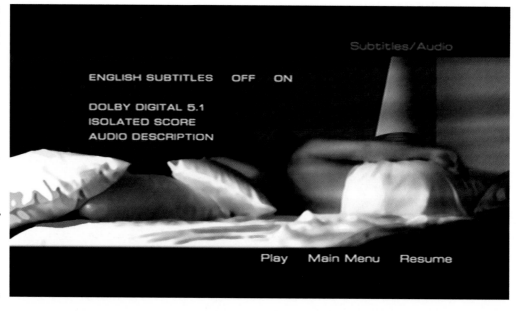

A submenu in the "Sexy Beast" menu system, this screen contains options to select subtitles and soundtracks. The "Resume" button returns a viewer to his original place in the video. As with most submenus, there is a button to return to the Main Menu.

Non-standard button labels

If you need to use a non-standard button label in your project, you must make sure the viewer quickly understands that it's part of the navigation.

One way to do this is with *proximity*, or grouping the odd button alongside others that *do* use the standard terms. When the viewer comes across this unfamiliar term, she'll understand by association that it's a navigational choice because it's surrounded by buttons she's already familiar with.

Button shapes

If text labels aren't sufficient, another quite obvious way to call attention a button is to make it *look* like a button. In other words, use a shape or object that will attract the eye—something that looks like it can be mechanically toggled or pressed. A beveled or embossed shape with a distinct outline or shadow is instantly recognized as a button.

A literal button shape might be just too obvious for a more sophisticated menu design, but there's always the option to use a graphic or icon image. Unlike an abstract shape, icon buttons are representative of some concept in the video, such as an image of a leaf used as a menu button on a DVD about a forest. On occasion, menu designers create DVD projects that use icons exclusively, without any text labels. This approach can be visually interesting, but icons that aren't accompanied by text may confuse the viewer and leave him scratching his head wondering where the heck to click next.

From a usability perspective, a combination of icons and text labels produces menus that are the easiest to understand and use.

Subpicture highlights

Using a standard button label or a recognizable shape are both good ways to ensure that the viewer quickly identifies your DVD's navigational options. But the most defining feature of DVD navigation is the **button highlight.** Highlights are displayed as contrasting single-color graphics, superimposed over or alongside a button that has been selected by the viewer. It disappears when the button is no longer selected. A highlight provides necessary feedback to the viewer, confirming their selection of a particular button.

DVD button highlights are the most common type of **subpicture overlay,** a graphic layer positioned over a still or motion menu background. A highlight will only be revealed within the boundary of a *hotspot*.

A highlight can be displayed as one of 16 colors assigned in an authoring application. Highlight colors can also have variable **contrast,** with 16 tranparency levels ranging from zero to 100 percent.

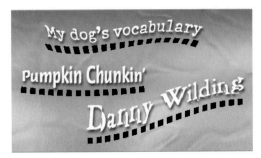

The black square shapes above are aliased and on a separate layer in Photoshop. When imported into DVD-authoring software, you can designate this layer as a subpicture and assign a "selected" color to the layer, then draw rectangular "hotspots" around the black shapes. In DVD format, the subpicture shapes are invisible until the button is selected.

Text buttons are effective in many situations, but there are times when you might want to insert a button that looks like it's clickable.

Each of the images above depicts a graphical button interface. Not only are they clearly labeled with text, but each contains a beveled shape that confirms its navigational role to the viewer.

A viewer should never be confused as to which button is highlighted. Use a highlight color that provides a distinct contrast between itself, the unselected buttons, and the menu background. Designers frequently use a bright color like yellow for highlights because the contrast is usually noticeable, but it doesn't apply in every case. Choose a contrasting highlight color that makes sense for the palette of your menu.

Each button highlight can be assigned up to three distinct modes of appearance.

Normal state: The button is not selected and the highlight remains invisible to the viewer.

Selected state: The viewer has used the player's remote arrow keys to select the button, which then will appear with a contrasting highlight color.

Activated state: This appears very briefly after the viewer has already selected a button and goes on to activate it by pushing the "enter" key on the remote. An activated button should highlight in a color that's different from the *selected state* highlight color.

A highlight often conforms to the shape of the button it overlays. A commonly used and effective method is to make the letters of a text label highlight when selected. This isn't your only option though—there are many other creative ways to highlight.

A highlight is a completely separate element from the menu background it overlays and it doesn't have to conform to the underlying text or button shapes. Possibilities for unique highlight shapes include underlines, arrows, bullets, or more complex pictographs.

Don't plan to create anything complex—subpictures are only *bitmap* graphics. Still, if you want to get creative, you can make each highlight display up to four colors when selected. Because of their low-color nature, menu highlights often have rough aliased edges that are most noticable in curved shapes and angles. This apparent lack of quality is no accident—the DVD specification requires subpictures to be low-color graphics, intended to take up less disc space.

Image-swap buttons

Aside from subpicture highlights, the other way to indicate the selection status of a button is to use an **image-swap.** Sometimes referred to as *active buttons* or *Photoshop-layer buttons,* this highlight method doesn't use subpictures. Instead, when an image-swap enabled button is selected, the entire menu background is swapped with another image.

The visual benefit is that the selected button graphic changes more dramatically than with a simple highlight. It's similar to the way some web sites use JavaScript to change the appearance of a button when it's moused-over by swapping the button image.

The difference is that DVD menus can't be sliced into pieces like web graphics. When the swap method is used on a DVD, the entire background has to change just to update the appearance of a single button graphic.

Hollywood DVDs rarely use this technique because it's noticeably slower than subpicture highlights and takes more time to create—each button needs three different menu graphics to display the various button states. Most importantly, menus that use *image swap buttons* can't be accompanied by audio because a single soundtrack can't span a range of menus. Audio can only be associated with individual highlight menus because image swapping is not required for this method.

Auto-activation

A DVD that will be used in an interactive public kiosk needs to navigate independently of the regular remote control functions. A kiosk DVD requires a viewer to make menu selections with a **touchscreen display.** Viewers use their fingers to physically touch the display to select buttons, instead of using a remote or mouse. An auto-activated button will carry out its pre-assigned function immediately after a viewer touches it. You'll need to set the buttons to **auto-activate** in your authoring software to make a touchscreen work with your DVD.

Touchscreen kiosks don't require a remote or mouse to make menu selections. A simple touch of the finger to the screen over the desired menu item "auto-activates" the button and initiates navigation to another section of a DVD.

Plan button routing to work intuitively with the arrow keys on a remote control.

Button routing

When you author a menu with multiple buttons, you need to determine the highlight order, or **button routing.** This describes the pre-set paths the viewer uses to cycle through the button list.

This may not be a concern for people watching the DVD on a computer—they can use their mouse to directly select any button they want. But the majority of people who watch the DVD on a set-top player will have to use the built-in remote features to navigate. This means that a viewer will cycle sequentially through the menu buttons using the remote's arrow keys, which have the options of *up*, *down*, *left*, or *right*.

To keep the navigation easy for the DVD viewer, avoid creating complicated button routes. Your button arrangement should be logical and easy to cycle through with the arrow keys. This isn't hard to accomplish when there are fewer buttons and they're stacked in a linear way, but if you've placed buttons in random locations around

your menu screen, you'll need to create a predictable selection sequence. The user will expect the *up* or *down* arrows to highlight the button directly above or below the one they're on. The left and right arrows should move the highlight to the next available button on either side of your current location.

A stack or row of buttons should have its routing set to **wrap,** which means the buttons are selected in a linear, circular path. For example, if the viewer uses the *down* arrow to arrive at the bottom button in a stack, another *down* click will move the highlight around to the top button and the path will repeat in a continuous loop. The same goes for the opposite direction or left and right. This circular path method avoids making the viewer "back out" of their selection and switch to the *up* arrow key.

Avoid *dead* clicks—every press of an arrow should move the highlight position. A click that does nothing will confuse the viewer.

Pay attention to your button routing—the order in which a set of buttons are highlighted by the arrow keys on a remote. Routing should be configured in a consistent, logical manner. Most DVD authoring software provides the tools necessary to establish a routing sequence.

*A **single column** uses only the "up" or "down" arrow keys on a DVD remote.*

*In a **multiple column design,** the routing options are more complex, making movement possible in all directions. Make sure the routing sequence is logical.*

Single column

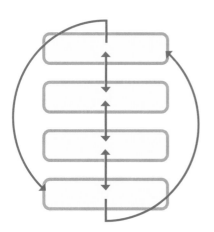

Multiple columns

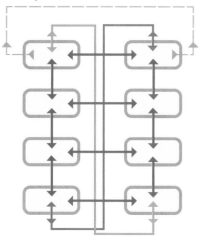

*The gray dotted line indicates where the left or right arrow should route—if a viewer is pressing the right arrow, at the end of the row it should circle around to select the first button **in the same row.***

Horizontal arrow buttons should always route horizontally, and vertical buttons vertically.

Menu Design Styles

Design directions for DVD menus

There's so much depth to the technical aspects of DVD that we could probably spend another two or three hundred pages explaining the gory details. Still, in the end, the story wouldn't be complete without a thorough explanation of *menu design*.

The DVD format is so technical that most literature written about it tends to treat menu design as something of an afterthought. However, from a designer's perspective, the visuals are the most important part—the underlying technical structure is simply the canvas on which to paint creative ideas.

In this chapter we'll take a break from the techno-speak, relax, and focus our attention squarely on menu design. We'll cover the basic visual concepts and stylistic directions most often used by designers to shape the viewer's experience.

Design Directions

Previous chapters focused on the practical characteristics of DVDs and described how they're put together and function. Important stuff to be sure, but structure is only part of the DVD story. Understanding how to make a menu system look great and communicate well is the other half of the equation.

As a visual medium, the ultimate success of any DVD rides on how well those visuals are presented. If we assume that the video on a DVD is worth watching, then the supporting menu system should be equally engaging to look at. That's where you come in.

A designer's job is to ensure that the menu system lives up to, or maybe even exceeds, the visual standards set by the main video content. Of course, that's easy to say, but often harder to achieve. You're probably wondering just where to start. While there isn't a magic formula for creating a perfect menu system, there are guidelines that will help point you in the right direction.

Authoring a DVD is not necessarily a simple task, but it does have the virtue of being a specific, sequential process, much like following a recipe. Menu design, on the other hand, is a far less structured undertaking that relies on intangibles like creativity and inspiration. Your inspiration can come from many sources, but the best place to start is with the video content on your DVD.

Content sets the tone

Video content will be the number one influence for the type of menu system you design. It sets the tone for the entire DVD presentation. Take the time to view the full video so you can learn how a typical viewer might feel when watching the movie. While you watch, take note of your own reactions. What kind of emotional response does it spark? Does it make you feel light-hearted, serious, humorous, or even sentimental? Is it factual or fanciful? Dark and edgy? Whatever the emotional tone, you'll need to consider how to incorporate this mood into your menu design.

The League of Gentlemen Series II
Menu design and animations
©2003 The Pavement
Client: BBC Worldwide Ltd.

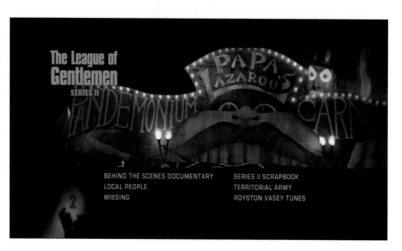

A DVD menu should establish the emotional tone for the entire viewing experience, preparing the viewer for what is to come within the movie presentation.

This menu for The League of Gentlemen *is dark, mysterious, and creepy—evoking a sense of foreboding in the viewer.*

User Experience

The kind of menus you create will be based on general themes from the video content, but filtered through your own unique creativity. The combination of a menu system and its associated video content makes a cumulative emotional impression on a viewer, known as the **user experience.**

To shape the user experience, a designer needs to establish a visual environment that prepares the viewer for the movie they are about to see. Within this environment, menus make the first impression. It's critical that the menus provide the right cues, so by the time the viewer begins to watch the video, he has already correctly sensed the emotional tone. For example, a dramatic thriller should be preceded by menus that have a serious and somewhat tense attitude. It wouldn't be appropriate to use humorous imagery and a comical soundtrack because they would give the wrong impression. You should make sure that your menus are consistent with the theme of the video and don't create any confusion for the viewer.

Menu Styles

A DVD user's experience will be formed by one of three basic menu styles: **utilitarian, derivative,** or **conceptual.** Each style reflects a different approach to menu design, but all are valid options depending upon the circumstances. In the following pages we describe these design directions and provide reasons why they might be appropriate for a project.

Fatboy Slim: Big Beach Boutique II
Menu design and animations
©2003 The Pavement
Client: Eagle Vision

These screens are part of the menu system for the Fatboy Slim: Big Beach Boutique II *DVD. The visuals work together to create a virtual carnival atmosphere for the viewer. There is a definite sense of place and purpose—a massive concert event at the beach. Without seeing a single frame of the video, the viewer is immersed in an exciting and fun experience.*

Utilitarian Menus

A utilitarian menu exists solely to provide navigation for the content on the DVD. In its most basic form, it displays little or no intent to acknowledge the disc's content either visually or conceptually. It's the straight-arrow personality among the menu crowd. Utilitarian designs have a no-nonsense attitude that can be appropriate for some DVDs and inadequate for others.

Utilitarian navigational screens are the very antithesis of the kind of menu systems that most designers would want to create. You might consider them to be boring, but they're not a complete waste of disc space. They do have their place and are sometimes the best choice for the job.

You will typically see utilitarian menus used in non-commercial projects such as home movies or corporate DVDs intended for internal use. They're not much to look at—often just text buttons on a single-color, motionless background with no sound. You can create utilitarian menus without heavy design expertise, but even the most austere menu should be a competent effort rather than an embarrassment to the main video.

Reasons for utilitarian menus

A DVD author may choose to go in this minimalist menu direction for a number of reasons, but it usually comes down to the factors of time, budget, effort, talent, and practicality — described in the points below.

Indifference: Sometimes the author just won't care about how the menus look— they'll cobble something together in the least amount of time possible. The author may consider the video content to be only thing of importance and could be uninformed about the value of well-designed menus.

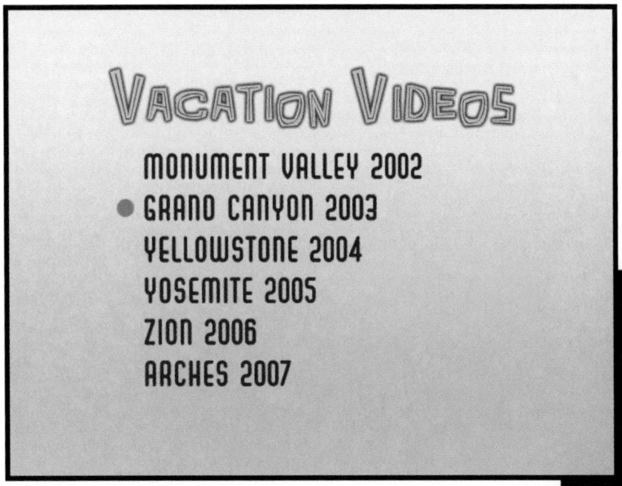

VACATION VIDEOS

MONUMENT VALLEY 2002
● GRAND CANYON 2003
YELLOWSTONE 2004
YOSEMITE 2005
ZION 2006
ARCHES 2007

Like the examples shown here, utilitarian menus aren't out to make a strong design statement. Their sole purpose is to provide a means to navigate the video content, but this doesn't mean that all design sensibilities should be thrown out the window. Like any other user interface, utilitarian menus should provide ease of use and adhere to basic design principles (see Chapter 9 for more on usability).

Family Greetings

David Rohr	Mary Jane Rohr
Matthew & Amy	▶ Julius Rohr 1
Fran Powers	Julius Rohr 2
Rich Powers	Joan Wren
Leonard & Alan Feit	Mike Wren
Rich Feit	Rachael Wren
Rich & Alan Feit	Chris Wren
Murray Ulin	Jacob Wren
Sheila Ulin	Josh Wren
Maureen Rodriguez	Caleb Wren
Annabelle Smith	Wrens/Rohrs Sing
Main Menu	*Next Menu*

Lack of skill: If a DVD author doesn't have the design skills necessary to produce visually interesting menus, he'll choose a bland, but safe path. This kind of author is aware that his menus could be more exciting, but he does his best with a limited aesthetic sensibility.

Limited time: A DVD project may be on a strict deadline with limited time for the author to spend on menu design. With the emphasis on the video content, the overall visual presentation may not be particularly important to the target audience.

Limited money: An underfunded author may also choose to make do with basic menus rather than lose money designing something more extravagant. She might be fully capable of doing more elaborate work, but the available budget doesn't justify the effort.

Practicality: Is it practical for an author to spend the time to create better menus if it really doesn't matter to the target audience? An elaborate menu system would be a waste of effort for some projects. If the video on a DVD is used for internal business purposes and will be seen by only a few people, there's no need for the menus to be anything more than utilitarian.

It's also possible you occasionally may want a single menu to contain a large number of navigation buttons. With so many elements on the menu, it can be impractical to squeeze in other decorative graphics. You're better off keeping it simple and clean.

Appropriateness: Utilitarian might be considered a non-style, but in some specific cases, it's the right approach for the audience involved. Certain situations demand a no-nonsense approach, such as the use of a DVD to display video evidence in a courtroom. The intended audience needs only to focus on the evidence at hand and wouldn't appreciate the distraction of colorful motion menus and a blaring musical soundtrack. For serious presentations, remember that less can be more.

Simple yet elegant

Just because a menu is simple doesn't mean it has to be *ugly*. If you are required to create a simple utilitarian navigation screen, don't let your apathy result in a bad design. Even the most basic utilitarian menu can benefit from a thoughtfully selected typeface and background color. The end result may not be spectacular, but it will at least be easy to use and perhaps even display a quiet elegance.

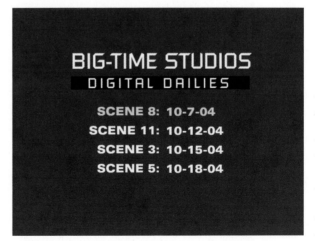

DVDs created for purely functional reasons don't need elaborate menu designs.

This example shows a simple interface to allow playback of dailies for a movie studio's internal use.

Derivative Menus

The most common type of professional menu design is the *derivative* style. This means that the majority of the graphic and video elements used in a menu composition have been lifted or *derived* from the main video content of the disc. There's a deliberate, literal connection between what you see in the menu system and the video itself. This can be in the form of still images, key motion clips, or audio extracted from a movie and used as the basis for a menu background.

Most Hollywood DVDs use derivative menus in some form. They function as a kind of preview for the video content and usually depict some of the most exciting or representative scenes. It's the most obvious way to ensure a meaningful connection between the menu system and the movie. The easiest way to obtain high-quality ingredients for your menus is to mine the source movie for material.

Derivative menu designs are found everywhere from the best Hollywood DVDs to the most humble home-grown productions. Many entry-level DVD applications allow you to incorporate derivative clips into your own menus, which often serve as motion backgrounds or buttons that display motion excerpts of the video content to which they link.

As a designer, you can make the most of the derivative style by doing your homework—carefully review the video content. Look for recurring themes throughout a movie and make a list. Take note of dominant imagery in the video, whether it's people, environments, or objects. Be on the lookout for action scenes with interesting movement. You may want to use these strong visual images in some part of your design composition.

Derivative menu designs borrow visual elements from the main DVD video, often arranging them in a new and interesting way. This type of design usually provides a preview of characters and themes from the main content.

As demonstrated in this menu from the 007 movie You Only Live Twice, *the visual imagery showcases the primary characters and places them within a context that is unmistakably derived from the mythos of James Bond.*

Any video clip worth watching will contain some kind of key incident that sums it all up. It could be the moment when the bride and groom share a wedding kiss. Maybe it's the part where Uncle Bob reels in a giant marlin—or an old tire. How about the scene with Billy sliding into home base? Any pivotal moment could provide an interesting basis for a derivative menu background.

Reasons to use derivative menus

There are several reasons why a derivative menu style may be the best choice for your DVD project. Derivative menus are so popular because it's hard to go wrong with visual elements from the main content. Take a look at these scenarios and see if any of them match your DVD design goals.

Consistency: Probably the best argument for derivative menu design is the consistency it provides for the DVD. The menus provide a glimpse of the interesting things a viewer will see in the main video presentation and unify the entire visual experience.

Convenience: A designer who chooses the derivative style will have no problem locating suitable material to include in her menu system. She won't need to look any further than the main video for all the pieces needed to construct menu layouts.

Cost: Using existing content from the main video is much less expensive and time-consuming than creating original graphics or video clips.

Visual interest: Assuming that the movie itself has appeal, menus that feature selected excerpts will be inherently interesting to the viewer. The best derivative menus take visual elements from a variety of characters and scenes. This new combination provides an interesting perspective on the soon-to-be familiar visual elements from a movie.

Derivative menus should tease the viewer with interesting scenes without giving too much away. Sure, you'll want to make your menus exciting, but don't use *all* the good parts from the video. Try to hold back the best parts and keep the surprises within the video where they belong.

Dinotopia
Menu design and animations
©2003 The Pavement
Client: VCI/Channel 4

In this menu from Dinotopia, *images of various dinosaurs have been extracted from the main content and are placed dominantly in this composition. The design leaves no doubt in the viewer's mind that this DVD has something to do with dinosaurs. The "chiseled in stone" text enhances the prehistoric theme.*

Conceptual Menus

The most ambitious design style for DVD is the **conceptual menu,** which requires more effort to create, but often provides the most interesting visual experience. This style consists of original visual elements conceptually and thematically related to the disc's content. The new imagery is suggestive of the overall character and spirit of the video, but unlike *derivative menus*, doesn't use extracted elements to get the point across. Conceptual-style visuals are unique to the menu system itself and you won't see them repeated anywhere in the video content.

Conceptual menus are both fun and challenging to create because you're not obliged to use pre-existing visuals. You can let your imagination run wild to create fresh imagery that expands and builds on the themes presented in the movie itself.

Because of the amount of effort, time, and money it can take to create original visuals for a conceptual menu system, you'll mainly see them in commercial Hollywood DVDs. Still, if you have the time, determination, and creative spark, you'll enjoy taking this direction for your own projects.

Menu environments

Conceptual menu systems can take many forms: from the simple to the painstakingly complex. One of the most interesting and complicated approaches is to create a virtual world that contains your DVD navigation. These worlds, or **menu environments,** use a visual metaphor of three-dimensional space in which the DVD viewer can move around and interact. Navigational buttons are made to appear as an integrated part of

Conceptual menu designs have a strong thematic connection to the content on the DVD, but don't necessarily reuse the visual imagery.

The DVD that accompanies this book uses a conceptual menu design to provide a unified theme to a largely dissimilar group of content elements.

the virtual scene, rather than superimposed over a background image. For example, if the environment is designed as the interior of a futuristic spacecraft, the menu buttons might be shown as 3D toggle switches arranged on a high-tech control panel.

For the environment to be effective, the scene should have some connection, however loose, to something present in the main video content. The spacecraft interior would only make sense if the movie had something to do with space travel, whether real or imagined. It could be a futuristic sci-fi movie complete with creepy aliens, or a present-day psychological thriller that has a character who only imagines that he can pilot a spaceship. In either case, DVD viewers would "get" the connection once they watch the movie.

These examples describe environments that have a more literal connection to a movie's plot, but a virtual scene doesn't necessarily have to reflect a specific place from the video—as long as the audience understands how the imagery relates to the video theme.

Conceptual menus can be based on 3D animations, still photographs, motion graphics, or even hand-drawn illustrations. The best DVD designs use a visual style that's well-matched with the content to inspire and delight the audience.

Each of these conceptual designs are virtual menu environments— fabricated worlds in which the navigation buttons are integrated into the virtual space itself.

Kansas Device Voice Drum
©2002 Song and Dance, Too, Inc.
Menu design and animations: Scott Long, MPL Media, Nashville

Finishing Post DVD Showreel 2002
© 2002 Finishing Post Television Facilities Ltd., U.K.

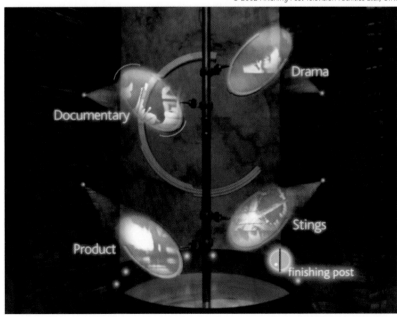

Reasons to use conceptual menus

Designers who are short on both time and money will probably avoid creating original conceptual menus, but for everyone else, there are compelling reasons to adopt this style.

Creativity: Of the three basic menu styles, the conceptual choice is often the most original, giving a designer more freedom to innovate.

Enhances perceived value: DVD viewers enjoy "fresh" visual images in their menus instead of recycled scenes from the video. Original imagery enhances the DVD's perceived value to the viewer.

Provide a theme: The conceptual design direction is an excellent way to establish a unified visual theme for a disc that contains a mix of unrelated video elements.

Suited to the content: An epic movie demands a menu system that equals its grandeur. Conceptual designs are usually the most complex and expansive, providing a good balance to blockbuster content.

Conceptual menu templates

Conceptual menus can show up where you'd least expect them. Although they're a far cry from the grand Hollywood 3D menu environments, the *generic menu templates* found in entry-level DVD authoring software are also considered conceptual designs. Generic menu templates are often theme-based and depict a representative scene such as a snowy landscape, a beach, a travel passport, or a birthday cake with candles—each one designed to coordinate with a distinct type of home movie.

Generic templates fall into the conceptual category because their main function is to suggest the themes in a home video, but they don't rely on extracted video elements. Sometimes a template will be so generic and abstract that it won't bring anything in particular to mind. Abstract textures or background shapes might help define a conceptual menu, but if the design is devoid of a specific theme, it's probably more of an enhanced *utilitarian* style.

These conceptual designs are menu templates from popular consumer DVD authoring applications. While neither is an original concept, both convey strong themes that relate nicely to the video content on the disc.

Combined Styles

We've described each of the three menu styles as they'd appear in their purest form, but in real-world practice, they're often used in combination.

For instance, a *utilitarian* menu will contain derivative elements if motion video clips are used as buttons. *Derivative* menus often display conceptual graphic elements that don't appear anywhere else in the movie. Even *conceptual* environments will integrate derivative video excerpts from the feature movie to reinforce the thematic connection. The combination of elements from each of these styles provides a designer with more creative options and often results in a better menu system.

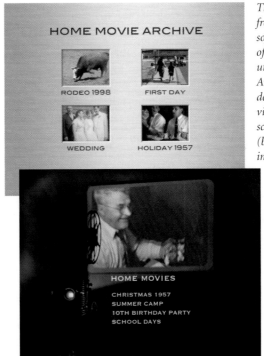

These examples of templates from entry-level DVD authoring software present combinations of menu styles. The mostly utilitarian "Home Movie Archive" (left) has some added derivative elements in the form of video thumbnails. The conceptual scene of an old movie projector (below) contains a derivative image from the video content.

Motörhead 25 & Alive Boneshaker
Menu design and animations
©2003 The Pavement
Client: SPV

The Motörhead DVD displays a menu system that is mainly conceptual in style, but mixes derivative video elements for added interest.

Original Menu Content

One of the most interesting options for DVD design is when a designer shoots original video specifically for use in his menus. Whether it portrays a familiar location presented in a unique, never-seen-before angle, or enlists the help of one of the actors in the movie, this combination of conceptual and derivative elements can make for DVDs that blur the boundaries between *menus* and *content*.

Familiar objects and props seen in a video can take center stage in the associated menu system to provide continuity and interesting visuals. A DVD with home movie footage of a boy learning how to ride his bike might have a menu that incorporates stylized photographs of the bicycle itself.

One of the best examples of this approach features one of the main video characters being aware of menu navigation and interacting with it. The character might appear to physically hold the buttons (as in the example below), provide some humorous instructions on how to use the DVD features, or could occasionally chide the viewer to hurry up and make a selection. In other cases, the character may not be aware of the navigation, but will still have original dialogue customized for the menu. He might do and say characteristic things while the viewer makes a button selection.

This menu design uses original footage of actors from the video content. The footage has been shot specifically for use in the menu so the actors are perceived to "participate" in the navigation process.

Menu Design Process

Helpful guidelines for DVD menu design

What does design really matter to members of the DVD-viewing public? Do they notice if the graphics are innovative and beautiful to behold? Can they tell the difference between motion or still menus? Is the pursuit of creative DVD design really worth the time, money, and effort?

These are all valid questions, considering most people rent or buy a DVD solely to watch the main video content and bonus features. Only designer-types or hard-core fans would *anticipate* watching a menu system. The rest of the viewing public won't even think about menus at all until the moment they first pop the disc into the player.

Faced with this reality, you may doubt that menu design has any impact at all. Not to worry—we're here to tell you that design is critical to the success of a DVD. This chapter provides some practical design guidelines, along with reasons why DVD design should matter to you, your clients, and the viewers.

Idea Generation

Whether you work with print, web, CD-ROM, or DVD, the creative process begins with inspiration. It's not so much the "lightning bolt out-of-the-blue" kind of inspiration where a fabulous idea just pops into your head from nowhere. It's more the type where ideas evolve organically from your own imagination, coupled with a solid understanding of the concept you're trying to get across. The imagination part may be instinctive, but *understanding* can only be gained through education. In DVD design, this means not only educating yourself about the content of the disc you're designing for, but also about the kinds of things other menu designers have already accomplished.

Educate yourself

If you're new to DVD, or interactive design in general, you'll need to get up to speed on the possibilities before trudging off into the menu design wilderness. Take the time to review a broad cross-section of DVD menu systems to get a feel for what other designers have done with the medium.

The best way to get started is to run down to your local video store and rent a stack of DVDs from all different categories. Dramas, comedies, sci-fi, animated features, concerts, documentaries—this broad selection of titles will provide inspiration and add to your visual vocabulary. Blockbuster movie titles are often the most interesting because they are more likely to have big budgets for extravagant menu systems, but they won't necessarily contain better designs than any other DVD.

Regardless of the kind of titles you review, be sure to take note of the features you admire, and also things you feel could have been better implemented. Pay attention to how well the menus relate to the movie itself and whether the designer took a *derivative*, *conceptual* or *utilitarian* design approach. See Chapter 7 for details about these design styles. You'll want to train yourself how to *think* like a menu designer. If you need suggestions for great DVD menus to review, see the sidebar for a short list of titles we admire for their creativity. Also, look at Chapter 12 for a showcase of amazing professional menus.

Preview the video

When you've seen what the professionals have done with DVD menu design, you'll be more than ready to create your own. Every DVD menu project should begin with a thorough review of the main video content. You'll want to watch the video all the way through at least once and take notes about the visuals (key characters, background scenery, video angles, and transitions). Most importantly, try to get a read on the emotional pulse of the project—What is the overall theme? How does this video make you feel? Specifically what did the designer do to make you, the viewer, feel this way?

Your role as designer is to interpret the imagery and themes of the video content, distilling it all into a single, unified menu system. The time you spend in video research will allow you to make informed decisions when it's time to select the visuals for your menus.

Method

People tend to have their own ways of doing things, so the process to create DVD menus is different for each designer. There's not really a *right* or *wrong* way to create, as long as the end result is effective. Still, if you want to save time and avoid frustration and mistakes along the way, we'll list a few suggestions that might help you with your menu design projects.

Research

As we mentioned earlier, the first step is to make sure you do enough research to become familiar with the subject matter of the video. It would be hard to create an appropriate menu system if you hadn't first seen the video. The best designer is informed and understands what he needs to communicate before he ever lifts a finger to create.

If you're new to DVD design, it's a good idea to do your homework before you begin your first project. You'll want to get a feel for the kinds of ideas other designers have already implemented on commercial DVDs.

Run down to your local video store, rent a handful of DVD titles and have yourself a great time studying the menus. And please, don't forget the popcorn!

Planning

Every DVD project should be carefully planned to determine how the content and menu sections will relate to each other within a common structure. This type of planning is known as **information architecture,** and the end result is typically an outline or flowchart that diagrams the way the various elements on the disc will connect. A flowchart is useful to a designer because it identifies all of the necessary menu screens and transitional videos for the DVD. In addition, the architecture will make the navigational options clear and allow the designer or authoring team to select appropriate button labels for each link. See Chapter 13 for more about planning and information architecture.

Project Reviews

Unless you only produce personal DVD projects, you will likely work with other people in the creative process. Whether it's a client or a full authoring team, you'll need to make sure what you do is compatible with the needs and interests of the others.

If your part is only menu design, it's important to collaborate early with the people who will be authoring the disc to ensure that you understand their requirements. Technical directives (such as NTSC or PAL, widescreen or fullscreen) need to be followed to the letter because any mistakes will be hard to fix at the end.

Get input from your client at each critical stage of design. Make sure they have given signed approval for every aspect of the menu system. Even smaller details like the choice of button labels or soundtrack music need client sign-off just as much as the menu graphics. Don't wait until the last minute to find out what they dislike.

Sketches and storyboards

Once the disc architecture has been set, the designer is free to create **thumbnail sketches** of her design ideas for both navigation and transitions. Simple hand-drawn sketches are a good way to quickly visualize a number of possible menu interface concepts before you begin the actual work in Photoshop.

When it comes to planning for complex motion graphics, menu transitions, or 3D animations, a designer needs to go beyond individual sketches and create **storyboards.** A storyboard is a sequential group of rough sketches that depict key frames of action in a proposed video or motion graphics segment. It serves as a reference for everyone involved in the project, as well as a way for the client to understand what is proposed and voice an opinion at an early stage. While a storyboard isn't a mandatory step, it's a good precaution to prepare one if you intend to incorporate motion menus and transitions into your DVD. It's better to work out the kinks on paper rather than in the thick of production.

Before you start on Photoshop work, first make rough thumbnail sketches of your menu concepts.

Create storyboards for your menu transitions (below) to work out the sequences before starting actual production work.

Design

If the sketches and storyboards are approved, the next step for the designer is to gather the necessary video, photographic, and sound assets and start to mold them into the various pieces of the menu system. Your menu designs will need to hold up under the weight of numerous expectations from your client, your audience, and yourself. To meet those expectations, read the tips on the following two pages.

You may want to initially create just a few representative mock-ups of a menu or animation section to show your client. This way you won't go too far with the finished designs until you know that everyone involved is happy with the way it's going.

Test your concepts

Don't wait until your menus are completely finished before you check their appearance on an ordinary interlaced scan television (instead of a computer screen). This is extremely important to determine if your intended layout, text sizes, and color selections are accurately represented outside of the computer they were created on.

At the point when there's something *real* to look at, it can also be helpful to begin limited usability testing and find out if the navigation makes sense to the average person. Any feedback you receive at this stage will allow you to make adjustments and move ahead with the rest of the menus and associated elements. You'll want to conduct a final round of usability testing after the authoring stage—before the DVD is committed to disc.

Effective Menu Design

Effective menu design is more than just a way to make things "look good." The visual aspects are important, but don't forget there are other factors that will determine the ultimate success of your designs. The following concepts are helpful guidelines to consider while you create your menus.

Unified experience

Try to develop a unified, cohesive DVD experience. That is, avoid stark differences between menu and video content. The viewers should feel that they're engaged in a single visual presentation that makes no stylistic distinction between a menu and the movie. Menus should introduce and echo the themes in the video content.

Simplicity

Remember to keep your menu compositions simple and don't overload them with too many buttons. Generally, four to six distinct button choices per menu is a manageable number and won't overwhelm the viewer with too much information at one time.

Ease of use

Keep your priorities straight and remind yourself that you need to create an interactive interface *first* and a killer visual design *second*. Practical considerations like legible text, logical button arrangement, and prominent selection highlights will make your menus easy to use and keep the viewer happy.

Accessibility

You should remember that some DVD viewers are hard of hearing or visually impaired. Design your menu artwork so that viewers with diminished vision will be able to identify the navigational choices. At the very least, keep your button labels and other menu text reasonably large.

If you design menu-based interactive games, don't rely on audio instructions alone. Make sure that play instructions are included as text or subtitles. At the authoring stage, you can make the content more accessible by including features like Closed Captions, subtitles, or a narrative soundtrack.

Speed

Menu transitions can easily wear out their welcome if they're just too darn long. Don't forget that a transition is only the journey— video and menus are the destinations. Viewers want to get to their destinations as quickly as possible, so make sure your transitions do their thing within about two seconds, and then politely go away.

Aesthetic appeal

Because DVD is such a visual medium, great-looking menus are a must. All viewers appreciate interesting, well-designed menu artwork. Graphics, text, and colors should be well-balanced and work well together, following proven design principles.

Quality

The notion of **quality** is one of those intangible concepts that greatly affects the viewer's experience, but is often hard to describe—"you just know it when you see it." By its very nature, DVD is a quality medium, widely applauded for delivering the best possible video picture to the masses.

For our purposes here, DVD quality can be achieved by three factors: expertise, effort, and control. *Expertise* implies that the author mastered the tools necessary to create a DVD. *Effort* means the designer/author took the time to do things right and went the extra mile to add features or perfect minute details. *Control* means the author used software and hardware tools that provided the necessary features to achieve his DVD goals.

Creativity

Viewers also enjoy menus with unique creative concepts. A clever theme or unique graphic arrangement provides a certain intellectual appeal and can possibly make viewers think about the movie in a different way.

Enhances perceived value

The concepts of quality, ease-of-use, and aesthetic appearance combine to influence the way a viewer feels about a particular DVD. When each of these things are done well, the menu system will be regarded as a unique asset and will enhance the disc's perceived value in the eyes of the viewer.

Stanford Creative Promo DVD
Menu design and animations
©2002 Ron Stanford
www.Stanford-Creative.com

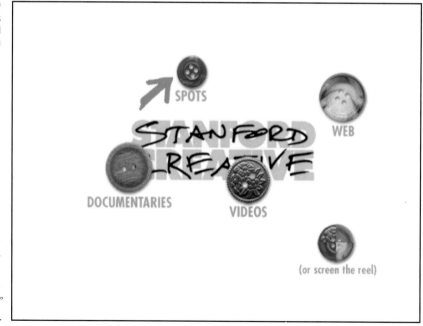

Viewers enjoy menu designs that go the extra mile to present DVD navigation in a clever way. This example from Stanford Creative literally uses "buttons" as the menu buttons.

Design principles

If you've never studied graphic design, it will benefit you to learn how the visual elements on a menu (or printed page) can be arranged for optimal communication. The concepts of *contrast, alignment, repetition,* and *proximity* are the foundation to construct solid, user-friendly menu compositions. Details on how these principles can enhance usability can be found in Chapter 9.

Visual hierarchy

Among all the design guidelines for DVD menus, pay extra close attention to the concept of **visual hierarchy,** a subset of the principle of "contrast." The basic premise of visual hierarchy is that the viewer won't know where to look first if all the elements on a screen are the same size and carry the same visual weight. For optimal comprehension and smooth visual flow, the size of objects in a menu should vary according to their overall importance. This is particularly important when there are numerous elements on a menu and potential for viewer confusion.

In practice, visual hierarchy means the largest graphic element conveys the most essential information and the other visuals appear progressively smaller according to their overall relevance to the viewer.

When you establish a visual hierarchy, you make it easier for the viewer to locate a starting point. The human eye naturally focuses first on the largest item and then tracks smaller items in descending order. For a typical menu, this means that you'll likely design so that the viewer's attention is first drawn to a representative visual that sets the tone and then to the navigational buttons. Other small elements will be noticed last.

While it's normal for viewers to focus first on the largest item on a screen, there are exceptions to this rule. A graphic that appears in the brightest, most contrasting color will draw the viewer's attention first, whether it's the largest or smallest element on a menu.

Design Reference

Are you new to graphic design? If so, some of the concepts mentioned here may sound completely foreign and even a bit intimidating.

It takes time to be a great designer, but if you want a friendly and easy-to-understand introduction to the basic concepts of graphic design, check out The Non-Designer's Design Book, second edition, *by Robin Williams. It's published by Peachpit Press.*

Sexy Beast
Menu design and animations
©2003 The Pavement
Client: VCI/Film Four

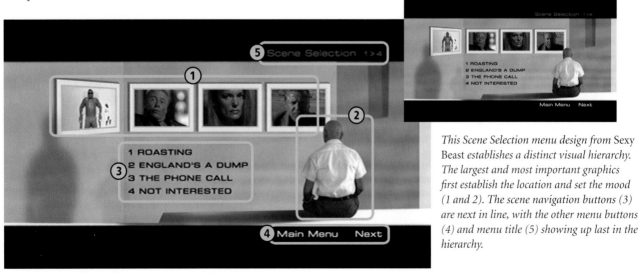

This Scene Selection menu design from Sexy Beast *establishes a distinct visual hierarchy. The largest and most important graphics first establish the location and set the mood (1 and 2). The scene navigation buttons (3) are next in line, with the other menu buttons (4) and menu title (5) showing up last in the hierarchy.*

Menu design guidelines

As you've seen, there's a lot to consider when creating DVD menus. To sum it all up, here's a list of the most important design guidelines.

▼ Understand that the main video content is the most important aspect of a DVD. The menu system exists only to support the video and make it look good.

▼ Create a unified experience. The menus should be an extension of the video—both visually and conceptually.

▼ Entice the users—make them excited about the feature video and provide visual incentive to explore the rest of the content.

▼ Provide easy, intuitive navigation to all the content on the disc. Don't make the viewer think about how to navigate.

▼ Keep the interface simple; don't clutter it with too many visual elements.

▼ Design your menus with prominent navigational choices. Viewers should be able to easily identify their options.

▼ Make sure your button highlights are easy to spot. Their colors should contrast well with the background image.

▼ Watch your speed—each video transition should execute within two seconds.

▼ Remember your priorities—functional interface first, clever design second.

▼ Don't assume anything about how the viewer will use the disc. Make the navigation work for all conceiveable situations.

▼ Include accessibility features whenever possible. Remember that some DVD viewers are hearing or vision impaired.

▼ Establish a visual hierarchy for your menus. The most important elements should be the largest.

▼ Follow established graphic design principles of contrast, alignment, repetition, and proximity.

▼ Preview the video content before you begin to design a menu system. You need to make *informed* design decisions.

▼ Plan your design approach before you attempt to produce the menus. Thumbnail sketches and storyboards are helpful ways to pre-conceptualize your plans.

▼ Test early and often. Find mistakes before it's too late in the development process.

DVD Menu Usability

Guidelines for good menu design

Usability refers to how easy it is for a user to interact with a system, and use it to complete a task, such as exploring a DVD's content effortlessly. Put another way, is the DVD simple explore? Users will likely judge your DVD menu designs more on usability than visual creativity and originality. No one cares how cool-looking the menu is if he can't find what he's looking for immediately.

Usability issues differ somewhat depending on the task being evaluated: navigating a DVD, a web site, a computer system, or a VCR, for example. But the basic concepts are universal: simplicity, effiiciency, consistency, effectiveness, and user satisfaction. These basic concepts may seem like ordinary common sense, but designers sometimes ignore common sense and go for the thrill of designing menus that are stunningly beautiful, original, and *not* as usable as they should be. Not to worry. It is possible to do both.

There can be a significant gap between how you think someone will interact with your DVD and how she actually does. An example of this is the true story of a guy who mailed his parents a home movie DVD he created. After a week or two he asked his mother how she liked the DVD. She responded with rave reviews, but he realized later they had only seen the main menu and had no clue there was anything more to it!

As DVD creators, we need to realize that many people are still unfamiliar with the basic functions of a DVD. Folks are used to stuffing a tape into the VCR and pressing "Play." By comparison, operating a DVD seems quite complex. Don't assume anything about the end user and their level of technical knowledge.

This chapter addresses the most common usability characteristics that affect DVD menus and suggests some usability guidelines to keep in mind. Even if you plan to stretch the envelope of menu design, the goal is consistent, intuitive design and ease of use.

Usability Starts with Understanding the Project

Assets: The content that's to be included in a DVD project, such as audio, video, slideshows, PDF files, and any other content that is to be included on the disc.

Evaluating a project's goals and *assets* and identifying a target audience will help you choose a design approach that will enhance the users' experience. A full understanding of the project and what it hopes to accomplish will also contribute to better usability.

When you develop a DVD project for a client, get as much information as possible about the target audience: age group, education and computer/technical experience levels, lifestyle and role-model preferences, and physical limitations that may require using techniques such as extra-larger type or subtitling. These are all factors that could influence your design thinking.

Think "user-centered" design

What passes as *usable* design can differ dramatically between projects and between users. Your responsibility as a designer goes beyond making menus that are good looking. You must also create menus to which a target audience can relate. An obvious example would be to compare a skateboarding DVD to a golf lesson DVD. Each target audience enjoys its own culture which is reflected graphically by their publications, labels, clothing, etc. Designing to the accepted or perceived preferences of a target group is referred to as *user-centered design*.

User-centered design also addresses the issue of simplicity vs. complexity in design and menu organization. The nature of a project and its audience will help determine how basic or complex the design should be. For instance, a DVD project that's meant to be used as a showcase of creative work by an advertising agency could justifiably go overboard with motion menus, entertaining transition menus, or unusual navigation design. But a project that's to be used as a no-nonsense training tool should be clear, concise, simple, and direct in its design.

This menu design for a DVD archive of old family photos and 1960s movie footage makes a blatant attempt to appeal to the family's youngest generation.

Most of your projects will fall somewhere between these two extremes, giving you plenty of opportunities to be creative and have fun. But always keep one fact in mind: most DVD users prefer clarity, familiarity, and convenience over creative menu behavior.

Basic Design Principles Can Improve Usability

If you approach menu design using the four basic design principles described in *The Non-Designer's Design Book*, by Robin Williams, your usability score will improve. Other books about design may list more complex principles or they may use other terms for similar concepts, but they generally agree that these are important things to consider. Our four principles of design are *contrast, repetition, alignment,* and *proximity.*

The principle of *contrast*

The term *contrast* applies to more than just the shades and tints of color. Elements on a page can also contrast in *size.* Or even in *style.* For example, if most of the elements in a design reflect a Victorian style, some other element in the design with a psychedelic '60s style will create contrast in the design. Contrast helps add *visual interest* to a design and *emphasis* to specific design elements. It also adds clarity to the visual hierarchy of a design.

Guideline for the use of contrast: For menu backgrounds or less important design elements, use darker, lower-contrast graphics to subdue visual impact and subordinate their importance to the design. For foreground elements, such as buttons and main visuals, use lighter, higher-contrast visuals to emphasize primary, focal-point elements.

Usability result: Contrast improves visual organization, reduces graphic clutter, and enhances menu clarity by emphasizing important elements.

continued . . .

The text colors in this menu do not have enough contrast to separate from the background.

This version of the menu uses text colors that have a lot of contrast with the background. To emphasize the contrast even more, a dark gradient darkens the right side of the background. Also, a shadow is placed directly behind the small text to create a soft, dark outline around the letters, making them pop from the background.

Design Tip

Design guidelines are useful as a safe starting point for design, or to help justify certain subjective design decisions, but they're not absolute or infallible in all design situations.

For that reason we prefer to call them "guidelines" rather than "rules."

Contrast Tip

The next time you drive down a busy street that has a lot of franchise restaurants, notice that a high percentage of them have signage that use dark colors for the background and lighter colors for the restaurant name. The few signs that have light backgrounds with dark lettering practically disappear in the maze of signage, visually overwhelmed by the others. Sometimes you need a lighter background, but be aware that contrast is often more effective when used in reverse mode (light foreground elements on a dark background).

The principle of *repetition*

The use of repetition is a powerful and useful design technique. You can repeat graphic elements in a single menu to reinforce their importance, or repeat elements among multiple menus to create visual continuity across menus and a sense of familiarity.

When you repeat colors, textures, font styles and sizes, or spatial relationships of design elements, you strengthen the unity of your design. You want your menus to seem familiar and predictable, rather than creative puzzles that slow down disc navigation.

Guideline for the use of repetition:

Repetition is a design tool that unifies multiple pages or screens, but it doesn't mean that everything looks the same! It simply means there are repetitive elements that tie the separate pieces together. Feel free to add variety within the unity.

Usability result: Repetition reinforces a sense of menu consistency, navigation simplicity, and thematic unity.

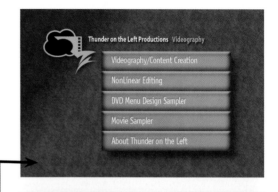

Each of the buttons in this menu links to a submenu that mimics the main menu in every respect except for the textual content. After one click a user can feel comfortable with the navigation.

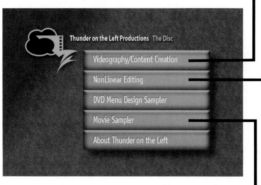

Any of these submenu buttons (the examples on the right) could link directly to content or to another submenu that provides more menu choices. Too many identical menus can be monotonous, so a variation of this design approach would be to use different background colors for each submenu hierarchy to help maintain user orientation and visual interest.

The principle of *alignment*

Navigation buttons should not be positioned arbitrarily in a menu design, but should have a visual connection to the other buttons in the menu. Alignment creates a strong cohesive unit of separate button elements. In addition to visually organizing the navigation buttons, alignment makes the buttons on a DVD remote controller predictable.

Guideline for the use of alignment: Use strong alignment of menu buttons to create a clean, organized interface.

Usability result: Strong alignment of navigation buttons makes remote control menu selection easy, intuitive, and predictable. Clear alignment helps avoid confusion about which menu button will be chosen when the user presses the left, right, up, or down key on a remote control or on a computer keyboard.

The principle of *proximity*

Proximity is another technique for organizing content. When items are close to each other, a relationship is implied. Items that are in close proximity are seen as one grouped unit rather than several separate items. Such visually organized information is easy to comprehend at a glance. Random information clutters the screen.

Guideline for the use of proximity: Use proximity to organize menu information.

Usability result: When a menu design needs to include lots of options and choices, proximity helps to visually organize the various elements into related groups that a user can comprehend quickly and easily.

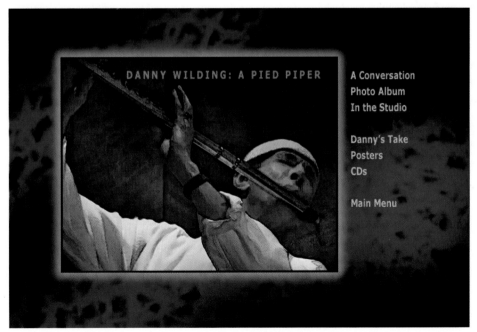

Simple vertical **alignment** of menu items (such as flush left) makes navigation with a DVD remote control easy. In this menu it's not immediately clear why certain items are grouped together, but **proximity** makes it obvious that items have been carefully chosen because they relate to each other in some way.

Characteristics that Enhance Usability

Usability can be subjective. Two different people using identical DVD discs may disagree about how usable they are due to personal preferences, past experience, or personal expectations. Apart from unpredictable personal preferences, there are a number of usability characteristics that should always be considered when you design DVD menus.

Some people make careers of studying and analyzing usability. You may find other lists of usability characteristics that differ slightly from this one, or they may use different terms, but you'll find there's a great deal of similarity in accepted usability concepts. Our list includes the concepts of *simplicity, consistency, forgiveness, accessibility, feedback, speed, customization, versatility,* and *predictability.*

Simplicity

Think *simplicity* when developing an organization and structure for a menu's information architecture. Careful organization of disc contents into a simple, easy-to-understand, and easy-to-navigate menu is one of the most important challenges of DVD design (see Chapter 13: Create a Plan).

Think twice about your target user before designing navigation that's overly clever and unique. It's better to have a simple, intuitive navigation than an inspired design that takes extra effort to figure out.

If a menu or submenu looks confusing or cluttered because it has too many options (buttons/links), simplify the number of choices by reorganizing the menu into a couple of separate menus.

Use as few menus as possible. If a DVD project's navigation and structure can be made clear and understandable using just one menu, and it provides easy access to all of the disc contents, be content with just one menu. Don't increase the number of menus if it's not necessary.

If several different menus have less than three navigation items each, consider combining the items into a single category. Fewer menus can result in easier navigation and better usability.

Arrange navigation links in horizontal and vertical rows to make navigation easier and more intuitive. TV remote controls and computer arrow keys require navigating up and down or left and right. Oddly positioned buttons in the menu design will force users to guess which button or key to use. See the examples on the following page.

The concept of simplicity doesn't mean you have to create *simple* designs. You can create visually rich and complex designs that are still uncluttered and well organized, and that clearly present the disc's content structure and available options.

Consistency

Be *consistent* in design throughout a DVD project. Use the same font style and color scheme for buttons and use a similar style of highlights on all menus to create a sense of familiarity and user-comfort. Even if some elements need to change from one menu to another, retain some similarity to reinforce the design's thematic unity. If a DVD project uses a design change for different areas of content, make it an obvious change rather than a subtle one.

Use consistent navigation organization, graphic style, and structure throughout a project to enhance usability.

Forgiveness

Navigation that seems simple and easy to you may be confusing to someone else. Go figure. But it's a fact and users are going to get lost or make mistakes and want to go back to a familiar place. *Forgiveness* is the usability concept that makes it easy for users to change their minds and return to a previous menu.

Always provide a button to return to the main menu or to the most recent menu. Most DVD authoring programs allow you to program a menu so that at any time you can press the *Return* key on a computer or the *Enter* button on a DVD remote control to access the main menu or any part of the disc content you want to specify.

This menu maintains consistency while allowing some variation of design in the submenus. In the main menu, above, the selected link, "Costa Rica," is indicated by showing a subpicture overlay highlight (the horizontal line). The Costa Rica submenu, above-right, uses the same basic design, but with a smaller text size for the buttons.

Submenu selections (shown in the example on the right) are highlighted in the same style and technique as the main menu. To make the small type more legible, the contrast was increased by adding black shapes behind each item.

The inclusion of a "Main Menu" button makes it almost impossible to get lost in the navigation. More complex submenus that are several levels removed from the main menu may choose to provide links to the most recently visited submenu rather than take the user all the way to the top menu level (the main menu).

Accessibility

Accessibility refers to the ease with which users can access disc features and content—the most frequently used features and content should be easiest to access.

Menu architecture and organization determine how easy it is to access all areas of the disc. In addition to designing links to different areas of content, consider providing *chapter markers* (see sidebar) throughout movies so users can skip ahead to specific scenes.

DVD authoring tools let you draw invisible rectangles (buttons) on top of menu graphics: these buttons can be programmed to jump to another menu, a video, or some other form of content on the disc.

If you make these rectangle buttons too small or try to make them fit too precisely around a graphic element, it can make selection of menu items using a mouse more difficult than necessary. Make selection buttons more accessible and easier to click by giving them a larger area that does not require expert aim and precision clicking.

Some people have physical challenges that can be aided with assistive technologies and techniques, such as audio navigation, subtitles, or extra-large type. To learn more about assistive technology visit www.Assistive.com.

Chapter markers
Chapter markers designate certain points in a video to which users can jump instantly when they activate a particular menu button. Most video editing software and DVD authoring applications provide tools to create chapter markers.

Usability Tip
Captions and subtitles are not just for people with hearing problems or for language translations. They're also a great solution for discs that may be shown in noisy bars, at rowdy parties, in quiet waiting rooms, or any place sound is an issue.

Feedback

Buttons in a DVD menu use *highlights* to make navigation selections obvious. The highlights also give the user *feedback* about what is happening or what is going to happen with the current menu selection.

Providing immediate feedback to user actions is important. When you select a button it should highlight or change in some way so users know the button is active and ready to be selected. Without this sort of feedback, users have to guess what's going to happen when they press the Enter key or select any button.

DVD authoring software enables you to program menu buttons with at least one highlighted state to provide feedback that a button has been *selected*. The user might select a button with either the controller buttons on a remote control, the arrow keys on a computer keyboard, or a mouse.

Some software lets you program buttons with an additional highlighted state to indicate the button is *active* (the user pressed the remote control's *Enter* button or the computer's *Return* key).

The official DVD specification provides these highlights as part of its *subpicture overlay* capability. However, because these built-in highlights are somewhat limited in color choices, a designer might occasionally choose to use another technique that can look more sophisticated, but is much slower (see the following page). But remember, users appreciate speed more than beauty.

Speed

In menu design, *speed* is a very good thing. Users want to access content, and a pause of several seconds can be annoying. There are two ways a DVD designer can affect the access speed:

1. The **type of menu highlight** used affects the speed of content access:

   ▼ DVD specifications provide a very fast built-in method (usually less than a quarter-second) of highlighting called *subpicture overlay* which lets you position an invisible button shape over a specific area that will highlight when selected. However, this type of built-in highlight provides limited color choices and visual effects.

   ▼ To have complete control over the appearance of a highlighted selection, you must create a completely new graphic for the entire menu. Use Photoshop to create any kind of highlight effect you can imagine, then use your DVD authoring software to instruct the invisible button overlay to *swap the menu graphic* when the button hotspot is selected. However, unlike a web page design in which a button can be a very small slice of the entire graphic, DVD menus cannot be sliced into smaller pieces. Instead, the *entire* menu graphic must be swapped to create a highlight effect, and this is *very slow* by comparison. This method requires one to two seconds to display the new menu graphic, which usually ruins the highlighting effect you tried to achieve, in addition to slowing down the speed of accessing content.

2. The **method of transition** used to jump between menus and to selected areas of content affects the access speed of your menu design:

   ▼ A *direct jump* to the selected content very fast. This is the simplest method to access content.

   ▼ You may decide to use *motion transitions* to bridge between menus or between a menu and the content to which it links. Motion transitions are short videos (usually with a duration of one to four seconds) that play when a menu button is activated. This creates a transition between the current menu and the next item (either another menu or content such as a movie). If your motion transition has a duration of four seconds, a user is forced to wait four extra seconds to access the selected content.

Transitions serve as thematic bridges between menus and video content. You'll often find them on entertainment DVDs, such as Hollywood movies.

Creative motion transitions are entertaining but may lose their appeal after the first showing when the user just wants to access an area of the disc. Your DVD authoring software may enable you to disable a transition menu after it plays once, allowing a direct jump to the selected content. Speedy menu response is important and makes for a better user experience.

Design motion transitions to have short durations of one to four seconds.

Customization

One of the advantages of DVD media is the potential to customize settings for certain features, such as choice of language, audio settings, captions, or even different camera angles. Include access to important customization options on the main menu, then ensure that all menus have an easy and quick link back to the main menu.

Versatility

Whenever possible, add versatility to content selection by offering optional ways to view or navigate the content. For instance, if a menu provides a link to an area that includes multiple subsections, provide users with Next and Previous navigation buttons so they don't have to return to the section's main menu to access the other content. Include chapter markers in lengthy movies so users can jump forward or back in the video.

Predictability

If you incorporate the other usability guidelines into your menu design, you automatically accomplish *predictability*.

Users feel comfortable if they know what to expect. A consistent design approach, along with simplicity, feedback, and forgiveness, gives a project a sense of predictability and familiarity.

Test Your Disc for Usability

As the creator of a DVD, you have an intimate understanding of a project's menu structure that may mislead you into thinking it's easier to use than it really is. Let average users test your DVD. Watch them try to use your menu and see how intuitive it is to them. Can they easily find all the content and move from section to section without getting lost or confused? Ask them to navigate to a specific section of content. If you've provided customization features such as audio language choices or language options for captions, ask them to change a customization setting to see if it's an easy task or confusing.

If you tell testers what to do or explain anything to them, you ruin the test and the opportunity to see design flaws exposed. Just watch and learn.

If testing shows any technical or navigational problems with the disc, you need to address whatever technical or design flaws are discovered by the testers.

When your project is ready for testing, burn it onto a *rewritable* DVD disc, either *DVD-RW* or *DVD+RW*, depending on the format supported by your DVD burner (see Chapter 1 for more information about disc formats). After testing you can erase the disc and use it over and over again for future tests, saving a lot of money on test DVD-R or DVD+R discs which can be burned only one time.

Graphics for TV Screens

Using Photoshop to create broadcast-safe menus

DVD menu design includes some idiosyncrasies that relate directly to the world of video technology. **Broadcast-safe** menus adhere to some basic TV technology guidelines to ensure that the menus will display correctly on a television.

Some DVD authoring applications include beautiful, professionally designed menu templates that are great for many projects, especially personal projects that you want to complete as quickly as possible. But other projects, such as those you may develop for clients, demand original, customized menus.

This chapter illustrates the use of Photoshop (about $600) or Photoshop Elements (about $100) to design *broadcast-safe* DVD menus.

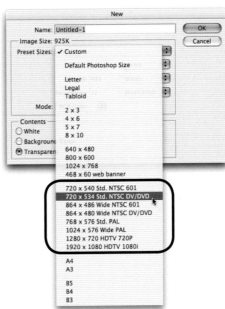

A sign of the times: when you create a new document in Photoshop or Photoshop Elements, notice that the "Preset Sizes" pop-up menu contains sizes specifically for video design.

Choose "720 x 534 Std. NTSC DV/DVD" to design a menu in the common 4:3 aspect ratio (fullscreen).

Choose "864 x 480 Wide NTSC DV/DVD" to design menus in the 16:9 aspect ratio (widescreen).

The "NTSC 601" options are for "D1" projects, a high quality video format used by some video professionals.

We predict future versions of Photoshop will include even more features for the coming tidal wave of video mavens.

Video Factors that Affect DVD Graphics

DVD menus that you create in an image editing program must conform to specific sizes and *aspect ratios* (proportions) that are determined by certain video specifications and standards. Some of the idiosyncrasies of DVD design stem from the fact that DVD discs and players are designed to work with televisions and TV technologies. For many designers, that's unfamiliar territory, so we'll touch on a bit of video background information and the main factors that directly affect how you'll design DVD menus.

NTSC and PAL video standards

When you open a movie in a nonlinear editor or when you use DVD-authoring software, you'll be asked to choose a video standard, either NTSC or PAL. Your choice will be based on the format that was used to capture the original video.

NTSC and PAL are the two video standards used around the world that define parameters for video creation and broadcast: **NTSC** (National Television Systems Committee) is the standard used in North America and Japan. **PAL** (Phase Alternating Line) is used in most of Europe.

We've included some information about the PAL format, but most of our comments relate to the NTSC format used in North America.

(One other standard, SECAM, is similar to PAL and is used in France and a few other countries, but it's a transmission-only standard that uses video produced in the PAL format.)

NTSC and PAL basics

When you design a DVD menu, you'll create a graphics file that uses either a *standard* aspect ratio or a *widescreen* aspect ratio. Usually you'll select an aspect ratio that matches the aspect ratio of the DVD's video content, although it's not mandatory from a technical standpoint.

▼ NTSC *standard* format has an aspect ratio of 4:3 (fullscreen format).

▼ NTSC *widescreen* format has an aspect ratio of 16:9 (widescreen format).

All graphics files that you create for DVD menus should have a resolution of 72 ppi (pixels per inch).

A video clip shot with a 4:3 aspect ratio (fullscreen).

A video clip shot with a 16:9 aspect ratio (widescreen).

Interlaced video

Another aspect of video that affects some menu-design decisions is **interlacing.** Both NTSC and PAL use *interlaced* scan lines to display video on a TV monitor.

Each frame of video on a TV screen is made of hundreds of horizontal scan lines (shown on the right in a simplified fashion). Interlacing is a technique in which the video scan lines are divided into two fields (odd and even numbered) and each field is alternately redrawn at a rate of 30 times per second on NTSC monitors (25 times per second on PAL monitors). The rapid redrawing of the two alternating fields creates the illusion of a steady and constant image on the screen. Only half of the image is displayed at once (the odd field or the even field), which can cause image quality problems such as *flickering.*

If your movie uses an editing technique known as **freeze frame** (where a single frame of video plays for a chosen duration), the single frame image might flicker because only half of the image has been captured by the single freeze frame and it needs to be **de-interlaced.** Video editing software often has a de-interlace filter you can apply to the image which fills in the missing scan lines with a duplicate of the existing scan lines. Or, you can open the freeze frame image in Photoshop and apply a de-interlace filter (go to the "Video" submenu of the Filters menu).

If you have some jerky video footage from an outside source, it may have been created using a **field dominance** that's different from the rest of your video clips. Field dominance determines which of the two interlaced fields (upper or lower) is displayed first. If necessary, use your video editing software

to reset a clip's field dominance. NTSC camcorders, players, TVs and other hardware usually use *Lower Field Dominance* (also referred to as *Field 1* or the *Even Field*).

An increasing number of video cameras, TVs, and DVD players can also accommodate **progressive** scanning, a video technology that displays all horizontal scan lines 60 times per second on NTSC TVs, 50 times per second on PAL TVs. Progressive scanning creates smoother video with fewer motion artifacts. Progressive-scan DVD players can display progressive video on digital HDTVs (high-definition TVs), but will display as interlaced video on analog TVs.

The example above simulates interlaced video scan lines and how they are divided into two fields (indicated by light and dark stripes). The two sets of fields are referred to as "upper" and "lower fields," or sometimes as "odd" and "even" fields or "Field 1" and Field 2." Because the two fields alternate, only half of the picture data is visible at any point in time.

This closeup of a single video frame shows the effects of interlacing, especially in areas where motion is more dramatic. It also gives an indication of how many horizontal scan lines are being redrawn every 1/30th of a second.

Quality-check Tip

Images can look dramatically different when viewed on both a computer monitor and a television screen. Many colors that you create on a computer cannot be displayed accurately on a TV screen. The differences in TV and computer display technologies can result in unwanted color shifts. Graphics that look good on your computer may show colors bleeding into adjacent pixels on a TV screen, or a flicker problem may be apparent that wasn't visible on the computer monitor. Try connecting a TV monitor to your computer so you can see problems such as color shifts, flicker, or unreadable type as soon as possible. Broadcast professionals use very expensive NTSC monitors, but even a small portable TV can be very helpful.

Square pixels vs. non-square pixels

Once you've chosen the aspect ratio for your DVD menu, you can create a new Photoshop file to design a DVD *static* menu. If you plan to use the standard NTSC aspect ratio of 4:3, you should size the new file to the standard DV/DVD size of 720 x 534 pixels.

But beware! TV screens use **non-square pixels.** While computers display images on a screen using square pixels, NTSC TVs use rectangular pixels that are taller than they are wide. PAL TVs use pixels that are wider than tall. An image that looks correct in Photoshop will be distorted on a TV screen unless you resize it prior to DVD authoring.

To compensate for the non-square pixel distortion (shown at bottom), you must squeeze the image vertically in Photoshop. Use the procedure described on the next page.

Pixels on a computer screen are square.

Pixels on an NTSC TV screen are non-square and tall.

Pixels on a PAL TV screen are non-square and wide.

This menu graphic was created in Photoshop using the standard DV/DVD size of 720 x 534 pixels. It's made of square pixels and looks correct on a computer monitor.

When the same menu graphic is displayed on an NTSC television screen (without first being vertically squeezed), the result is the undesirable effect shown to the left. NTSC's non-square, tall pixels stretch the graphic vertically out of proportion.

If the same graphic is displayed on a PAL television screen, PAL's non-square, wide pixels stretch the graphic horizontally (not shown).

The original graphic, created at 720 x 534 pixels.

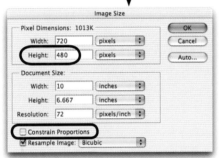

Resize the finished menu to a new height of 480 pixels in Photoshop's "Image Size" window to create a "squeezed" version of the image (shown below). Uncheck the "Constrain Proportions" checkbox so only the vertical aspect of the image is changed.

To design a menu that uses the standard NTSC 4:3 format: (720 x 534 pixels):

1. Use Photoshop to create an original graphics file, sized at 720 x 534 pixels, with a resolution of 72 pixels per inch. Choose the RGB Color Mode.

2. When you've finished the design work, resize the image file: From the Photoshop "Image" menu, choose "Size…" to open the "Image Size" window (shown left). Uncheck "Constrain Proportions."

3. Change the "Height" measurement from "534" to "480," then click OK. The image now appears vertically squeezed (bottom-left).

When this image is used on a DVD, it will display correctly on a non-square pixel device, such as a TV screen.

For NTSC DV/DVD widescreen menu designs (16:9 format), work in an original graphics file that is 864 x 480 pixels, then resize the final file to 720 x 480 pixels. Make sure the aspect ratio setting in your DVD authoring software is set to the 16:9 format and your widescreen menu will display correctly.

Pixel Tip

Some DVD authoring software may require that you create the master file of a graphic as a 640 x 480 pixel file. In such cases the software takes care of correctly resizing the graphic to compensate for non-square pixels. Check the manual for the software you're using.

This is the resized, squeezed graphic, displayed with square pixels on a computer monitor.

When shown on an NTSC monitor, NTSC's tall pixels make the squeezed graphic look correctly proportioned.

Avoid thin horizontal lines

A thin, horizontal line that falls completely within one horizontal scan line will appear to flicker on a TV screen because it is actually visible just half of the time. To be safe, make sure horizontal lines in your design are at least three pixels thick. If a line must be thin, anti-alias it so it will span more than one scan line.

Be wary of patterns

Small patterns such as small checkerboards, polka dots, or parallel lines can sometimes cause video to look jittery or vibrate. This may be caused by the interlaced scan lines or issues of creating colors on a computer that cannot be displayed properly on a TV screen.

The high contrast of adjacent colors that typically appears in patterns can also cause jittery video. The easiest solution is to avoid small patterns. Or apply anti-aliasing to small patterns to minimize flicker/jitter problems.

Small type and serif fonts

Small type is more readable on a computer monitor than a TV screen. In addition to the usual low-quality display of a TV screen, interlacing can cause havoc with very small type and with fonts that have thin serifs. Most menu designs should use fairly large, readable type. Type that is at least 20 points is a good place to start, although the design and readability of a particular font may allow you to use a smaller size or persuade you to use a larger size. In any case, always test your design and type choices on a TV monitor.

If the structure and organization of your menus requires so many text buttons that only small type will fit all the links to the page, rethink and reorganize your menus. For more about menu typography, see pages 166–167.

We used Adobe Photoshop Elements to create the layout below. The differences between using Photoshop and Photoshop Elements to design DVD menus are not critical. Photoshop Elements has an interface that is slightly different from Photoshop (meant to be more user-friendly for non-professional designers). Elements doesn't let you create folders (see page 165) in the Layers palette, and it doesn't include the soft-proofing capability described on page 163.

This menu design uses 96-point Spring for the main title font and 28-point Officina Sans for the smaller text. We chose the script Spring because its thin strokes are thick enough to avoid video problems. We chose the sans serif font, Officina Sans, because the even-weighted medium strokes and sans serif design are very legible and avoid any flicker problems that thin strokes or serifs sometimes create.

The small inset images are placed in the Photoshop file to help make design decisions and to show the client for approval of the menu design. In final production, the small images will be removed and scaled-down video clips will be positioned on top of the menu graphic in the video editing software to add motion to the menu.

Broadcast-safe colors

If you know that your DVD project will never be viewed on a TV screen, you don't need to worry about using *broadcast-safe* colors (or *title-safe* areas as discussed on page 164). Since that's unlikely, you need to remember that TV monitors use a different color space than computers.

When working on a personal project meant for friends and family, the broadcast-safe color issue may not be critically important to you. However, if you're producing a DVD for a client, you'll want the final product to look as professional as possible.

By using colors that fit within *broadcast-legal* limits, you can avoid quality problems such as *bleeding* (bright or oversaturated colors bleeding into adjacent pixels), or *clipping* (a form of video distortion in which colors

are eliminated and a loss of detail occurs). Non–broadcast-safe colors may create a *flicker* or *jitter* visual effect on the screen. Colors that are too bright can even create a hum in the video's audio track.

Because TV sets usually have the color saturation (color intensity) set at a high level, you should lower the saturation of bright colors in your menu graphics. Even muted colors look more saturated on a TV monitor. Reds and light yellows are known to be difficult—reds tend to bleed, and yellows can shift to unpleasant variations.

Subtle variations of dark colors are difficult to distinguish on a TV screen. Make sure your menu designs have enough contrast between hues and shades of color to be legible.

continued . . .

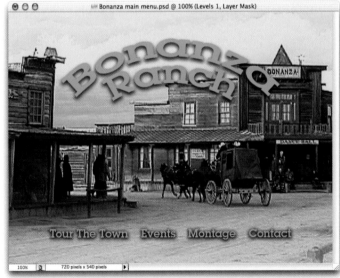

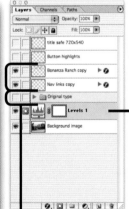

The colors have been brought to within the broadcast-safe range by creating a "New Adjustment Layer" and changing the "Output Levels," as shown on page 162.

We placed the original, editable text layers in a folder (shown above) named "Original type." If we need to alter the menu wording in the future we can open this folder and make text changes. We made copies of the original text layers (just above the folder) and then rasterized them (changed from editable text to pixels) in order to apply Photoshop's "NTSC Colors" filter to them, as described on the next page.

Convert colors to "NTSC color"

To bring colors within the color range of a TV monitor, Photoshop includes a video filter called "NTSC Colors." **To apply the filter to your design:**

1. Open a menu design in Photoshop.

2. From the "Filters" menu, choose "Video," then from the pop-up submenu, choose "NTSC Color."

Black and white levels for menu graphics

This filter usually ensures video-legal colors *except* for blacks and whites. The Photoshop file that contains your menu design should have its "Color Mode" set to "RGB" (red, green, blue).

On a computer monitor RGB colors are described as three sets of numbers ranging between 0 and 256 that define the amount of luminance of each of those three colors. When the RGB number is 255, 255, 255, all

three colors are combined at full strength to create *pure white* on the screen. When the luminance of each color is turned down to zero (0, 0, 0), the resulting color is *pure black*. Because neither of these colors are broadcast-safe, you need to bring the blacks and whites of your design into video-legal range.

For a **safe black** the RGB value is 16, 16, 16. For a **safe white** the RGB value is 235, 235, 235. In Photoshop you can create an adjustment layer that will bring those colors into this 16-to-235 range:

1. Open a menu design in Photoshop.

2. Select the layer whose values you want to adjust.

3. Click the "New Adjustment Layer" icon at the bottom of the "Layers" palette (circled below), then from the submenu, choose "Levels...."

4. In the "Levels" window (opposite page), set the "Output Levels" to 16 and 235, then click OK.

This menu design contains blacks that are too dark for video, and the white glare of the candles is too bright.

Click the icon circled to the right to create a "New Adjustment Layer" in which the black and white levels can easily be adjusted to broadcast-safe levels. Choose "Levels" from the pop-up menu.

After setting the new levels (as shown on the following page) you'll see the whites turn to a very light gray and the blacks turn to a very dark gray.

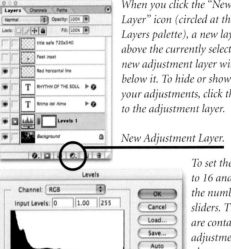

When you click the "New Adjustment Layer" icon (circled at the bottom of the Layers palette), a new layer appears just above the currently selected layer. This new adjustment layer will affect all layers below it. To hide or show the effects of your adjustments, click the "Eye" icon next to the adjustment layer.

New Adjustment Layer.

To set the Output Levels to 16 and 235, type in the numbers or drag the sliders. These settings are contained in the new adjustment layer shown above and can be changed or hidden at any time.

Soft-proof your design

If you don't have a TV monitor connected to your system to check colors, you can get an idea of how your adjustments look on a TV screen by using Photoshop's **soft-proofing.** A soft-proof is an on-screen preview of how a document's colors will look when output on a specific device, such as an NTSC monitor. Soft-proofing enables your computer to simulate the appearance of the selected color profile. The results can vary due to the quality of your monitor and the ambient light in your work area, but it's worth a look to better understand the shifts in color and saturation that occur. **To soft-proof your Photoshop file:**

1. Make sure "Proof Colors" is selected in the "View" menu.

2. From the "View" menu, choose "Proof Setup."

3. From the submenu, choose "Custom." In the "Proof Setup" window, shown right, choose the "NTSC (1953)" profile.

Photoshop's title bar identifies the soft-proof profile you've chosen.

Action-safe and title-safe areas

When you design a DVD menu and display it on a TV screen, approximately 10 percent of the outside edges of your design will either not be visible or may be distorted due to something TVs do called "overscan." To ensure that the important elements of your menu design remain visible and undistorted on a TV screen, place an *action-safe* and *title-safe* layer in your Photoshop file (shown below).

The outside lines show the action-safe area. Anything outside of this area may not show on a TV monitor.

The inside lines show the title-safe area. Keep menu text within this area to ensure that the text is visible, undistorted, and doesn't crowd the edge of the TV screen.

A Photoshop file (named TitleSafe.psd) of the title-safe area shown below is available in the DVD-ROM section of the DVD disc included with this book.

To place the title-safe graphic in a Photoshop file containing your menu design:

1. Open a 720 x 540 pixel menu design file you created in Photoshop.

2. Open the supplied "TitleSafe.psd" Photoshop file and find the layer named "Title Safe."

3. *Shift-drag* that layer from the "Layers" palette and drop it on top of your open design document.

Holding the Shift key while you drag causes the layer to be centered in your document when you release the mouse.

The "Title Safe Area" graphic will appear as a new layer in your document's "Layers" palette.

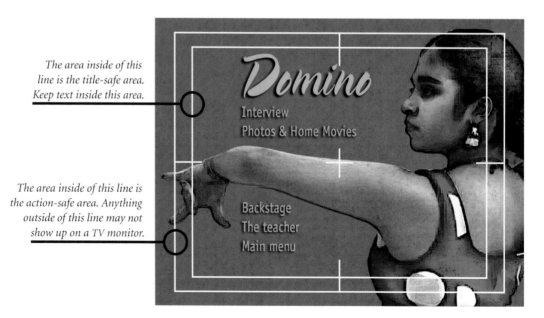

The area inside of this line is the title-safe area. Keep text inside this area.

The area inside of this line is the action-safe area. Anything outside of this line may not show up on a TV monitor.

The Power of Layers

Photoshop's powerful tools go beyond just image editing, sizing files, and saving them in the proper format. Use Photoshop's "Layers" palette to keep all your menu assets organized and together in one place. It can be very frustrating to search for a dozen different design files from a year ago.

Most DVD projects require a main menu and multiple submenus to organize and navigate to the various areas of content on the DVD disc. Each menu and submenu may contain multiple text items and graphic elements. Having each item on a layer is great for altering, manipulating, and experimenting with the design, but the number of layers can become overwhelming and difficult to navigate.

The "New Set" icon at the bottom of the "Layers" palette (the circled folder icon, below) lets you create folders in the Layers palette into which you can add new layers or drag existing ones.

In the example below, we created a "New Set" folder for the main menu and for each of the submenus. Set folders have "disclosure" triangles next to them so you can hide or show the collection of layers.

To place elements from another Photoshop file into your current Photoshop file, first open the other file. Then drag the Set Folder that contains the elements you want and drop it on top of the current open Photoshop document window. The entire Layer folder and all its contents will be automatically placed in the "Layers" palette of the current document.

Always keep your original layered Photoshop file in case you may need to make changes to your DVD project in the future.

Unfortunately, Photoshop Elements 2 does not include the Layers Folder feature.

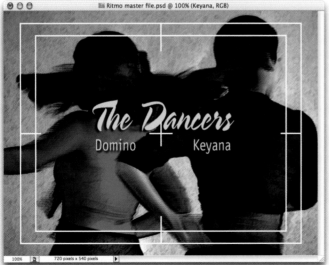

Click the folder icon to create what Photoshop calls a "new set," which is actually a new folder into which you can drag one or more layers. To hide or show a whole collection of layers, click the "eye" icon next to the folder. To toggle the visibility of the layers within a folder, click the small "disclosure" triangle next to the folder.

Typography for TV Screen Display

Some of the main issues concerning type legibility on a TV screen are mentioned on page 160. Following are some additional thoughts about typography and menu design, along with some examples.

Type styles

Generally speaking, sans serif fonts that have a uniform medium or heavy weight are more readable on a TV screen than fonts that have thin strokes. Large text can be readable in almost any font style as long as the serifs or thins strokes remain at least three pixels thick.

Open letterspacing also helps the legibility of text on a TV screen. Extra-tight letterspacing, especially when used on smaller type, is much harder to read.

Type sizes

In print design, very small type can look sophisticated and trendy. In a DVD menu it can look really ugly when shown on a TV screen. Lean towards the large size for type. Using all large type can look clunky and heavy-handed, so strive to use enough contrast of text sizes to add visual interest to your design.

Fancy, fun, goofy, grungy, and weird fonts are always harder to read than traditional fonts. Because they're less legible, be extra careful to make them a size that's easy to read. And use them sparingly for best effect. Of the thousands of fonts available, there are very few that can't work as long as they're large enough to avoid flicker problems.

This menu, designed for a presentation to be projected from a computer, uses smaller text—and more text on a single menu—than we would normally recommend. In this case we wanted one simple menu to link to 19 different videos. The font used for the menu buttons is ITC Highlander Bold Italic, sized at 20 points. The uniform weight of the font, the plain, solid color background, and the generous line spacing help ensure legibility, even at a rather small point size. Always test your font style and size choices on a TV monitor.

This design emphasizes the contrast between typographic elements. The size and boldness of the Corporate Compressed Regular title (size: 100 points) contrasts with the smaller, serifed font, ITC Lubalin Graph Book (size: 36 points). There's also plenty of color contrast between the text elements and the abstract textured background. Even though the Lubalin Graph font is in a fairly light weight, the large point size makes strokes and serifs thick enough to avoid the problems of thin lines in video.

More menu design tips

Be as brief as possible with the text on a menu. **Less text** on the screen makes a more appealing menu design that's easier to read. Text buttons don't have to be overly descriptive. A viewer needs to be able to scan the menu quickly to get a sense of the content and then make a selection without having to read descriptive copy.

It's possible you could have a situation in which you want a full page of text, such as a narrative text introduction to a slideshow you've included on the disc. In that case, you should still avoid giving the viewer too much to read on one screen by breaking the text into two or more visuals. You can also use your video editing software to create a video scrolling text page.

You'll also need a lot of text on the screen when you want to include credits and acknowledgments on your DVD. Keep in mind the readability problems caused by using type that is too small, and TV screen display issues, such as *interlacing*, that can cause small type to flicker.

Colorful text that looks beautiful on your computer's color monitor may not have enough **contrast** on a TV screen. Different colors (hues) positioned next to each other may actually be close to the same *value*. When viewed on a TV screen or by someone with color-blindness, this lack of contrast can hurt the menu's legibility. **To test your design for contrast,** convert it to grayscale mode in Photoshop. Check it for legibility and make sure the design elements are clear and easy to see.

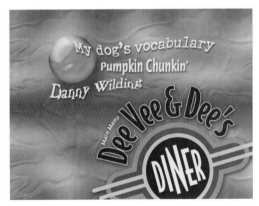

When the DVD disc contains an eclectic collection of material that's not related to any one theme, an abstract menu design is a good solution. For this disc, the unifying theme is the diner logo and the gradient background. The diverse font styles of the menu selections at the top are subtle hints that each movie is different and unrelated. The various elements were carefully sized to ensure that thin strokes were at least three pixels thick, including the yellow outline around the logo title (Dee Vee & Dee's).

To test a menu design for contrast, convert it to grayscale mode: From Photoshop's "Image" menu, choose "Mode," then from the submenu, choose "Grayscale." In this example the outside ring of the Diner logo doesn't have much contrast with the background, but it's not interfering with the overall visual comprehension of the design. You may assume that your disc will never be seen on a black-and-white TV screen, but remember that many people have varying degrees of color blindness that make low-contrast menus hard to read.

More Photoshop Tips

It seems you just never stop learning things about Photoshop. Here are a few extra tips that may be useful.

Annotate Photoshop files

Select the "Notes Tool," then click in a document to create notes to yourself or associates. If you have a microphone connected to your computer you can create audio notes. You can export the file as a PDF to share with associates who don't have Photoshop, and the Notes remain intact.

Double-click one of the little yellow note icons in the Photoshop or PDF document to read it. Click a note's close box in the upper-left corner (gray circle) to minimize it down to a "note" icon.

The Notes Tool and the Audio Annotation Tool.

Power Blur

The Blur tool, which can be used to touch-up graphics and smooth edges, is more versatile than many people realize. When you select the Blur tool, the "Mode" pop-up menu in the upper tool bar is set to "Normal," but you can get dramatically different results by changing the mode to "Lighten" or "Darken."

No blur applied.   *Lighten Mode.*   *Darken Mode.*

Stamp layers

As you work with multi-layered files, you may want to merge certain layers but keep the original layers intact. This procedure is called *stamping layers*. **To stamp layers in your file:**

1. Enable the visibility of layers whose content you want to copy into a target layer. The eyeball icon appears next to visible layers.

2. Select a target layer to which you want to transfer the contents of all visible layers, or create a new layer to use as the target layer.

3. Press Shift Control Alt E (Windows) or Shift Command Option E (Mac).

All the contents of the visible layers are now copied to the target layer (shown below as a layer named "Stamped"). Any text layers that are copied to the target layer are rasterized and no longer editable. But the original layers remain in the Layers palette untouched.

After stamping, the target layer (shown highlighted) contains the merged contents of all the layers whose visibility was enabled.

Designing with Motion Graphics

Use video compositing techniques to create motion menus

Motion graphics are literally *graphics in motion.* They are usually short clips of video (30 to 60 seconds in duration) that play repeatedly (called *looping*) to create special effects, set a mood, or add pizzazz and non-stop visual interest to a menu. They can also act as introductions to content or as transitions between menus or video tracks.

Motion graphics may be animated abstract shapes moving around on the screen, or a video clip playing in the background of a menu. They often appear as miniature video clips inset into a menu to provide video previews of content.

Including motion graphics in menu design enhances the entire DVD experience by adding entertainment to the navigation process. Motion menus aren't necessary—or even appropriate—for all projects. For instance, motion menus would look silly on a DVD developed for a lawyer who will use the disc to present evidence in a court room. But for most projects, motion graphics are one of DVD's most compelling features.

You can create them in animation and compositing software such as Adobe After Effects, Apple Shake, or Discreet Combustion. These specialized video compositing applications create amazing, high-quality effects and animations, but you can also create motion graphics using the video compositing capabilities that are built into NLE software such as Adobe Premiere or Apple Final Cut Pro.

Video Compositing

Video compositing techniques are used to create video special effects for both movies and *motion menus*. A motion menu usually is a short movie (30 to 60 seconds) that loops (repeats endlessly). The movie that is used as a menu can also contain other movies that have been resized to fit within the menu's viewable area.

Whether you use a specialized video compositing application, such as Adobe After Effects or Discreet Combustion, or use the compositing capabilities built into your NLE software, the basic techniques of compositing several video clips into one are similar.

To create basic video-composite effects for menu designs:

- ▼ **Place** the various elements of your menu design on separate video layers in your video compositing software (see the layer example on the following page).

- ▼ **Size** the various video clips that are to be included in your menu. To resize a video clip in video compositing software, drag a corner of the clip (shown below). Then move the resized clip to any position in the frame.

- ▼ **Export** the project as a single movie file (MPEG-2) and place it in your DVD authoring software as a *menu*.

The layer in the timeline that contains the river clip is above the layer containing the beach clip, hiding the visibility of the lower layer.

After the river scene clip is resized (as shown on the left), the beach scene on the lower layer shows through the transparent areas of the frame.

To resize a video clip in video compositing software, drag a corner of the clip inward towards the center. Items on lower layers will show through the empty areas of the frame, creating a composite video.

The power of video layers

Video compositing programs use *layers* (just like the blend mode found in Adobe Photoshop) to assemble separate video components into a single motion graphic. Items on each layer can be modified individually, and each layer's *blend mode* can be modified to affect how that layer blends with other layers.

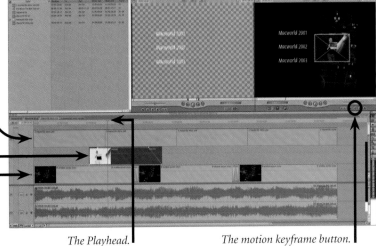

In Final Cut Pro, the Canvas window shows a preview of the composited video, consisting of the three transparent video layers in the timeline.

Video Track 3 contains text that will serve as buttons.

Video Track 2 contains a scaled-down video clip that fades in, then out.

Video Track 1 contains a scaled-down video clip that repeats.

Default black background color.

The Playhead.

The motion keyframe button.

The "checkerboard" pattern in the diagram above indicates transparent areas of the video frames. The tracks in the timeline that hold video clips are transparent unless completely covered by a video clip. These video clips have been scaled-down, leaving transparent areas for items on other tracks to show through.

Mini-videos for menus

Video compositing software lets you create effects such as multiple mini-videos on the screen at the same time, perfect for showing small previews of movies in a menu, or just to add visual interest to a design.

The motion menu on the right was created in Final Cut Pro using the techniques shown on this page and the previous page. It contains a movie background and three inset movies, all in motion.

To create mini-video clips for a menu:

1. In your video compositing software *place a video clip* on the the bottom video track (layer) in the timeline. The video on the bottom layer serves as the menu background (the beach scene in the example below).

2. Create a new video track (layer) in the timeline—on top of the background layer—and drag another video clip from the list of project assets to the new track, as shown on the left.

3. *Select* the new video track to show it in the preview window, and *drag the corner* of the clip toward the center of the screen until the clip is as small as you want (shown on the previous page).

4. *Drag the scaled-down clip* to the desired position in the menu composition.

5. *Repeat* this procedure for each video clip you want to place in the menu as a mini-video.

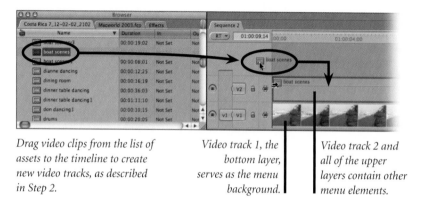

Drag video clips from the list of assets to the timeline to create new video tracks, as described in Step 2.

Video track 1, the bottom layer, serves as the menu background.

Video track 2 and all of the upper layers contain other menu elements.

Video Track 5: text.

Video Track 4: a scaled-down movie clip.

Video Track 3: a scaled-down movie clip.

Video Track 2: a scaled-down movie clip.

Video Track 1: a beach scene.

The composited video for the menu above consists of five video layers, as shown on the left. The video can be exported as an MPEG-2 movie file, then placed in DVD authoring software as a menu. DVD authoring software allows you to draw invisible button shapes on top of the three mini-video shapes and assign links to other movies on the DVD.

Keyframe animation

Video compositing enables you to *modify properties* (size, position, opacity, and rotation) of menu elements over a designated period of time. For instance, you can have a video clip or a graphic that's on a separate video track follow a path across the screen by setting **keyframes** at certain points along a timeline. A keyframe marks a point in the timeline at which a change in a video clip's property takes place.

In the example below, we want to make the center inset clip move to the top of the screen. We select the center clip and set a keyframe for it by clicking the "motion keyframe" button (circled below) in the NLE preview window.

Next we move the playhead forward five seconds in the timeline, drag the clip to a new position in the preview window, then set another keyframe for the new clip position.

During a preview playback, the center clip starts its move to the new position when the playhead in the timeline reaches the position of the first keyframe marker. Because we set the second keyframe five seconds beyond the first keyframe, the move will take five seconds to complete.

The *motion path* is indicated by a straight line (shown below-right). To alter the path or to create a smooth curve, click one of the points on the line and drag the path, creating a curved path.

You can create very complex paths if desired. You can also modify any other attributes, such as opacity. For example, a video clip could fade-in, fade-out, rotate, or change size as it travels along its path. You could also apply a filter to a clip over a period of time determined by the position of keyframes in the timeline. The possibilities are unlimited.

The playhead.　*The motion keyframe button.*

The example above shows the motion path created by setting two keyframes: one at the starting position, and another at the ending position, five seconds later in the timeline.

Compositing Software

Applications that *specialize* in video compositing and special effects enable you to create motion graphics that until recently were possible only for big-budget movies. These applications use *layers* to *composite* various video elements into a single visual, and *keyframes* to *modify* element properties at certain points in a timeline, such as changing an element's position, size, or opacity. Two examples of popular software programs for motion graphics and effects are **Adobe After Affects** and **Discreet Combustion.**

Adobe After Effects

After Effects, shown below, is very popular on both Mac and PC platforms. You can save motion graphics in several formats that your NLE software can import or that can be transcoded as an MPEG-2 file to import into your DVD authoring software.

The Composition window shows a preview of the composited layers.

The Project window contains all the imported assets of your project.

In addition to importing graphics into After Effects, you can create all sorts of graphic shapes and lines in the Composition window and animate them by modifying their properties in the timeline.

To modify the behavior of an item in the timeline, click the triangle to reveal the properties that can be modified. In this example, we set many keyframes to adjust the opacity of the lightning bolt between 100 and 0% to simulate lightning flashes on the "bolt" layer (circled on the right).

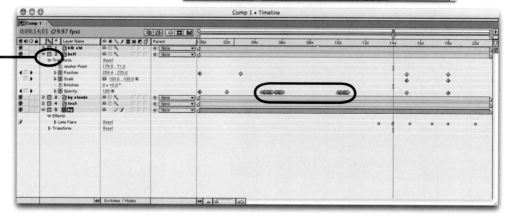

Discreet Combustion

Combustion is an award-winning paint, animation, and 3D-compositing application for graphic motion designers. The elegant interface, shown below, provides a wealth of professional tools, including a *particle* system for creating effects such as explosions, smoke, and snowstorms. The character generator lets you format and animate text.

In addition to the traditional layer-based view of the workspace, you can also view your project as a tree-type diagram, or in a schematic view which lets you visualize and organize your compositing project as a visual flowchart. The high-end features are too numerous to name. Combustion is fully compatible with other effects systems by Discreet, such as **flame** and **inferno,** and it also works well with industry-standard products like Adobe Illustrator and Adobe Photoshop.

Switch between Toolbar and Workspace modes.

Click the appropriate tab to the timeline and other settings and controls.

Player controls.

"Save" Tip

After you create a video animation or composite in After Effects or Combustion, save the sequence in an uncompressed video format. This will provide the highest-quality source file possible for encoding into the required MPEG-2 file format.

PC: *Choose "Video for Windows (AVI)" set to "no compression." Or "Save" using the "Animation" QuickTime setting if QuickTime is installed on your computer.*

Mac: *Save using the "Animation" QuickTime setting.*

Always size the final composited video to 720 x 480 pixels (NTSC) or 768 x 576 pixels (PAL).

Motion Graphics Examples

Although motion graphics are not *necessary* to provide menu navigation, they add entertainment and sophistication to menu design. The vast majority of entertainment DVDs include motion graphics. The examples shown here demonstrate some of the creative techniques used by other designers.

Look on the disc

The menu examples below are included on the DVD disc in the back of the book. Look for the "Menu Samples" button in the DVD's main menu.

The Complete Jam
Menu design and animations
©2003 The Pavement
Client: Universal Music

You Only Live Twice
©1967 Danjaq, LLC and United Artists Corporation. All Rights Reserved.
007 Gun Symbol Logo
©1962 Danjaq, LLC and United Artists Corporation. All Rights Reserved.
Artwork and Design ©2003 MGM Home Entertainment Inc. All Rights Reserved.

Menu design and animations:
designed by The Pavement

This James Bond DVD menu uses a dramatic fireball motion graphic for a transition to the selected movie.

A spontaneous, youth-culture look is achieved with this motion menu that has a flickering, jittery, motion.

David Blaine
Menu design and animations
©2003 The Pavement
Client: VCI/Channel 4

The David Blaine menu uses subtle motion for visual interest. Blaine, an incredible street magician, stands almost motionless, shuffling cards. At the end of the clip, an ace of spades floats down and across the screen.

Fatboy Slim:
Big Beach Boutique II
Menu design and animations
©2003 The Pavement
Client: Eagle Vision

This audio customization menu shows an enthusiastic, cheering crowd in the background with dramatic clouds crossing the sky. The motion is subtle but more interesting than a static image. The gray bars create a nice separation of the main menu buttons from the audio option buttons that are part of the motion graphic.

Motörhead 25 & Alive
Boneshaker
Menu design and animations
©2003 The Pavement
Client: SPV

The Motorhead main menu looks both mysterious and curious with a pendant swinging ominously in the middle circle and strange images fluttering in the outside shapes.

Royalty-Free Video Tip

Deadlines, budgets, and lack of expertise may prevent you from creating sophisticated 3D and textured motion graphics.

But you can buy the same royalty-free video clips that are available to professional editors and producers. High-quality clips are not bargain-priced, but they are still quite reasonable when you have a client with a deadline.

Explore these royalty-free web site resources:

www.12inchDesign.com

www.DigitalHotcakes.com

www.Eyewire.com

www.Veer.com

www.ArtBeats.com

Packaged Motion Graphics

Motion graphics often appear in the form of abstract or organic textures that undulate on the screen, creating a sense of motion that adds visual interest. These *motion textures* are sometimes combined with *masks* that enable you to include other video clips in combination with the texture video. Designers create texture videos using video compositing software, 3D-animation software, or a combination of the two. If you don't have the time or expertise to create your own motion graphics in Adobe After Effects, Discreet Combustion, or Apple Shake, there are a couple of other options available.

Royalty-free motion graphics

If you need a cool, rotating, 3D, organic shape to use as a menu background or as an element in your design, consider *buying* some motion graphics. There are many resources on the Internet for high-quality, **royalty-free** motion graphics. Royalty-free graphics and video clips can be purchased for a one-time buy-out price, then used as you want—with some restrictions, such as not being permitted to re-sell royalty-free items. Check with individual vendors for details of usage permissions. The sidebar tip on this page lists a few of our favorite stock-video sources, or you can search the web for "royalty-free video."

Software templates

Many of the most popular NLEs and DVD authoring programs include motion menu **templates** you can customize for your projects. For example, Apple iDVD (shown below) includes professionally designed theme templates that offer a variety of styles. In the iDVD example shown below, our custom video has been placed in an existing template. The background textures and shapes vibrate and tremble in a hip, contemporary style. The title text and button text is editable. Just drag a video clip into the *Drop Zone*, (shown below) and iDVD automatically creates a composite video menu.

The Drop Zone.

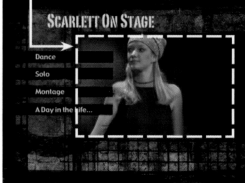

This is one of the motion menu templates that are included with iDVD, the Macintosh entry-level DVD authoring program.

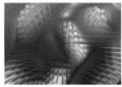

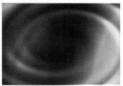

These motion graphics are from one of the Digital Hotcakes collections. Look in the ROM section of the DVD disc in this book for a Digital Hotcakes PDF brochure and a couple of royalty-free motion graphics video clips.

Section Three

DVD planning, encoding, authoring, testing, and duplication vs. replication

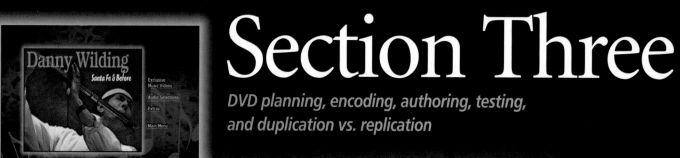

Danny Wilding, from the Danny Wilding DVD.

You might be a DVD designer if . . .

▼ you max out your credit card for an
MPEG-2 encoding card.

▼ you know what an MPEG-2 encoding card is.

▼ you know the Region Code for Kazakhstan.

▼ you care about GOPs, VOBs, and BUPs.

▼ you have a tattoo that says "Born to Mux."

Professional DVD Showcase

Menu design inspiration

Inspiration fuels the design process. It can originate anywhere: brainstorming sessions, casual conversations with friends, visual observations, random chance—practically any situation that exposes you to new ideas or fresh perspectives. A DVD designer's best intentional source of inspiration comes from observing what other designers have accomplished in their projects. Novice and veteran designers alike benefit from exposure to a wide variety of DVD menu styles. Observation is helpful not only to review visual techniques, but also to understand where your work stands in relation to the standards set by the pros.

This chapter provides a showcase for a broad range of DVD menu styles. All the examples have been designed for commercial purposes, which include movies, concerts, and self-promotion. The following pages exhibit menus in a variety of aspect ratios (proportions) due to the fact they were created by designers from many countries. These examples include fullscreen, widescreen, NTSC, and PAL. They'll give you insights not only to creative menu solutions, but also to the high level of sophisticated design awareness around the world.

We hope this amazing collection of menus inspires you, gets your creativity flowing, and most importantly, motivates you to show the world what *you* can do with DVD.

Our thanks to the companies and individuals who not only submitted examples, but jumped through hoops to obtain legal permissions for us to use them. Many other designers submitted menu designs, but were not able to obtain permission for reproduction in a book. Odd, isn't it, that although the DVDs are showing up on televisions and computers and web sites all over the world, we can't show them in a book.

Design: **Finishing Post**

Finishing Post is a London-based digital post production facility that caters to the television industry. Their stated philosophy is to provide the very best in editing, graphics, DVD authoring, and design. Judging from the quality of this DVD showreel (digital portfolio) they created, it's clear their work lives up to those standards.

Right from the beginning the viewer is immersed in a futuristic mechanical environment, complete with fanciful equipment and mysterious technology. This edgy, techno environment sets the tone for the showreel content, establishing the impression that Finishing Post is on the cutting edge.

Finishing Post DVD Showreel 2002

©2002 Finishing Post Television Facilities Ltd., U.K.

The opening animation sequence for the Finishing Post DVD presents a futuristic techno environment which turns out to be an elaborate setup to display the menu selections.

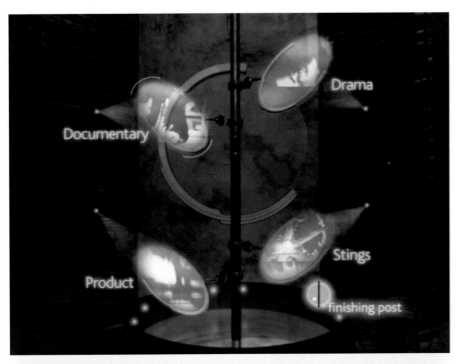

The refective mirrors in the futuristic device show motion images that are ghost-like and blurry. This creates a mysterious, out-of-the-ordinary menu environment that piques the viewer's curiosity about what lies beyond this menu.

The typography's glowing effect makes it an integral part of the visual, rather than just text on top of a menu.

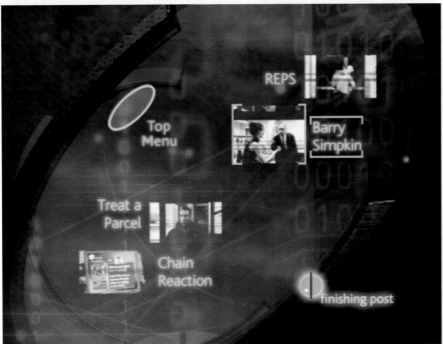

After the introduction animation is over, the main menu and submenus retain the techno theme with edgy graphics and interesting random background motion.

The use of brackets for highlights that appear around selected menu items adds an unexpected and stylish touch to this original design concept.

Design: **MPL Media**

Kansas: Device Voice Drum

The first concert DVD produced for the progressive-rock band Kansas was filmed in Atlanta in the summer of 2002. The disc not only contains an amazing concert performance by Kansas, it also provides interviews with band members and a "Making of DVD" featurette.

One particularly interesting design aspect of this disc is the use of two original 3D animation sequences. Designed by Wayne Lytle of Animusic, the animations depict a fanciful music device hovering in outer space and playing a broad array of instruments.

After the 2002 *Kansas: Device Voice Drum* concert was filmed and edited (by Reel to Real in Atlanta), Scott Long of MPL Media in Nashville was asked to create the DVD. While Long produces many DVD titles for a variety of clients, this experience was especially enjoyable because he also happens to be a long-time fan of Kansas and their music.

Since its release, *Device Voice Drum* has won the enthusiastic approval of Kansas fans and critics alike. Long agrees, adding "The concert and performance were right on."

While many DVD projects are a collaborative compromise between client and designer, the Kansas DVD was different in that Long enjoyed the full confidence of the band and was given free reign to create. Kansas drummer/manager Phil Ehart describes the extent of the creative process: "There was no collaboration, Scott put the menus together and I OK'd it." Long appreciated the group's trust in him, "Phil allows people to stretch out and do what they do best."

Long's creative freedom paid off for the *Device Voice Drum* DVD. It presents a unique conceptual menu environment that loosely combines elements of the concert footage and introductory animation with original artwork. Seamless transitions help the viewer perceive the menus as an integral part of an interactive virtual experience, rather than as independent video screens.

Kansas: Device Voice Drum
©2002 Song and Dance, Too, Inc.
Menu design and animations:
Scott Long, MPL Media, Nashville
(www.MPLmedia.com)
Introductory Animation: Wayne Lytle,
Animusic (www.Animusic.com)
Images courtesy of Phil Ehart and
Kansas: www.KansasBand.com

The Kansas: Device Voice Drum DVD displays a conceptual theme for its menus, placing them within a futuristic space station environment that just happens to double as a mechanical music device.

The introductory animation depicts a lone space station drifting above the Earth, but it still ties into the musical theme of the DVD because of the presence of a fantastic musical device that mimics the instruments of the band. Note the metallic truss in the background.

The menus themselves are designed as an extension to the same space station environment as seen in the introduction.

You'll notice that still more trusses appear in the background.

While the actual DVD concert has absolutely nothing to do with a space station, the menus still make sense because of the shared visual and thematic threads. The now familiar metal trusses appear here too—this time as part of the stage set. The truss element serves to visually tie the menus and content together in a subtle, yet logical way.

Design: **Marek Doszla**

Within the following paragraphs, Paris designer Marek Doszla shares his creative thoughts about DVD, After Effects, and his innovative demo reel.

"I work in a small, but talented and very creative studio in Paris, France called La F@KTORY which specializes in multimedia and digital video. After several years of creating CD-ROMs, we are continuing with the wonderful technology of DVD-Video. Personally, I use Apple DVD Studio Pro for DVD authoring and Adobe After Effects with Maxon Cinema 4D for DVD motion menus and CGI animations.

In my DVD demo reel entitled "After Effects Experiment," I show the awesome possibilities of After Effects in creating CGI animations only from stills and using numerous creative techniques and effects with plug-ins either from Adobe or a third-party such as Alias Maya PaintFX or The Foundry's Tinderbox.

When I came to design the motion menu for my DVD, I wanted to use a special technique for animation that is driven by "expressions," which is possible in After Effects, instead of animating by keyframes as usual. Expression is a little program that can create physical movements of, for example, a spring. I ended up with a looped motion menu in which five

Marek Doszla Showreel for La F@KTORY
A self-promotional DVD that showcases the designer's expertise with After Effects.

Marek Doszla
La F@ktory, Paris France
©2002 Marek Doszla
www.LaFaktory.com

springs are in endless movement dragging small videos representing the content. The expression parameters for each spring are different so the motion menu has a complex and attractive appeal.

My criteria for creating an effective DVD Menu design is derived from creating CD-ROMs. With each project, we had to invent a new layout and interactivity suited to the universe of the content. With the DVD we can do even much more, thanks to the technology of MPEG-2, which plays video at its best.

I try to author in such a way so that there is always a seamless transition after a menu button selection. Good planning and tricky programming with DVD Studio Pro can challenge "Hollywood authoring" on much more expensive systems.

I always render my After Effects composites in a lossless animation codec before encoding to MPEG-2, thus I get a sharp look on DVD.

Marek Doszla's demo DVD contains an eclectic and innovative mix of After Effects animation projects.

These two pages present designer Ron Stanford's first-hand account of his motivations and process for creating the clever Click on a Button *menus.*

Design: **Stanford Creative**

I really made this DVD from scratch, to use my mother's cooking jargon.

As a newly independent creative director, I was getting used to the unpredictable rhythm of the freelance work cycle. At the beginning of what turned out to be a three-week dry spell, I decided to learn how to make myself a DVD reel. Up to that time, my only experience with the medium had been as a renter.

I already had most of the assets, and that's as it should be; I've been producing documentaries and corporate films for almost thirty years and web sites for the last five.

I quickly learned that the great thing about DVDs is that you can include all kinds of material—and lots of it.

I felt that I should do more with my DVD than just present a catalog of video clips and web projects and that I should do for myself what I try to do for my clients: create a visual and aural environment that makes a viewer want to keep watching or clicking.

Then why all the buttons?

I just think that the way we in the interactive world use the word "button" is funny. Are we talking about a button on a radio?

Click on a Button
Stanford Creative Promo DVD
Menu design and animations
©2002 Ron Stanford
www.StanfordCreative.com

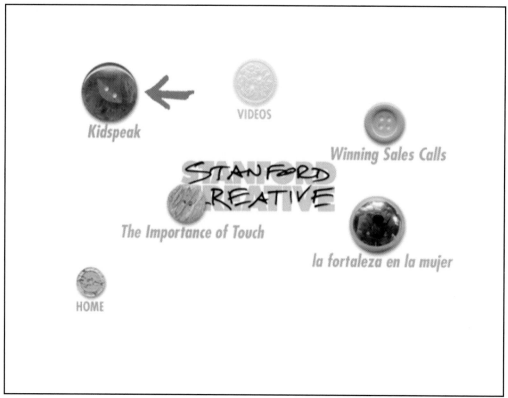

Designer Ron Stanford of Narberth, Pennsylvania, created this self-promotional DVD to showcase his interactive and video portfolio.

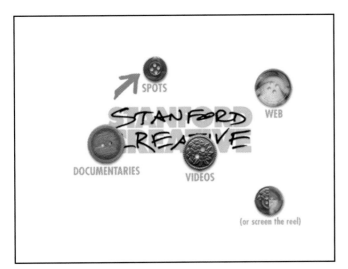

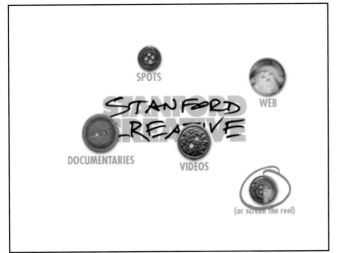

On a telephone? On a dashboard? In a missile silo? We want people to navigate around our CD-ROMs and web sites using these peculiar graphic inventions, whether they're cheesy, tasteful, 3D, beveled, blinking, spinning, embossed, or rolling over.

For some reason, in my mind's eye I've always pictured real buttons: shirt buttons, coat buttons, all kinds of clothing buttons. Unfortunately, I've never gotten the idea past my clients. So here was my chance.

How I made the DVD

It was really striking to me how easy it was to make a DVD. I thought that if I had to learn one more piece of software, my head would explode, but as it turned out, DVD Studio Pro was easy to learn, at least compared to the other programs I use regularly: Final Cut Pro, Photoshop, QuarkXpress, and Freeway (a Mac-only web tool). It was probably my struggles learning those programs that helped me with DVDSP. Plus I had a quick lesson from a video editor friend, Geoff Yoskin, and he taught me the basic concepts.

I probably use less than 5 percent of the program's capabilities, but then that's all I need right now. The DVD I made is simple. There's an introductory title frame with one big button. The title tells the viewer what to do. *Click on a Button.*

There's a brief animation that introduces my areas of work: videos, documentary, spots, web. I put this together entirely in Photoshop and Final Cut Pro. I just put a bunch of buttons on my scanner and pretty much used them all. I layered and mixed the music in Final Cut Pro using some cool jazzy sounds I downloaded from several talented musicians in Canada. They let me use the music free if I promised to give them some credit and maybe some paying work one day.

My menus all feature several buttons, each representing a different piece of film, video, or web work. You have several choices within a given category of work: video, documentary, spot, or web. The variety of motion picture work is represented by clips that last from 15 to 60 seconds. Of course, I could have included longer pieces, but I really wanted to leave the crowd wanting more.

As for the web work, I didn't link to my web sites from the DVD because I thought it just might not work technically for everyone. The web menu links to examples that show a succession of pages, each with a different music loop.

Click on a Button is supposed to be the opposite of mysterious. I don't want the viewer to have any question about what to do. I even put big honking arrows pointing to the buttons you can click on. In case there's any doubt, I always included the trusty old "back" and "home."

Design: **The Pavement**

The Pavement is an award-winning DVD production facility based in London, acclaimed for its creative designwork and innovative approach. As you can see by their own showreel interface and the many subsequent examples that follow, The Pavement clearly has a passion for the DVD medium and is driven to push the boundaries of the format in every way possible.

When asked to describe a few of The Pavement's guiding design principles for DVD, Creative director Lloyd Shaer comments: ". . . DVD design can be led by many factors, from the client and artist's involvement, budgets, time, region, to one's own principles.

Uppermost in our mind must be how the potential user/purchaser (age, fan base, etc) will navigate through the disc. Sometimes it is easy to forget that we are creating what is essentially a set of functional information screens that the user needs to easily understand and act on. So hopefully we can find a middle ground where creativity and function work together harmoniously.

[We try to] take each disc to the next level in development, whether this is a technical step or a design concept."

The following pages contain menus exclusively designed and produced by The Pavement. Many of them are accompanied by comments from The Pavement producers providing background context for that particular project. While the designs look great in print, you'll appreciate them even more in their intended DVD environment. See the DVD that accompanies this book for selected motion examples.

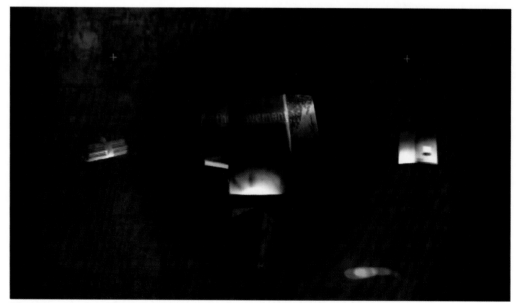

The Pavement Demo Reel
Menu design and animations
©2003 The Pavement
London, U.K.
www.The-Pavement.com

The main menu from The Pavement's Showreel DVD. You need to see it in motion to get the full impact of the concept. It's the kind of menu that makes you wonder, "How'd they do that?"

The Pavement wanted to create a showreel/demo disc that not only showed off their work, but also demonstrated what can be done with DVD in terms of both design and functionality. The disc uses what The Pavement refers to as "time-based navigation" (tbn) in the main menu.

Also presented are superb interactive examples of work, the traditional showreel, and hidden content (Easter eggs). If you hit "enter" upon seeing a flash frame of a green hand within the transition from Main Menu to Navigation, you can find The Pavement's "Head Hunter" game and get a chance to shoot the staff in a randomly programmed game.

Win this and unlock a video called "Behind the scenes at The Pavement."

Fatboy Slim: Big Beach Boutique II

The Pavement team heard that Fatboy Slim was planning his second free beach party and was keen to be involved if a DVD was going to be part of the production. This DVD was aimed at young, techno-dance–friendly consumers and has received excellent reviews.

The designs reflect the carnival nature of the massive event on Brighton Beach. The games were based on classic pier games with a Fatboy twist. Plenty of hidden extras and an excellent edit that captures the vibe of the day makes this a blinding DVD.

Fatboy Slim: Big Beach Boutique II
Menu design and animations
©2003 The Pavement
Client: Eagle Vision

The design above show a series of screens from one of the carnival-style interactive games. Each graphic is designed to provide feedback to the viewer, depicting a particular stage in the game.

Client perspective

In the words of the client, "The *Big Beach Boutique II* has been our biggest DVD project to date. We wanted to create a DVD with young, techno-friendly consumers in mind. I had seen the work that The Pavement had done on the Orbital and Underworld DVDs and was very impressed. We arranged an initial meeting to discuss the project and was amazing by the amount of forward planning they had already done. One of the Pavement's designers had even been down to Brighton the day before to take photographs for possible menu designs. Now that's what I call service!

Additional designs continue the graphic concept of looking at images through a coin-operated telescopic viewfinder—a theme established in the main menu (previous page).

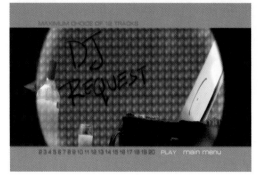

Fatboy Slim: Big Beach Boutique II
Menu design and animations
©2003 The Pavement
Client: Eagle Vision

The Pavement was also actively involved at the event on the day itself, filming extra footage specifically for the DVD.

I think the finished product is fantastic; the menu designs really represent the feel of the event. I especially like the way that some features are not necessarily obvious to the consumer; the fun is that things are hidden and surprises are to be found the more you explore around the disc.

I am very pleased with all the hard work that everyone at The Pavement has done."

Stephanie Lee, Eagle Vision

Dinotopia

The Pavement created an extensive menu system for the TV miniseries *Dinotopia*.

The Dinotopia menus rely heavily on derivative images from the video to present a strong and compelling theme.

The viewer is provided with a distinct sense of place and is reminded at every turn that dinosaurs are principle characters in the movie.

Dinotopia
Menu design and animations
©2003 The Pavement
Client: VCI/Channel 4

The designers have used convincing 3D menu environments to place the viewer squarely in the world of Dinotopia.

Many are motion menus that show 3D animated dinosaurs walking past and often curiously inspecting the navigation.

To further reinforce the sense of place, each menu features stone background textures or rock elements. Even the menu text seems to be chiseled in stone. Combined with the dinosaurs, this visual environment effectively portrays an ancient locale.

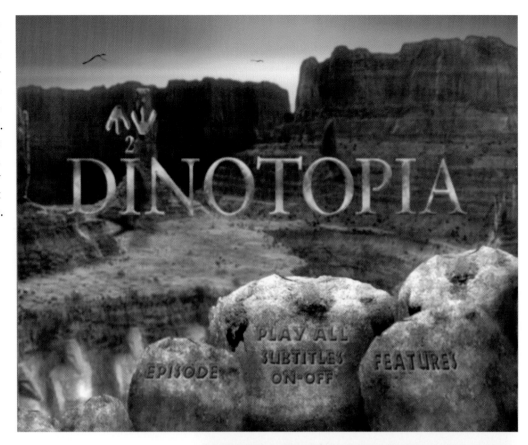

Additional menu screens for the Dinotopia series.

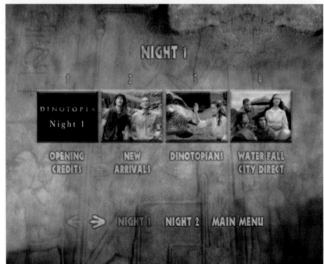

Dinotopia
Menu design and animations
©2003 The Pavement
Client: VCI/Channel 4

The *Special Features* screens are unified with the image of the ancient city illuminated by a towering beacon of light. While each menu is different in purpose and composition, the beacon image lets the viewer know they're all part of the same section.

Jamiroquai— Live in Verona

An excellent concert with Jay Kay in fine form. This entertaining DVD includes five multi-angle video tracks, hidden loop outs (hidden content that viewers try to find) and a 360° spin-cam (virtual 3D movie) on the DVD-ROM section of the disc. The menu composition is simple, allowing the video to dominate the screen and mesmerize the viewer.

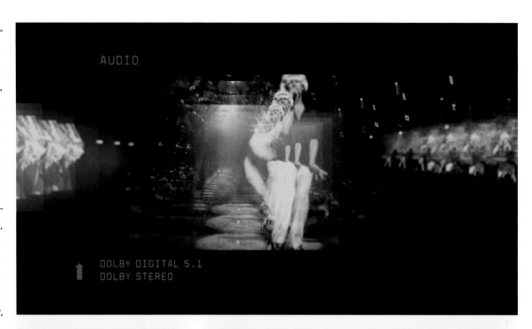

Jamiroquai—Live in Verona
Menu design and animations
©2003 The Pavement
Client: Sony Music

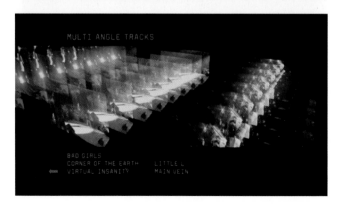

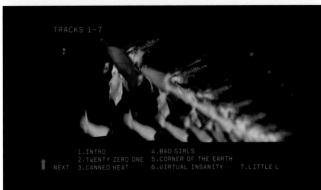

While the menus incorporate recognizable concert footage, their presentation is far from ordinary. At times the video appears to contain hundreds of repeating video frames that strobe in ever-changing patterns. This "larger-than-life" effect prepares the viewer for a dynamic concert performance.

The League of Gentlemen Series I

The Pavement has worked with *The League of Gentlemen* since their first DVD in 2000 when the League was considered a "cult" TV show. The first DVD won a DVD-A Award for Excellence that year.

The initial menu designs depict a rolling, nearly deserted landscape to underscore the remoteness of the fictional town of Royston Vasey in Northern England. The main menu presents an interesting image of an old stone building against a stark landscape. Its colorless, dreary appearance sets an ominous tone.

The League of Gentlemen Series I
Menu design and animations
©2003 The Pavement
Client: BBC Worldwide Ltd.

Subsequent menus focus on one of three primary topics: the location, the characters, or the cast. Each menu (except for Scene Selections), uses a single photographic or video image that represents some unique aspect of the series.

A series of content menus allows the viewer to become better acquainted with the various characters, their unique personality traits, and unusual quirks. Visuals taken from the video adeptly capture the essence of each character and the locale.

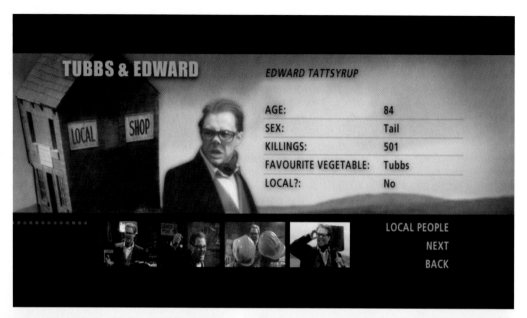

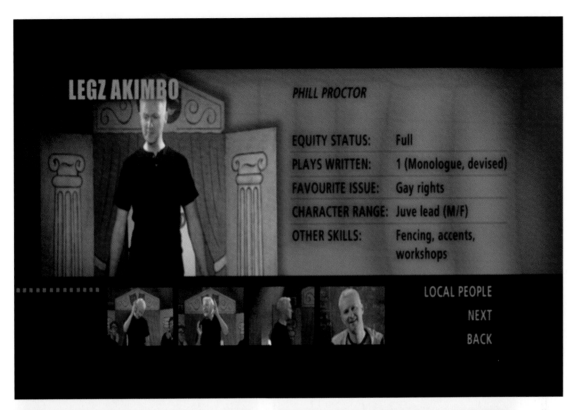

While the screens with character biographies each present a unique photographic image of a particular character, they are all visually connected. The same black bounding bars appear above and below the photos. Navigational buttons are consistently placed and a common type style is used throughout; these examples of repetition unify the various screens.

The League of Gentlemen Series II

As their popularity grew in the UK, the subsequent DVDs became more imaginative and complex with various Easter Eggs including a phone number access code in Series 2, unlocking the cast's own behind-the-scenes footage.

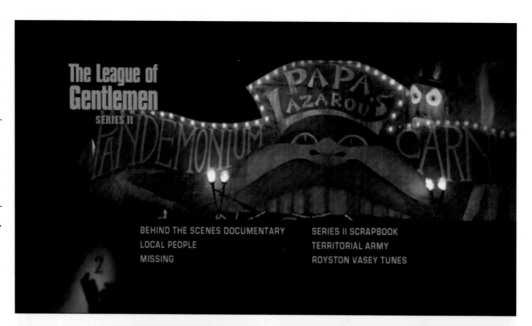

The League of Gentlemen Series II
Menu design and animations
©2003 The Pavement
Client: BBC Worldwide Ltd.

The black and white main menu depicts a creepy carnival fascade, but quickly transitions to color and reveals one of several submenu images.

Each submenu represents some unique aspect of the skewed world of the League of Gentlemen and its freakish inhabitants.

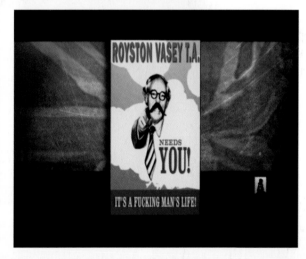

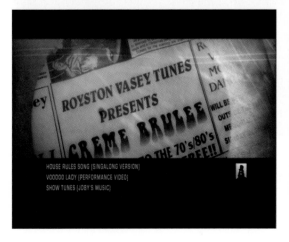

The League of Gentlemen Christmas Special

A series of rich, stylized menus and content screens support this Christmas-themed DVD for *The League of Gentlemen*.

The decrepit gothic-style designs evoke an uneasy feeling in the viewer—the sense that things are not quite right, despite the hint of holiday trimmings.

The presence of a hang-man game confirms the sinister tone suggested by the other menus. The game (shown left and below) required over 100 screens and advanced authoring to display all possible combinations.

The League of Gentlemen Christmas Special
Menu design and animations
©2003 The Pavement
Client: BBC Worldwide Ltd.

Motörhead 25 & Alive: Boneshaker

This title came with all the bells and whistles and hot pants. The band's 25th anniversary concert is presented in surround sound with Easter eggs* liberally scattered. These included sound bites of what Lemmy really thinks—never one to hold back his opinions.

Easter eggs are hidden treats; in software, the treats are digital.

The Pavement shot all the footage used in the menu designs, much to the enjoyment of the crew. They also worked extensively with Motörhead's most devoted fans, who contributed rarely seen photos, extensive creative concepts, and memorabilia, guaranteeing the title's popularity with fans worldwide.

Motörhead 25 & Alive: Boneshaker
Menu design and animations
©2003 The Pavement
Client: SPV

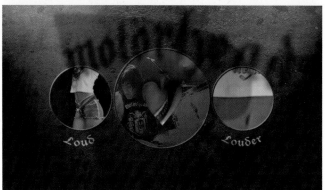

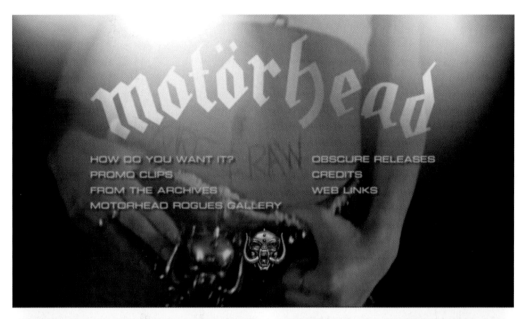

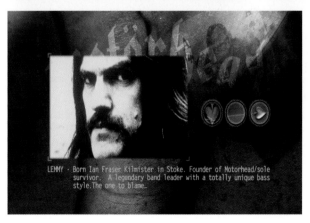

The *Motörhead* DVD menus combine images of the band with related artifacts designed to appeal to the fans. This mix of derivative and conceptual elements makes the menus more than a way to navigate— it also serves to define the unique identity of the band.

Black and white background imagery dominates most screens with contrasting color graphics used sparingly, which creates extra emphasis on those particular elements.

Sexy Beast

"This disc was designed in what we call a 'laconic Mediterranean style,' with the unusual extra feature of an isolated music score. With award-winning performances by Ben Kingsley and Ray Winstone, this DVD has sold extremely well. It's one of our favorites."

The Pavement

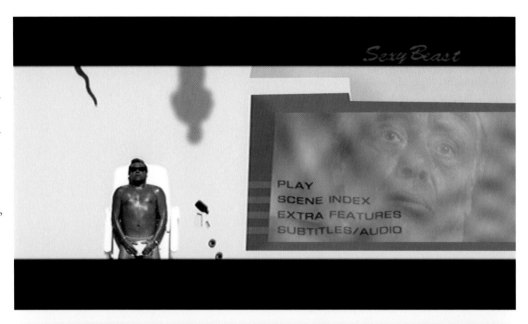

The designers have created highly stylized menus that use subtle motion, such as the ripples and the changing image in the pool, to create visual interest. The horizontal black bars provide a dramatic framing effect and give the main visuals an interesting, superwide screen appearance that looks unique and contributes to the strong composition in each menu. The placement of some menu items in the black bars creates a nice separation of main menu items from those that are specifc to the current submenu.

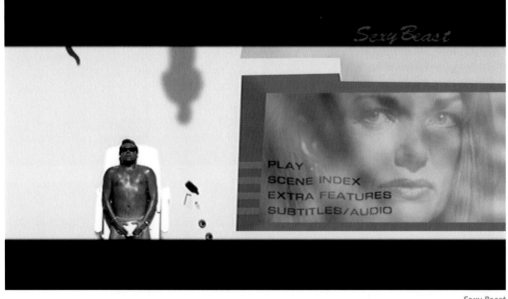

Sexy Beast
Menu design and animations
©2003 The Pavement
Client: VCI/Film Four

The menu selections in the upper bar are always red and other menu items are black or white, depending on which color provides the best contrast with the background image.

Simple, understated typography is combined with well-designed image compositions to create a classy and elegant visual presentation.

The Complete Jam

The Jam is one of the UK's most famous bands from the 1970s and '80s with Paul Weller as its lead singer.

The Pavement's designer was inspired by the Mod era typographics and The Jam's classic visual archives.

There was so much content in the double-disc set that the menu options had to be organized to allow users to select a year and go through the relevant playlists of that year's content.

The Complete Jam
Menu design and animations
©2003 The Pavement
Client: Universal Music

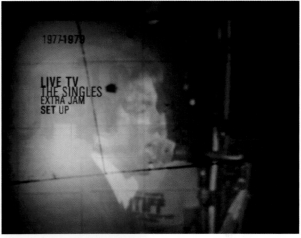

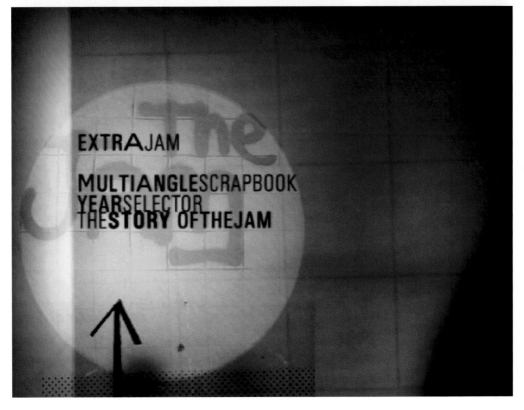

The design consists of multiple moving layers of text, uneven textures and sketchy video. It's all presented in subdued tones with very little color.

This edgy combination helps to reinforce the fact that the disc contains live "raw" concert footage.

The Terminator

MGM released *The Terminator* DVD in the UK prior to the US release, allowing The Pavement to take the lead on the graphics using elements supplied by the States. This title won the Home Entertainment Weekly Award for Best Overall DVD-Video in 2002.

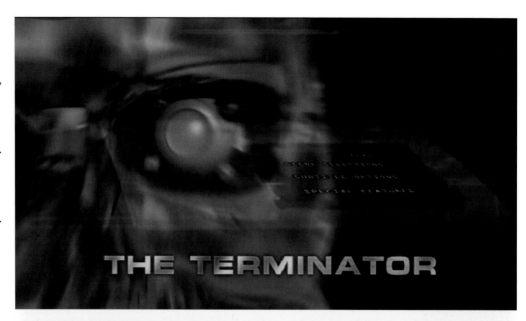

The Terminator
©1984 Cinema '84
A Greenberg Brothers Partnership
All Rights Reserved
Artwork and Design ©2001
MGM Home Entertainment Inc.
All Rights Reserved

Menu design and animations
by The Pavement

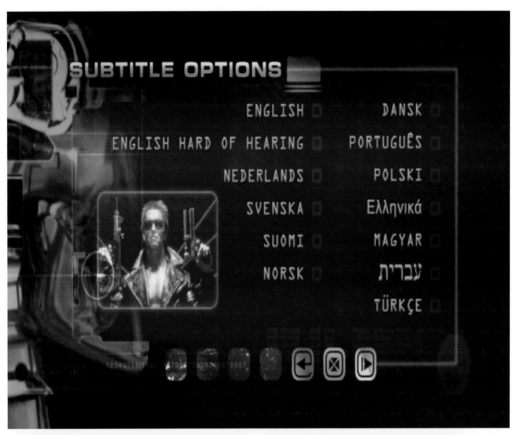

Everything about the menu design implies a futuristic and dangerous environment: the interesting but sterile typography, extreme closeups of menacing robotic faces, and a disturbingly muddy red and green color scheme. The overall darkness of the menus not only suggest drama, action and a lot of tension to come, but also provides excellent legibilty for the menu items.

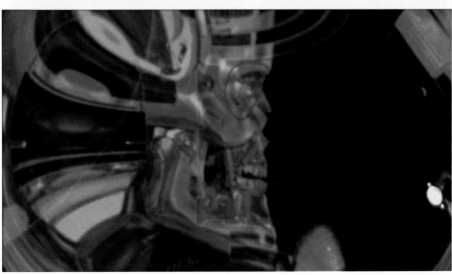

Spaced:
Series 1 and 2

Spaced, a TV sitcom developed for Channel 4 in the United Kingdom, plots the lives of Tim, Daisy, and their friends. Its creator, Simon Pegg, describes *Spaced* as a cross between *The Simpsons*, *The X-files*, and *Northern Exposure*.

The Pavement chose to use caricature for the menu's design theme, which conveys an overall tone of unusual and outrageous comedy.

"The disc itself is another story of dedicated endeavor and has been lovingly crafted by the good folk at VCI and The Pavement who did everything in their power to accommodate our inordinately geekish desire to exploit this medium to the fullest."

Simon Pegg
writer/performer

Spaced Series 1 and 2
Menu design and animations
©2003 The Pavement
Client: VCI/Channel 4

The *Spaced* DVDs are rich in content, including deleted scenes, photos, full soundtracks, cast biographies, raw footage, commentaries, and an "homage-o-meter."

Hidden surprises (Easter eggs) can be found on the DVDs by selecting hidden buttons or by pressing the "subtitle" button on the remote control until it selects a second set of subtitles.

Information screen styled menus provide the biographical information for the main characters in the series.

David Blaine Showman

The menus and navigation for this title were designed to reflect Blaine's street magic style. The Pavement shot footage around Shoreditch in East London for menus with Blaine. Then they created excerpts into a hidden feature called, "Making of the DVD," edited by The Pavement.

Dramatic, extreme closeups are composited with graffiti-style graphics to create interesting visuals that relate to the urban settings featured in the menus.

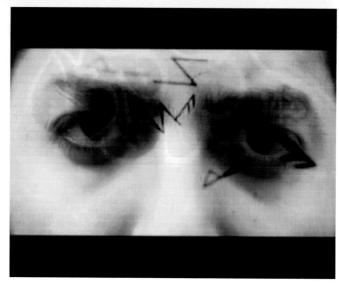

David Blaine Showman
Menu design and animations
©2003 The Pavement
Client: VCI/Channel 4

The main menu and subsequent screens show David Blaine in an urban setting, surrounded by walls covered in graffiti. This establishes the notion that Blaine's style is that of a street-wise magician.

The main menu is a motion clip of Blaine throwing individual playing cards. The cards appear to curve magically toward the viewer with each toss.

Streets scenes are the perfect menu environment for this street magician. The urban graphics set a mood, adding color and visual appeal to the presentation.

You Only Live Twice

The Pavement produced five James Bond Special Edition titles—all of which were multi-language with Dolby 5.1 sound and extensive special features. Menus are all consistent with James Bond themes and allowed space for localization.

You Only Live Twice
©1967 Danjaq, LLC and United Artists Corporation. All Rights Reserved.
007 Gun Symbol Logo
©1962 Danjaq, LLC and United Artists Corporation. All Rights Reserved.
Artwork and Design ©2003 MGM Home Entertainment Inc. All Rights Reserved.
Menus and animations designed by The Pavement

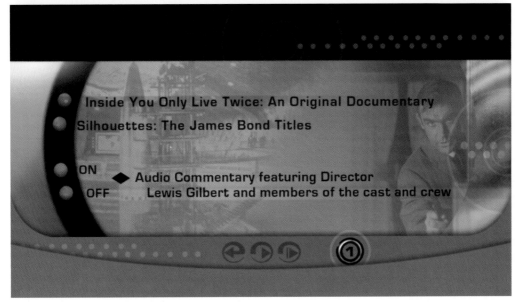

These menus are great examples of a design that makes the most of derivative elements from the video. The graphics undeniably represent the Bond style, but with just enough of a new perspective to give a fresh appearance to this classic movie.

A screen area that shows scenes and montages from the movie provides a unique and entertaining background and is a clever solution for providing a dedicated area for text information and descriptions.

Distinctive design elements such as the stylized control panel appearance of menu buttons, and the rich, black-and-gold color scheme of the background, work together to create a refreshingly updated look for the cinematic classic.

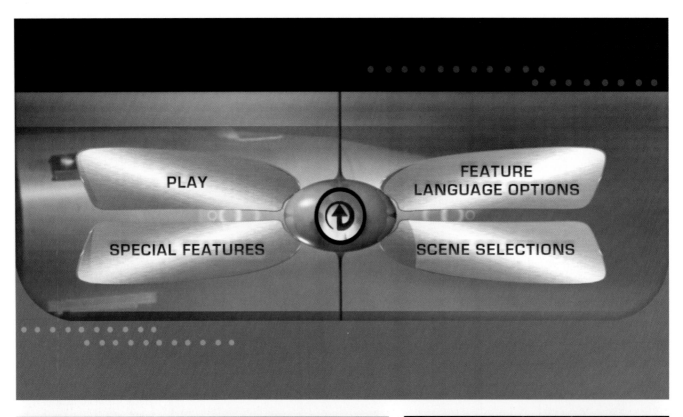

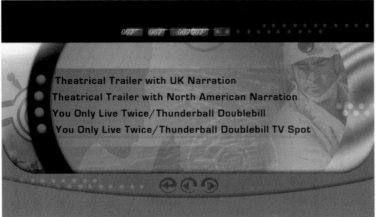

New conceptual elements like the propeller have been added into the mix, providing an interesting counterpoint to the familiar Bond images.

You Only Live Twice

Create a Plan
Planning and information architecture

13

Effective DVD menu design includes much more than just creating professional-looking, interactive visuals. It also includes careful *planning* and the discipline of *information architecture*. Planning includes the organization and scheduling of all phases of DVD development. Information architecture includes the organization of a project's content into categories and the design of a menu structure to make navigation of those categories easy and intuitive. Your mission as *information architect* is to get users from point A to point B effortlessly, maintaining a sense of familiarity about where they are, where they've been, and where they want to go. As the *project planner,* you must see that every phase of development stays on budget and on schedule.

Planning is the key. The more effort you put into planning your DVD project, the fewer adjustments and changes you'll have to deal with as the project progresses. Each project is unique, and the target users of each project are unique, so every plan pretty much starts with a blank piece of paper. You can lay the groundwork for a plan by asking several questions:

▼ What are the goals of this DVD and what should it accomplish?

▼ Who are the intended users and what do they want to know?
Or what do you want them to know?

▼ What existing content can be used?

▼ What content needs to be created?

▼ What is the scheduled delivery date?

▼ How many copies are needed and on what media?

With these questions in mind, you can start planning your project.

The Five Phases of DVD Development

For the sake of convenience, we've categorized the DVD development process into five sequential phases. Be aware that some tasks in different phases may overlap or may not fall into this order at all.

For instance, we've placed the "Bit Budgeting" information in the **Phase 1: Project Planning** category because it is an important part of planning. But you can't make bit budget calculations, which involves estimating disc storage space requirements for all assets, until you've completed **Phase 2: Asset Acquisition.**

Make a New Plan, Stan

The various processes of DVD development can be grouped into five phases:

1. **Project planning and architecture**
2. **Asset acquisition**
3. **Encoding**
4. **DVD authoring and multiplexing**
5. **Delivery**

The planning phase should address the scheduling and production concerns that are unique to each of the other development phases, described later in this chapter.

For small, personal projects, a formal plan may not be necessary, but it can make even a simple project more successful. We've hurried through personal projects in the past and invariably at some point have thought, "Woe is me. If I had planned better I could easily make those changes. A thousand curses!"

Put your plan in writing to avoid confusion later in the project about what was originally agreed upon. Get a signed client approval for as many stages as possible, such as flowchart development (see the following page), menu design, and project scheduling.

For client projects, a formal plan saves time and money for both you and the client, plus it makes you look smart, organized, and efficient—which you are, if you have a plan.

Phase 1: Project Planning and Architecture

Even a simple DVD project can be complex and confusing. Begin your planning by answering the questions on the previous page.

If you're developing a DVD for a client, get as much information from the client as possible. Make a list of content *assets* that the client wants to use, such as video, audio, photos, graphics or computer files to make available on the disc. Discuss how the various components should relate to each other.

The same client who can give you valuable input about the project is probably totally clueless as to how to present the content in an effective way. It's *your* job to take the available information and turn it into an *architecture of information* that can be easily accessed.

One of the first things you can do to start designing the organization of project content and information is to create a **flowchart.** A flowchart is an essential tool for visualizing the architecture of a DVD. It enables you to visually experiment with the organization of the content elements and how they link to each other. See the following page for more information.

Create a project flowchart

A flowchart is a diagram that shows all of the project's separate elements of content, how they're organized, and how they relate to each other. The flowchart is a visual map that makes it easier to see the project from the perspectives of organization and functionality. By studying the flowchart you can determine if critical elements have been overlooked or if some elements should be repositioned in the information architecture.

You can sketch a flowchart on a piece of paper or create one with sticky notes so it's easy to move elements around. You can use any software program that lets you draw shapes and lines, or you can use visualization and charting software intended for organizational charting. Three such programs are OmniGroup's OmniGraffle (Mac), Microsoft Visio (PC), and Inspiration from Inspiration Software (Mac and PC). These programs provide libraries of special shapes that you can label and connect, then move them around the document area without breaking the connections. Changing the connections is as easy as dragging a connecting line to a different shape. As decisions are made that affect your project, such as adding or removing content, it's especially easy to revise a flowchart that was created using visualization software.

Group your list of assets into a visual organization. Being able to see an overview of the entire project gives you and the client a better understanding of the structure and the relationships between various elements of content.

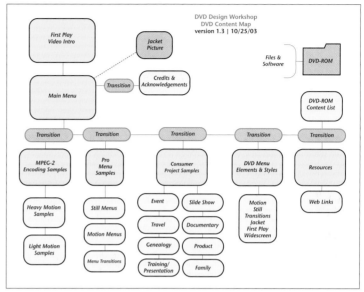

Dave used QuarkXPress to create the flowchart above for the DVD disc in the back of this book. A nice chart, but more trouble to revise than the one below.

John created the flowchart for a flamenco dance project in OmniGraffle, a Mac application from The OmniGroup. OmniGraffle can open Microsoft Visio files and can export charts as Visio files.

Microsoft Visio is a similar charting application for the PC platform.

Another popular visualization program for both Macs and PCs is Inspiration from Inspiration Software.

www.OmniGroup.com
www.Microsoft.com
www.Inspiration.com

Built-in Bit Budgeting

Many of the newer DVD authoring applications have built-in bit budgeting features. These applications display a running tally of all the imported assets so you can make decisions on encoding rates.

Bit budgeting

Video and audio have to be **encoded** into the proper DVD-compliant formats before they can be placed into DVD authoring software. Audio formats use specific **bit rates,** but video content can be encoded at various bit rates.

When you encode video, the bit rate you choose will affect the quality and the file size of the video clip. Higher bit rate settings result in better-looking video and larger MPEG-2 files. Your challenge is to encode the project video at the highest bit rate possible and still fit everything into the limited storage space of the final DVD.

To plan the bit rate for your encoding, you'll need to **bit budget.**

Bit budgeting is a mathematical process to determine how much space will be available for *video* storage on a disc after you've added up how much storage space is required for the *non-video* elements (audio, menus, DVD-ROM content, subpictures, etc.). If you subtract the amount of *non-video* data from the total disc capacity, you've calculated the amount of space available for *video* storage. You can adjust the encoding bit rate so the video will fill up the remaining space on the disc, enabling the highest possible video quality.

About 90 minutes of video fits on a single layer DVD if you encode at the bit rate of 6 Mbps (megabits per second). Raise the bit rate to 8 Mbps and you'll only have room for about 60 minutes. Even when there's enough space on a disc, high data rates can cause playback problems. DVD allows a maximum combined data rate of 9.8 Mbps for simultaneous streams of audio, video, menus, and subtitles, etc. (see **data rate budgeting** on the next page).

How to bit budget

The following example uses manual calculations, rounding down the number of bits per byte from 1,024 to 1000. *For a more accurate estimate, calculate using 1,024 bits per byte.*

1. **Determine the total storage capacity of your destination disc**
   A DVD-R holds 4.37 GB (technically 4.7 billion bytes).

Calculate the amount of storage (number of bytes) required by the following assets:

2. **Allocate some overhead space**
   Allocate 5 to 10 percent of the total disc space for overhead (see tip on next page).

3. **Calculate audio data storage requirements of each audio asset**
   When you encode an edited movie in the MPEG-2 format to place in DVD authoring software, the audio track of the movie is saved as a separate, synchronized audio file, usually as Dolby Digital Stereo whose encoded data rate is typically 192,000 bps (bits per second).

Use this formula:

audio duration in minutes x 60 x encoded data rate ÷ 8 = audio data storage requirement in bytes

When your project contains audio assets in another format, use the typical encoded data rates for those file formats:

Dolby Digital Surround
448,000 bps

DTS Surround (Half)
758,000 bps

DTS Surround (Full)
1,536,000 bps

PCM Stereo (AIFF or WAV files)
1,536,000 bps

4. Estimate subpicture storage requirements

Subpictures are graphic bitmap overlays that are used to create menu highlights, subtitles and captions. An average size for a subpicture is about 5 kilobytes (5,000 bytes).

Add 5,000 bytes for each unique caption or subtitle.

Use the following formula:

Number of subpicture graphics x 5,000 = subpicture storage requirement in bytes

5. Calculate menu storage

A *static menu* usually requires around 100 kilobytes (100,000 bytes) of storage.

Use this formula for static menus:

Number of static menus x 100,000 = static menu storage requirement

A *motion menu* contains video and is much larger. If you haven't yet created your motion menus and don't know what the menu durations will be, you'll have to estimate how many *total minutes* of motion menu video you'll include, and multiply that by an average video storage requirement of 40 MB per minute. Most motion menus have a duration of 30 to 60 seconds.

Use this formula:

Number of minutes of motion menu video x 40,000,000= motion menu storage requirement

6. Calculate DVD-ROM storage

If your project plan includes making files accessible in the ROM storage area of the DVD disk, add together the file sizes of the various items.

Use this formula:

total size of all ROM contents (in bytes) = ROM storage requirement

7. Calculate available disc storage

Add together the storage requirements from this list (numbers 2 through 6), then subtract the total from the original disc capacity (shown in Step 1). The remainder is the amount of disc space that is available for storage of the project's encoded video assets.

8. Calculate encoding rate

Calculate the average bit rate at which you must encode video files to *fill the remaining disc space*.

Use this formula:

Video space available (in bytes) ÷ minutes of existing video ÷ 60 ÷ 8 = average data rate to use for encoding

This is the average encoding value you'll use in your MPEG-2 encoding software to make the existing video fill the remaining disc space.

Data rate budgeting

Make sure that the combined **data rates** of simultaneous assets don't exceed the maximum data rate allowed by DVD specifications: 9.8 Mbps in a single *program chain* (a collection of programs that consists of cells or chapters—usually a video clip or movie). To check your data rate total, add the bit rates of the video and audio streams that will be combined in a video file. If the total exceeds 9.8 Mbps, use a lower encode rate.

Bit Budgeting Tip

When planning how much content will fit on a disc, plan to keep between 5 and 10 percent of the DVD's disc storage capacity available for "overhead" and "safety net."

When you finish a DVD project, content is saved in the DVD Video Object format as a VOB file. This format includes some DVD-specific data that makes the VOB file a little larger than the original content file. The extra data is referred to as "overhead."

"Safety net" refers to the fact that no plan is perfect and chances are you'll wish you had just a little extra room on the disc before you've finished the project so you can add one more video clip or reorganize a large menu into two smaller ones.

Commercial projects need permissions

Be sure you have written permission to use any content that you acquired from an outside source and whose copyrights may belong to someone else. For original content that you create, get written permission from anyone who appears in a movie or custom graphic.

Create a schedule

Create a schedule for your project, especially if a client relationship is involved. A written schedule can prevent misunderstandings. The phrase "as soon as possible" is always interpreted differently by the client and the designer.

A schedule should include time for:

▼ Preliminary client meetings to define goals, audience, budget, deadlines, concept, and to determine content requirements and resources.

▼ Flowchart design and approvals.

▼ Acquisition of existing content and creation of original content.

▼ Additional time for client approvals.

▼ Collecting legal permissions to use copyrighted material, if applicable.

▼ Asset encoding and extra time to re-encode if necessary (see next page).

▼ Menu design, testing, and approvals.

▼ DVD authoring and production.

▼ Simulation, emulation, and DVD disc testing (see Chapter 16 on testing).

▼ Reproduction of discs (see Chapter 17 on duplication and replication).

▼ Labeling and packaging (see Chapter 17).

Phase 2: Asset Acquisition

A DVD is basically a collection of **assets** (video, audio, graphics, and menus) that's made to work as a cohesive presentation of content. One of your biggest jobs will be to acquire all the assets of the project.

At least some of the assets may be given to you by someone else associated with the project. Video, audio, photos, or data files could come from clients, associates, or anyone. You may decide to buy stock video clips or audio files from a stock library (see the sidebar on the left). Good stock library content is not cheap, but it can provide content that would otherwise be unavailable.

Most designers start building a project before they've acquired all of the required content. You can start building the structure of your project in your DVD authoring software, using the flowchart you developed as a guide, and using short "placeholder" encoded videos or temporary menu graphics until you've acquired the actual content and finalized the menu designs in Photoshop. This enables you to build and test the project navigation while you're still acquiring assets or encoding them.

Phase 3: Encoding

Once you've gathered the finished content for your project, you must prepare it for DVD authoring by *encoding* it into formats that are compliant with DVD specifications. Read more about encoding in Chapter 14.

Phase 4: DVD Authoring and Multiplexing

DVD **authoring** is the process of *assembling* all of the finished content elements (edited movies, audio, and menus) into a form that makes all content easily accessible. You do this by using a **DVD authoring application** such as DVD Studio Pro or Adobe Encore DVD.

After you assemble all the elements together in your authoring application, the project content exists as encoded files of *elementary streams*, a general name for the encoded Dolby Digital audio files and the MPEG-2 video files. Before these files can be put onto a DVD disc and played in a DVD player, they must be **multiplexed.**

Multiplexing rearranges the files and puts them in a format that DVD players know how to use (see the example on the right). This process is also known as **muxing.**

When a project is multiplexed, the assets are reformatted and placed into two folders exactly like the ones on the right (AUDIO_TS and VIDEO_TS folders).

If you look inside the VIDEO_TS folder (right), you'll see that all of your MPEG-2 video files and Dolby Digital audio files have been reformatted into VOB files (Video Objects) and text files. This is the result of the multiplexing procedure. If you look at the contents of a Hollywood DVD on your computer, you'll see the same two folders: AUDIO_TS and VIDEO_TS.

Chapter 15 provides a more detailed explanation of authoring and multiplexing, plus an overview of some popular DVD authoring programs.

Multiplexed DVD project files in a typical VIDEO_TS folder.

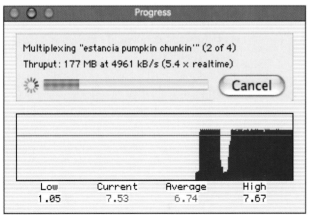

Multiplexing is fast. This progress window shows that the files of this project are being processed 5.4 times faster than realtime (the actual duration of the content that's being reformatted).

See Chapter 17 for an overview of packaging options and suggestions about how to professionally label your discs with custom graphics.

Phase 5: Delivery

The last phase of DVD development involves reproducing as many copies of your DVD disc as necessary and delivering them to your client, customers, or associates in a professional-looking package. Your project planning will include determining how copies will be made (below) and making arrangements for labeling and packaging. If you plan to reproduce large quantities, you may need to schedule a printer for the packaging design or arrange for storage and distribution.

Duplication and replication

To make copies of your project, discs can be duplicated or replicated.

Duplication is a *laser disc-burning method* used for smaller projects whose disc quantities are generally around 200 or less, and for projects that are small enough to fit on a DVD-R or DVD-5 disc format (a one-sided, one-layered disc). When you use your DVD drive to burn one or more discs, you're using the duplication method.

Replication is an *injection molding method* that's used when large quantities of discs are needed (usually above 1,000), or when a large amount of content contained in the project requires more than one layer on a disc.

Use of advanced DVD features such as file encryption (content scrambling) can also influence the decision of which process to use. See Chapter 17 to learn more about the two different processes.

Label design and package design

Your project's label design and packaging create an important first impression.

Commercial DVD titles that require the replication of large quantities of discs also require high-quality commercial printing of package inserts and labels.

Package design requirements are more demanding for large commercial projects that are distributed and sold through retail channels. The packaging for such titles usually includes UPC bar codes, Region Code identification, DVD logo branding, and other information describing the format and features of the disc.

If you need this level of packaging for your title, the replication facility will offer those services or help you find a solution.

Your projects at first will most likely be smaller, and distribution of discs will be local or regional, such as delivering a dozen training discs to a sales team, or a single disc for a trade show kiosk. It is possible however, even without much DVD development experience, that you could get involved in projects that involve large quantities and the services of a replication facility. Producing a DVD high school video yearbook or a church video directory could bring in orders from hundreds of students and church members.

Encoding

Compressing video and audio for DVD

The marvel of DVD is made possible in part by compressing very large, high-quality video streams into significantly smaller files that fit on a DVD disc. On the average, video files on DVD usually compress down to about six times smaller than their original source files. Amazingly, even at this smaller size, DVD video retains its broadcast-quality appearance. High-quality compressed video is made possible by the **MPEG-2** (pronounced *em peg two*) format.

Audio on DVD can also benefit from compression. Compared to video, original audio streams are much smaller to begin with, but if disc space is tight, compression will help conserve space. Audio is encoded differently from video, using either the **Dolby Digital (AC3)** or **DTS** format.

The process of compressing large video and audio streams into smaller DVD-friendly files is known as **encoding.** Next to authoring, it's one of the most important technical parts of DVD creation. This chapter covers the technology behind compression and provides an overview of software and hardware encoding products.

MPEG Formats

Video is an essential component for DVD but it must first be compressed into the MPEG format to be useful. MPEG compression, or **encoding,** is the first half of a two-part process: MPEG files are first **encoded** from an original source video and then later must be **decoded** by either a software or hardware DVD player before they can be viewed.

The acronym *MPEG* stands for **Moving Picture Experts Group,** the committee that originally developed the format. Their first effort was **MPEG-1,** a format that provides decent video for some purposes (like Video CD), but with an appearance that is well below broadcast-video standards. MPEG-1 has a resolution of 352 x 240 pixels, with a picture quality roughly comparable to that of VHS videotape.

The successor to MPEG-1 is the vastly superior **MPEG-2** format. At 720 x 480 pixels, MPEG-2 has nearly double the resolution, making it perfectly suited for use in DVD.

Either MPEG-1 or MPEG-2 files can be used on a DVD, but if you care about picture quality, MPEG-2 is clearly the superior choice.

Frame rates
for common video types
(numbers represent frames per second

24 Film

25 PAL video

29.97 NTSC video

MPEG-2 Compression

The next few paragraphs go "under the hood" to describe the inner workings of MPEG-2 compression and file structure. We'll try to make it as painless as possible, but we won't deny that it's a complex and mind-numbing heap of information. Consider yourself officially forewarned.

Both MPEG formats use a method known as **lossy compression** to achieve their small file sizes. The basic premise behind lossy compression is that it selectively eliminates, or *loses*, redundant information that the viewer wouldn't notice anyway. In the case of MPEG-2 compression, redundant visual information is eliminated within a series of individual pictures, or **frames,** as they're known in video terms.

An average MPEG-2 file has a 6:1 rate of compression. In other words, it's normally about six times smaller than the original source video, but your results may vary.

Frame rates

To fully understand how video frames are compressed, you should first know how they're arranged. All video and film formats are comprised of a progressive series of individual frames. The number of frames required to display one second of video varies with each original format. Motion picture film has a rate of 24 frames per second (fps), while PAL video is at 25 fps. NTSC video contains even more frames, with a data rate of 29.97 fps.

How MPEG-2 compression works

Prior to MPEG-2 encoding, an original *uncompressed* digital file will contain picture data for each and every frame of video. This will ensure that all the visual information is accounted for, but will make for a very large file. By comparison, the same video compressed with MPEG-2 is smaller because it doesn't need to contain complete picture data for *all* frames anymore—it only has full data for a few *selected* frames, and the others are saved in a kind of video shorthand method.

Video files encoded into the MPEG-2 format are subdivided into small sections of inter-related frames, each known as a **Group of Pictures** or a **GOP.** Each NTSC GOP usually contains about 15 frames, which accounts for one-half second of video. PAL GOPs contain 12 frames. If you do the math, you'll find that there are two GOPs in each second of MPEG-2 NTSC or PAL video. A full-length, two-hour movie could contain over 14,000 GOPs!

I, B, and P frames

The following can be mighty confusing, but don't despair. For most authoring jobs, the only thing you'll need to know about GOPs is that *chapter markers* can only be placed at the first frame of a sequence—never in the middle. But if you want to know more:

The first frame of a GOP is called an **intraframe** or **I-frame,** and it contains the complete picture (pixel data) for that instant of video. Each GOP can contain only one I-frame in a sequence. The I-frame image itself is compressed to eliminate redundant color information (similar to the way a still JPEG image is compressed). DVD menus and other still images are compressed as MPEG-2 still I-frames.

Subsequent frames in a GOP are known as **P-frames** (predicted frames) and **B-frames** (bidirectional frames). Neither P or B frames are complete pixel images, but rather containers for vector-based mathematical calculations that describe what has changed since the I-frame appeared. These frames are derived by assessing the state of the frame that directly precedes or follows.

The appearance of a *P-frame* is based upon the preceding I-frame or P-frame. However, a *B-frame* interpolates its appearance by checking both the preceding and subsequent frames.

Each GOP (Group of Pictures) in a MPEG-2 compressed video stream consists of 15 frames that represent a half-second of motion. There is only one complete image frame in a GOP, called the I-frame. The other B and P frames describe only what has changed in reference to the I-frame. The top example (IBP) shows a standard GOP sequence. The bottom IBBP sequence is another possible arrangement. The I-frame is always the first frame, but the B and P frames can be optimized in different patterns depending on the type of motion in the video.

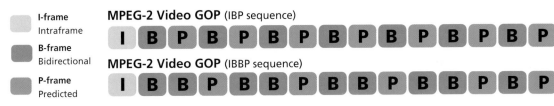

I-frame — Intraframe
B-frame — Bidirectional
P-frame — Predicted

MPEG-2 Video GOP (IBP sequence)

I B P B P B P B P B P B P B P

MPEG-2 Video GOP (IBBP sequence)

I B B P B B P B B P B B P B P

Maximum Bit Rate Tip

*The term **bit rate** refers to the amount of data that streams from a DVD in a single second. The maximum bit rate allowed for DVD is 9.8 Mbps. In order for a disc to function properly, the combined bit rate of all DVD data (not just video) must never exceed 9.8 Mbps at any point during playback.*

Combined bit rate data includes video, audio, menus, and subpictures—anything that will take up space in a datastream.

Bit rate

Encoding software lets you adjust the amount of compression applied to your MPEG-2 video to achieve the best balance between visual quality and file size. The amount of compression depends upon the **bit rate** you select when encoding. The DVD specification allows the use of MPEG-2 files with a bit rate up to 9.8 megabits per second (Mbps). In real-world usage, video streams should have a lower bit rate than the stated maximum to allow space for audio (see sidebar). Lower bit rate numbers yield a smaller file size, but at the sacrifice of image quality. Video with light motion can withstand more compression, while heavy-motion streams will require a higher bit rate to maintain quality.

Creating a *bit budget* will help you determine the optimal bit rate settings for your DVD project. See Chapter 13 for information on how to calculate a bit budget.

As a rule of thumb, you shouldn't go any lower than a bit rate setting of 3 or 4 Mbps, and no higher than 8 Mbps if you want to stay compatible with most consumer set-top players. Computer DVD players tend to have a harder time handling high bit rates than set-top players. If you're authoring a DVD aimed mainly at a computer audience, try to keep your bit rate at 6 Mbps or so to avoid the possibility of erratic playback.

You'll want to test encode short representative sections of video to determine which setting works best. A good median bit rate is 4 Mbps, but this will vary based on the compression algorithms of your encoder.

Your encoder will also give you the choice to select a **constant bit rate (CBR)** or a **variable bit rate (VBR)**. A *constant bit rate* applies the same level of compression to your entire video regardless of how much or little motion there is. A *variable bit rate* intelligently applies compression as needed for the type of motion encountered. High-motion segments are encoded at a higher bit rate and low-motion parts are set to a lower bit rate. Selecting a variable bit rate is the best way to encode the most efficient MPEG-2 file.

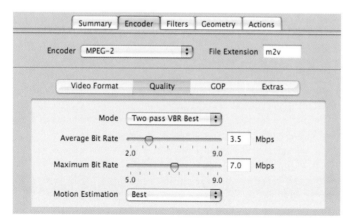

Apple's compression encoder provides controls that let users adjust the bit rate, alter the GOP structure, and apply video filters.

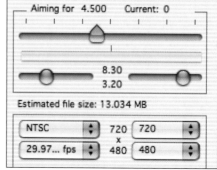

Innobits' BitVice has intuitive controls that allow users to not only select their desired average bit rates, but also set a minimum and a maximum for their MPEG-2 encodes.

Video Encoding

To convert a digital video stream into a genuine MPEG-2 file, you'll need to use a specialized tool called an **encoder.** A video encoder performs intensive analysis and number crunching, resulting in an efficient, great-looking MPEG-2 video stream. A good encoder will pre-analyze the video and automatically determine the points at which one GOP stops and another begins, based on the kind of motion contained in each frame. More advanced encoders feature color correction and various filtering techniques to improve poorly shot video.

Encoder types

There are two kinds of MPEG-2 encoders available—*software applications* or *dedicated hardware.* The settings for both software and hardware encoders are controlled using a software interface, but the actual encoding is handled differently.

Software encoders rely on combinations of coded compression algorithms and the processing power of the host computer. This is often a slow process, but it's way less expensive than using a hardware solution.

Hardware encoders do their work on specialized PCI expansion cards optimized for MPEG-2 compression. They are very fast but significantly more expensive.

Both types of encoders are capable of producing excellent results, depending on your needs. Base your selection on the solution that best fits your budget and project deadlines.

Input formats

Most encoders can accept a variety of original digital video formats, such as Windows AVI, QuickTime, or DV (miniDV or D1), but be sure to check before you purchase. Some Windows encoders will only accept AVI files and some Mac encoders will only accept QuickTime-based video.

Settings

The most prominent interface feature of any encoder is the settings panel with an abundance of pull-down menus and text boxes containing numeric values. A settings panel most often includes:

Output format: Select an output file format. MPEG-2 for DVD or MPEG-1(if you must).

Size and broadcast standard: Choose either NTSC 720 x 480 or PAL 768 x 576.

Aspect ratio: Assign a setting of 4:3 (fullscreen) or 16:9 (widescreen), depending your source video.

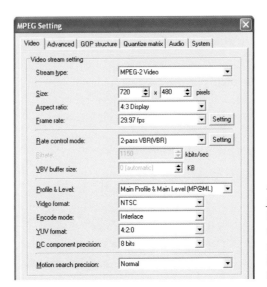

Transcoding

*The process of converting your original video source into a compressed MPEG-2 file is called **encoding**, but you may come across the term **transcoding** when using MPEG-2 software.*

*Sometimes these two terms are used interchangeably, but they do have different meanings. **Transcoding** refers to the process of taking a video file **already encoded or compressed** into one format and changing it into a different format. For example, when you convert a PAL MPEG-2 file into a NTSC MPEG-2 file, that's transcoding.*

A few applications specialize in transcoding between video formats, including MPEG-2. The most popular transcoders are Discreet Cleaner and Canopus ProCoder.

A typical settings panel from the TMPGEnc interface allows the user to adjust parameters like video size and format, bit rate, and even the GOP structure.

Compressionist

The task of encoding is much than just clicking a few software buttons. It's a true craft that requires expertise, perseverance, and a critical eye to produce a quality MPEG-2 video stream. A person who performs professional encoding is called a **compressionist.**

You may never consider yourself to be a compressionist, but it's important to have an eye for quality and do the best video encoding you possibly can because it directly affects the appearance of your DVD.

Interlaced or progressive input: Indicate if your source video was recorded as interlaced or progressive scan (see Chapter 10).

Field dominance: If your input is interlaced, choose either *top*, *bottom*, or *automatic*, depending on your source video format. If you aren't sure, choose *automatic*. MiniDV video uses the *bottom* field first.

Bit rate: A setting between 4 to 8 Mbps is a safe median range, with 4 or 5 Mbps considered the average. After you set your desired bit rate, select whether you want CBR or VBR (see page 236). If available, a two-pass VBR is the best choice because the encoder will do an initial pass to analyze the entire video before encoding. The second pass utilizes the data gathered in the first pass to optimize the video compression for each type of motion.

GOP settings: It's usually best to leave the GOP settings at their default value, but some encoders allow you to make adjustments to the sequence of I, P, and B frames (see page 235). A setting of 15 frames per GOP is standard. To avoid problems, don't mess with the GOP settings unless you really know what you're doing.

If you're presented with a choice of *open* or *closed* GOPs, pick *closed* unless you have a specific technical reason to choose *open*. Many authoring applications will only import closed GOPs.

Some encoders allow you to change the GOP structure, altering the frame pattern to optimize for a particular video stream. If you don't know what you're doing, leave these settings alone.

Elementary or transport streams: If your encoder offers you the output choice of **elementary** or **program** (multiplexed) streams, pick *elementary*. This produces two separate files, one containing MPEG-2 video and the other PCM audio. DVD authoring software requires the import of separate elementary video and audio assets.

Audio

The majority of MPEG-2 video encoders don't compress (or do anything with) audio tracks. Encoders will strip the audio away before encoding the video stream, saving the soundtrack as a PCM (AIFF or WAV) file. You can take this stripped audio track and encode it later into a Dolby Digital or DTS format. See pages 247–248 for more about audio encoding software.

Output extensions

Some encoders allow you to set your own output file extension suffixes, while others hard-code the extension into the software. The majority of DVD authoring applications will recognize a file with the **.m2v** extension as an MPEG-2 video file. If it doesn't, you can manually change the extension suffix to whatever suits your software.

Quality balance

Compress your video enough to conserve disc space but not so much that it sacrifices quality. Compressed video with bit rates set too low look blocky and pixelated.

When encoding video, keep in mind that image quality matters for both your motion menus and the main content.

Software Overviews

The following pages provide screenshots and brief feature overviews of some of the most popular software and hardware encoders on the market. We cover selected MPEG-2 video applications as well as encoders for Dolby Digital and DTS audio streams.

This is not intended to be a comprehensive listing of every encoding product available, but it does represent a good cross-section of the common features and user interfaces. We've focused mainly on affordable software that most authors could easily use.

All of the featured applications can produce high-quality encodes for every level of DVD authoring, but each has a slightly different set of features.

These overviews will help you become familiar with the available products, but you'll likely want further information before making a purchase. Be sure to visit each product's web site and download a trial version of the software, if available.

Web Links

For a list of links to the software mentioned in this chapter, go to our companion site for DVD Design Workshop *at:* www.MotionMenu.com

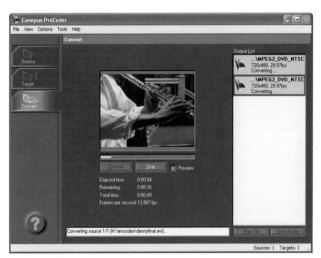

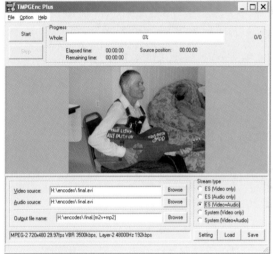

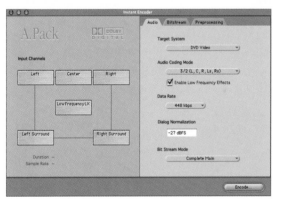

Whether it handles video, audio, or both, each encoding application has its own way of doing things and presents a unique user interface.

TMPGEnc Plus

Type: MPEG Software encoder

Platform: Windows

Manufacturer: Pegasys, Inc.

Input Format: AVI

Compression Mode: CBR and VBR

Output Formats: MPEG-2, MPEG-1 (elementary and program streams)

Audio Output: PCM

Special Features: Many expert controls for adjusting the GOP structure. Creates MPEG-2 stills which can be used as DVD jacket pictures.

Price: $48 or free version for non-commercial use (trial version available for download).

Web Site: www.Pegasys-inc.com www.TMPGEnc.net

TMPGEnc Plus

This Windows encoder may have an unpronounceable name, but it does an excellent job encoding MPEG-2 files. The original name was **Tsunami MPEG Encoder,** but it was shortened to **TMPGEnc** to make the name fit the old Windows 8-character naming convention.

Priced at just $48 for the downloadable version, you can't find a better encoder value anywhere, unless you count the free version intended for non-commercial use.

TMPGEnc Plus allows you to adjust your MPEG encodes to the nth degree, with probably more features than you'll ever need. It only accepts AVI (PC) files, but there's a freeware plug-in available that makes it QuickTime (Mac and PC) capable.

One special feature in TMPGEnc Plus is the ability to generate MPEG-2 stills, which you can use as DVD jacket pictures.

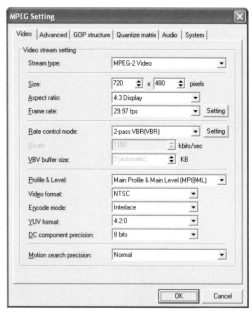

TMPGEnc offers extensive user control, allowing you to adjust nearly every aspect of the MPEG-2 video stream.

The TMPGEnc interface allows you to preview a video while it's encoding. A progress bar at the top indicates the percentage of completion.

BitVice

BitVice is a great option for Mac DVD authors who need a stand-alone software MPEG-2 encoder at an affordable price. Most of the other Mac-based encoders come bundled with an authoring application and are not available for purchase separately.

While it's fully Mac OS X compatible and runs on current G4 and G5 computers, BitVice can also be installed on older machines. It works with Mac OS 9.1 and up, and there's even a version optimized for older G3 Macs.

The interface is extremely straight-forward—all controls (except for preferences) are available within a single panel.

Although the presentation is simple, BitVice contains several advanced features such as video filtering, color correction, and 3:2 pulldown (a technique used by production houses to convert 24 fps video to standard NTSC 29.97 fps).

The output quality of BitVice is top-notch, particularly in the "High Precision" mode.

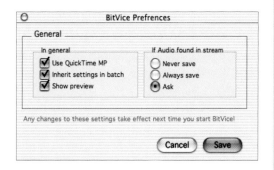

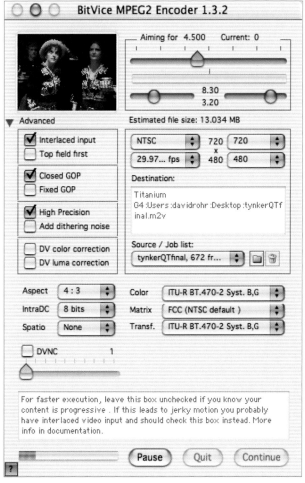

BitVice has a simple and concise user interface: all controls are available within this single panel.

BitVice

Type: MPEG-2 Software encoder

Platform: Mac G4 (G3 version available)

Manufacturer: Innobits

Input Format: QuickTime

Compression Mode: VBR

Output Format: MPEG-2

Audio Output: PCM (AIFF)

Special Features: Several video correction filters, batch processing, 3:2 pulldown only in full version

Price: $297 full version $56 lite version (trial version available for download)

Web Site: www.Innobits.se

Cinema Craft Basic

Type: MPEG Software encoder

Platform: Windows

Manufacturer: Cinema Craft

Input Format: AVI, DV, QuickTime

Compression Mode: CBR and VBR

Output Formats: MPEG-2, MPEG-1 (elementary and program streams)

Audio Output: PCM

Special Features: Expert controls for adjusting the GOP structure.

Price: $58 (trial version available for download)

Web Site: www.CinemaCraft.com

Cinema Craft Basic

Cinema Craft Basic is an affordable entry-level version of the Cinema Craft family of professional MPEG-2 encoders.

While the controls are more limited in Basic than in the high-end offerings, they will likely be more than enough for most DVD authors.

For an entry-level encoder, the output quality is still top-notch and suitable for use in nearly any personal or professional DVD project. If you ever need more control, you could upgrade to either the SP or Pro version.

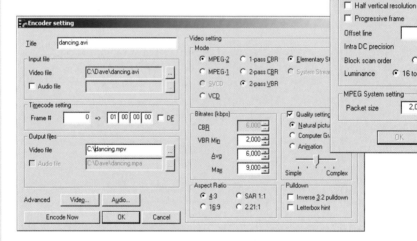

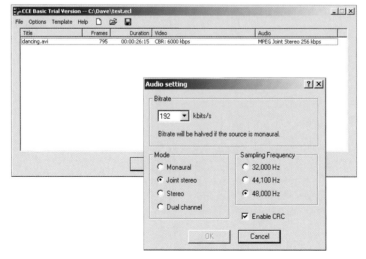

For an entry-level encoder, Cinema Craft Basic still provides many advanced controls for both video and audio output, including controls for GOP modes and PCM audio.

Compressor

Apple's Compressor is a stand-alone software encoder that comes bundled with DVD Studio Pro and Final Cut Pro. It's capable of producing professional-quality encodes at even the lower bit rate settings.

While offering a high degree of control, the user interface adheres to Apple's design philosophy of simplicity and ease-of-use. One of the most useful features is a split preview screen that allows you to view your original uncompressed video alongside a preview of the way it will look when compression is applied.

Compressor can also do batch processing, which allows you to encode several video clips at once without your constant supervision. It provides control of advanced settings such as GOP modes and video filtering.

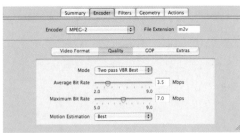

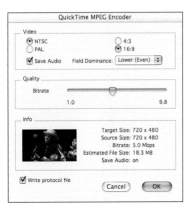

While Compressor is bundled with DVD Studio Pro 2.0, previous versions 1.0 to 1.5 came with the QuickTime MPEG-2 encoder. While this version does the job, it usually works best when set at higher bit rates (6 Mbps and over).

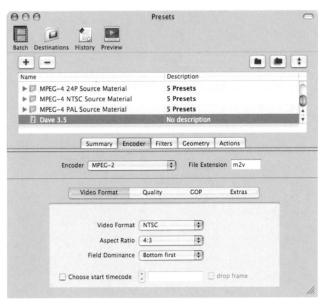

Compressor

Type: MPEG-2 Software encoder

Platform: Mac

Manufacturer: Apple Computer

Input Format: AVI, DV, QuickTime

Compression Mode: CBR and VBR

Output Formats: MPEG-2, MPEG-4 , QuickTime formats

Audio Output: PCM (AIFF)

Special Features: Split-screen previews, presets for different types of video, video filters, batch processing

Price: Not available separately. Bundled with Apple DVD Studio Pro 2.0 and Final Cut Pro 4.0

Web Site: www.Apple.com

The Compressor interface is representative of Apple's design philosophy—simple, clean, and intuitive.

It has a list of several preset configurations for different kinds of video and output formats. You can also customize the settings to suit your needs.

Adobe Encore DVD

Type: Built-in MPEG-2 Software encoder

Platform: Windows

Manufacturer: Adobe Systems

Input Format: AVI

Compression Mode: CBR and VBR

Output Formats: MPEG-2

Audio Output: PCM (WAV) and Dolby Digital 2.0, MPEG-2 audio

Special Features: List of presets for different types of video

Price: The video encoder is part of the Adobe Encore DVD package; $549

Web Site: www.Adobe.com

Adobe Encore DVD

Adobe Encore DVD is primarily an authoring application, but it can also do MPEG-2 encoding if needed. Encore DVD can import MPEG-2 video streams that are compressed by any compliant external encoder, but it provides the added ability to perform encoding (or *transcoding* as Encore refers to it) right within the application itself.

Encore 1.0 will only encode Windows AVI video files, but it's possible that a future release may support additional formats.

You can select from a list of several "transcode presets" or customize your own MPEG-2 compression settings.

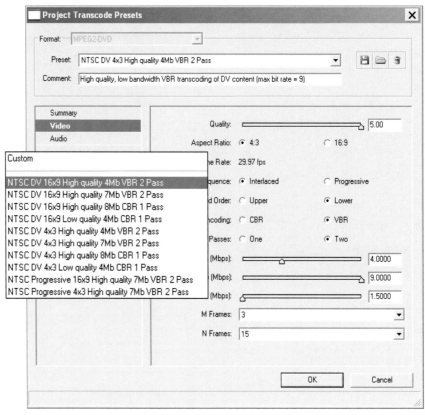

Adobe Encore DVD provides basic control for encoding MPEG-2 video. The "transcode" menu provides a list of commonly used preset parameters for different types of video. You can also customize your own settings and adjust the levels of bit rate compression.

ProCoder

ProCoder is a handy application to own if you need to frequently convert video from one format to another. It does many things well, but it's particularly good with MPEG-2 encoding and transcoding.

ProCoder isn't a dedicated MPEG-2 encoder, but it might as well be since the output is such high quality. Whether you encode an original DV stream or transcode between formats, ProCoder does the job quickly and effectively.

The user interface is different from most and may take a few minutes to understand, but once you get the idea, you'll appreciate the level of control it provides. You can make fine adjustments that balance the encoding quality with the amount of processing time. It can do "fast and good" encodes, but if you're willing to wait, ProCoder can produce MPEG-2 files that are downright excellent.

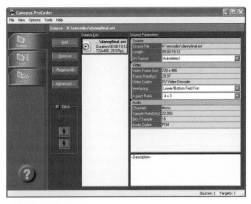

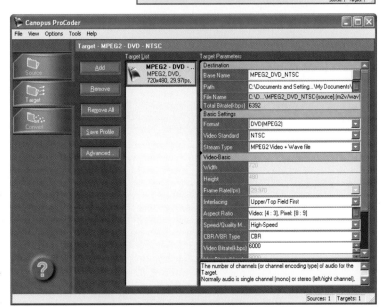

ProCoder displays an interface that may seem intimidating at first, but it won't take long to discover how much control it provides for your video encoding.

ProCoder handles many other video formats beyond MPEG-2 and is more expensive than encoders that only do MPEG. Still, the output quality is worth every penny.

ProCoder

Type: Transcoder/ encoder

Platform: Windows

Manufacturer: Canopus

Input Format: DV, AVI, QuickTime, many others

Compression Mode: CBR and VBR

Output Formats: MPEG-2, MPEG-1, many others

Audio Output: PCM (WAV)

Special Features: Can import and export many video formats, video and audio filters, batch processing, fast

Price: $599

Web Site: www.Canopus.com

Sonic SD-500

Type: Hardware encoder

Platform: Windows

Manufacturer: Sonic

Input Format: DV, AVI QuickTime

Compression Mode: CBR and VBR

Output Formats: MPEG-2, MPEG-1

Audio Output: PCM (WAV), Dolby Digital 2.0

Special Features: Can import and export many video formats, video and audio filters, batch processing

Price:
SD-500: $5,000
SD-1000: $10,000
SD-2000: $25,000

Web Site:
www.Sonic.com

Sonic SD-500 hardware encoders

Software encoders are fine for occasional DVD projects or light professional workflows, but if you create DVDs for a living and deadlines are a way of life, you'll need the speed and power of a hardware encoder. Hardware encoders consist of a PCI expansion card (the *hardware*) and a software interface to control the process.

Sonic offers three hardware encoder cards: the SD-500, SD-1000, and SD-2000. Each of these cards connects directly to an original video source and does realtime MPEG-2 and Dolby Digital audio encoding.

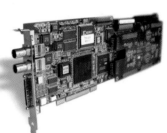

The SD-500 is the most affordably priced card in the group and has added with the ability to directly import DV via a standard FireWire cable.

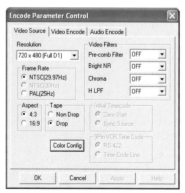

The SD-1000 and SD-2000 are both ultra high-end cards that accept SDI video input.

The SD-500 has an easy-to-use software interface that controls the encoding process.

You can import original uncompressed digital video streams directly from your deck or camcorder, or encode a file saved on the hard drive. The SD-500 also encodes Dolby Digital audio files on the fly.

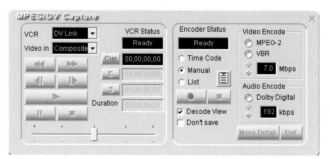

The SD-500 software provides precise controls for video and audio compression.

A.Pack audio encoder

Your encoding chores don't stop with video—you will often need to compress audio tracks so they will fit comfortably on a DVD. Apple's A.Pack is a Dolby Digital audio encoding application bundled with DVD Studio Pro.

It can compress regular uncompressed PCM audio files (AIFF or WAV) into smaller DVD-ready Dolby AC-3 files.

While it can produce full 5.1 surround files, it is just as capable with mono or stereo mixes.

A.Pack provides several advanced settings for noise reduction and customized processing based on the type of audio track (voice, music, etc.).

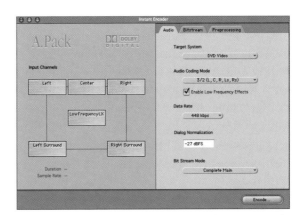

A.Pack's interface displays a layout showing the number of channels you wish to encode. To assign a track to particular channel, simply drag a source PCM file onto one of the boxes in the layout. A.Pack only accepts PCM files sampled at 48 or 96 kHz.

A.Pack

Type: Dolby Digital 5.1 encoder

Platform: Mac

Manufacturer: Apple Computer

Input Format: PCM audio (AIFF or WAV)

Audio Output Formats: Dolby 1.0 to 5.1 surround sound

Special Features: Noise reduction filters, compression presets

Price: Bundled with DVD Studio Pro 2.0, $499

Web Site: www.Apple.com

Adobe Encore DVD

Type: Dolby Digital encoder

Platform: Windows

Manufacturer: Adobe Systems

Input Format: PCM audio (WAV), AVI video soundtracks

Audio Output Format: Dolby Digital, MPEG audio

Price: The audio encoding is built into Adobe Encore DVD, $549

Web Site: www.Adobe.com

Adobe Encore DVD audio encoding

Adobe Encore DVD is an authoring application, but it can perform both internal MPEG-2 and Dolby Digital encoding. If an AVI video file has been set to "transcode" using the Dolby Digital codec, its associated audio soundtrack will be converted into Dolby at the same time the video is encoded into MPEG-2.

Encore DVD provides few options for adjusting the quality of the encode, but even standard Dolby Digital compression is still a valuable feature for your DVD authoring project.

Encore allows you to select Dolby Digital as one option for encoding your movie's audio track.

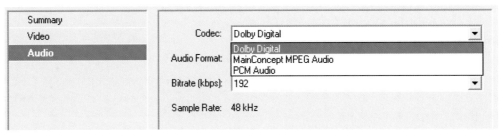

Surcode

Types: Dolby Digital encoder, DTS encoder

Platform: Windows

Manufacturer: Minnetonka Audio

Input Format: PCM audio (WAV or AIFF)

Audio Output Formats: Dolby Digital 5.1, DTS 5.1

Price:
Dolby 5.1 $995
Dolby 2.0: $599
DTS: $1995

Web Site:
www.Surcode.com

Surcode audio encoders

Minnetonka Audio publishes several high-end audio applications under the Surcode brand, including encoders that cater to the DVD market. Their Windows product line includes applications for both Dolby Digital 5.1 and DTS surround.

Surcode Dolby Digital produces AC-3 files with up to 5.1 surround channels. Similarly, Surcode DVD-DTS produces DTS surround files with up to 5.1 channels.

Both applications have an identical user interface that lets you easily assign a PCM audio file to any one of the six channels of the mix.

There are several controls to allow for fine adjustments, but by and large the process is straightforward and most functions are always visible.

If you don't require full 5.1 channel soundtracks in your DVDs, a less-expensive Dolby Stereo encoder is available.

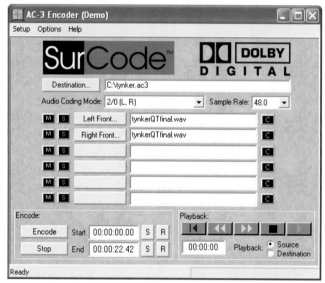

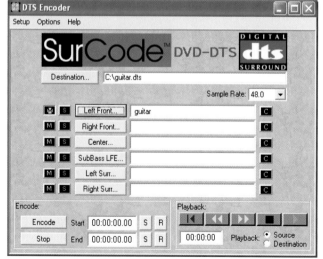

Surcode encoders sport a refreshingly simple user interface which presents all your options within the main control window.

Authoring

An overview of the DVD assembly process

15

Authoring is the digital crossroad in the DVD process where everything finally comes together. It's the step where all the individual media pieces are imported, arranged, and then merged into a single cohesive, exciting presentation. The current range of authoring software offers many different approaches to building DVDs, from simple programs with limited abilities to sophisticated applications with mind-boggling complexity and extensive control.

This chapter will help you understand the general capabilities of DVD authoring software and familiarize you with the most common features and settings. The final part of the chapter presents overviews of many popular authoring software packages, with brief descriptions and interface screens from entry-level to high-end. If you're in the market to buy an authoring application, this section will identify your options and assist you in matching the right software with your needs.

DVD Authoring Software

Authoring software is the essential hub of DVD production. It takes individual video, audio, and image assets and mixes them together into a DVD-ready file structure. The software not only assembles assets, it also controls how they display, interact, and function on the finished DVD.

Asset assembly and more

The main role of DVD authoring software has traditionally been as an assembly environment, with individual assets created by outside applications. But recently, some applications have blurred the boundaries by incorporating built-in features such as menu creation, video compositing, encoding, and subtitling. We'll show examples of these and other individual software applications later in this chapter.

DVD authoring software is available for every budget, ranging from free applications that come bundled with computer hardware, to professional programs that cost several thousand dollars or more.

Inexpensive entry-level software is easy to use and allows you to put basic video, audio, and images on a disc, but it doesn't provide full access to all the possible features of DVD. To get your hands on the good stuff, you'll need to move up to a mid-level or high-end software package, which will give you the kind of control necessary to create professional-level DVDs. Generally, the more you spend, the more access you'll have to the full features of the DVD specification.

The more crayons the better

It's like the example of two children, each with a box of crayons. Tommy has a small box with eight basic colors, while Sarah is lucky enough to have a set of 64. Both kids can use their crayons to draw as many pictures as they want, but Sarah's pictures will always be more colorful because she has more options to choose from.

It's the same way with authoring software. All authoring applications create DVDs, but the ones with more features allow you to produce more sophisticated projects.

Which box of crayons provides more creative coloring options?

Like a bigger set of crayons, the more features available in a DVD authoring application, the more sophisticated your projects can be.

Abstraction layer

Any software interface that shields humans from the harsh realities of computer code is called an **abstraction layer.** Most software user interfaces are considered abstraction layers, if they don't require the user to communicate in computer code. Users are usually most comfortable interacting with a system of easy-to-understand control panels and selection menus.

All DVD authoring applications use the abstraction layer concept, but with varying intensity. For example, entry-level software has a "thick" abstraction layer to simplify the choices and protect the user from being overwhelmed by anything considered to be too technical.

As you gradually move up towards the high-end authoring applications, additional advanced controls become available that allow you to more directly manipulate features of the DVD specification. These professional authoring programs tend to have a "thin" abstraction layer because users at this level understand what they're doing and require a high degree of control over the DVD specification and their authoring environment.

Some people refer to entry-level and mid-range DVD software as *abstraction layer software* because it's often simpler to use. High-end authoring software is sometimes called *spec software,* because it allows more direct control over the DVD specification.

Abstraction layer authoring software acts as a buffer, allowing you control the features of the DVD specification without the need to work directly with specification commands. This example shows the interface of Apple DVD Studio Pro 2.

Authoring Process

There's an abundance of DVD authoring software on the market, each with its own unique user interface, but all with a common goal: to build a DVD.

The basic premise of any DVD authoring software is to allow the user to perform three distinct tasks:

1. **Import individual assets.**
2. **Organize and manipulate the assets.**
3. **Merge everything into a DVD-compatible file structure (multiplex).**

Import assets

The first step of authoring is to import all of the selected media assets into your DVD software. All DVD applications accept video, audio, and still image files, but will not necessarily recognize every file format. Advanced applications often only allow the import of **elementary streams.** This means that video and audio tracks are separate self-contained units, not joined together.

Asset types

Video: Many advanced authoring applications require that video be pre-encoded into the MPEG-2 (.m2v) format. A dedicated MPEG-2 encoder can convert your video into this compressed format (see Chapter 14). MPEG-1 files are also allowed, but we don't recommend them because the quality isn't all that good when compared with MPEG-2.

Entry-level software often accepts original digital video streams and does the MPEG-2 encoding itself. These source video formats may include DV, QuickTime, or Windows AVI. If you do import files formatted in something other than MPEG-2, make sure they haven't already been compressed with another video format (like Cinepak)—re-encoding will likely result in poor quality video.

Audio: All authoring applications accept PCM audio files such as WAV (.wav) or AIFF (.aif), so long as they are sampled at 48 or 96 kHz. Audio sampled at 44 kHz (CD quality) won't work. More advanced applications will also accept compressed Dolby Digital (.ac3) or DTS (.dts) audio files.

Still Images: Still images used for menus, highlights, or slideshows can be saved in a number of formats, depending on what your software will accept. The most common still image formats accepted for DVD authoring are Photoshop (.psd), PICT (.pct), JPEG (.jpg), BMP (.bmp), and TIFF (.tif). You can use Adobe Photoshop or Photoshop Elements to pre-format your still images for DVD. See Chapter 10 for more about editing images in Photoshop.

Subtitles: Some authoring software allows you to import subtitles that have been created in an external subtitling program. There are many different subtitle formats, so learn what your authoring software will accept before creating the subtitle streams.

Organize assets

Once all the assets have been imported, organize them in the way you envisioned during the planning stages (see Chapter 13). This stage often involves a tremendous amount of detail work, depending on the amount of content and menus on your DVD. During this process you'll arrange the overall playback order, establish menu links to the content, assign button highlights, and insert audio tracks. You might also associate subtitles with video tracks and add some scripting to enhance interactivity. While you work, use the built-in preview mode to test and make sure things are working as you expected.

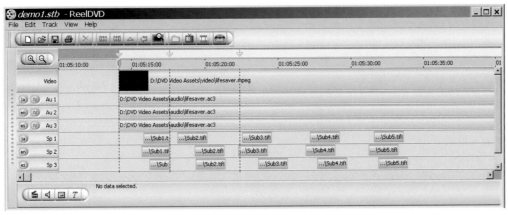

This timeline view from Sonic's ReelDVD displays the relationships of several imported assets including video with multiple audio tracks and subtitles.

Merge (multiplex)

After everything is properly arranged and you've tested as much as possible, it's time to compile your assets into a single unit. This merging of assets is known as **multiplexing,** or **muxing** for short (catchy, isn't it?). The end result is a set of DVD-ready files precisely structured to be recognized by any DVD player. These new files are ready to burn onto a blank DVD or DLT tape drive. Multiplexed files contain combined video and audio streams, as well as instructions that tell the DVD player how to play the disc.

File Structure

When a DVD project is multiplexed, the process saves two file directories (folders) to your hard drive or disc. These directories are always named **VIDEO_TS** and **AUDIO_TS,** which stands for *video title set* and *audio title set* respectively. When they're burned to a disc, both are located at the **root directory** level. If you're not familiar with the term, the *root directory* is the top directory in the DVD (or any) file system. This means if you were to put a DVD-Video disc in a computer, select its icon, and open it to examine the files inside, the first two things you would see are the VIDEO_TS and AUDIO_TS directories.

The AUDIO_TS directory is always empty—it would only contain files on a DVD-Audio disc, so its presence on a DVD-Video disc is mostly a technical formality. **Don't delete it though**—some players won't read your DVD correctly if they can't locate the AUDIO_TS folder.

The main action takes place inside the VIDEO_TS folder where all the multiplexed DVD files are stored. There are three kinds of files in this directory, with the suffixes of VOB, BUP, and IFO.

VOB or Video Object is a multiplexed file that contains an MPEG-2 video segment combined with its corresponding audio track.

IFO or Information contains instructions for control and playback for a particular VOB file.

BUP or Back Up is an exact copy of an IFO file, but always written to the opposite side of a disc. This is for error correction—if the DVD surface is scratched on one spot and the player can't read the necessary IFO file, it will then search for the corresponding BUP file.

The directories shown below contain files that were created during the multiplexing stage of the authoring process.

The root directory (above) must contain both AUDIO_TS and VIDEO_TS directories.

The VIDEO_TS directory (left) contains all of the vital DVD files. The VIDEO_TS.VOB file contains information about the disc and menus. VTS files contain segments of video and audio.

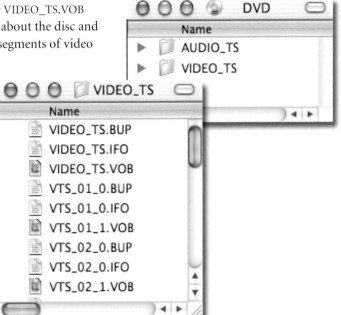

JACKET_P folder

The root directory of your DVD is required to contain both AUDIO_TS and VIDEO_TS folders, and may even contain an optional DVD-ROM folder. But there's a fourth type of directory allowed at the root level: the JACKET_P folder.

*The JACKET_P folder is not required, but if present, it contains three to six still images called **jacket pictures** that display a graphic title screen for the disc. See pages 25 or 117 for more information about jacket pictures.*

Anamorphic widescreen video

There are two ways to display a widescreen image on DVD. The first is to create a letterboxed video at a 4:3 ratio, with the bounding bars encoded as part of the video.

The other and best way is to create an anamorphic video that can work on both fullscreen and widescreen TVs.

Basic Authoring Options

When you use a DVD authoring application, the main challenge is to understand your available options and make intelligent choices. Making even a simple mistake could result in a wasted disc, or worse yet, an unhappy client.

You'll want to study the user manual of your chosen authoring software to become familiar with its unique interface, but all DVD software packages have many features in common.

The following text covers some of the basic options available in nearly all entry-level authoring software.

Basic disc settings

Disc name: Give your disc a title, but keep it short. DVDs follow the old Windows file-naming convention and limit the title name to eight characters or less. If you want to include a space between letters, use an underline character like this "_" because some file systems don't understand a blank space.

Video format: Choose either NTSC or PAL—it can't be both.

DVD-ROM directory: If you plan to include data files on your DVD, your authoring program needs to know where they are. Identify the ROM directory that contains the files on your computer's hard drive.

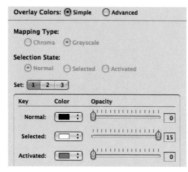

Authoring software provides controls to adjust settings for menu navigation, disc functions, and video playback.

This image shows a palette for assigning button highlights in DVD Studio Pro.

Asset attributes

Video tracks: As the primary asset on a DVD, a video track has several attribute controls in your authoring application.

Aspect ratio: Choose 4:3 if your video is fullscreen, or 16:9 if your video is widescreen. Anamorphic widescreen video (see Chapter 2) starts out at 864 x 480 pixels (NTSC) but is squeezed to the required 720 x 480 before encoding. You'll need to indicate that a video track is widescreen so the authoring software can set a flag to expand it to its rightful size during playback.

First play: A particular video track can be designated as the first item to display when the DVD is inserted into a player.

Chapter markers: Unless they've already been inserted in your NLE or encoding software, you can add video chapter markers during the authoring stage.

Audio tracks: You can associate one or more audio tracks with any video asset.

Menus: You can designate still images or motion video clips to function as menus. A single audio track can be added to either type of menu.

Buttons: Create button hotspots over menu artwork. Assign link commands to each one.

Highlights: Associate subpicture overlays with corresponding menu backgrounds. Assign highlight colors for each button state (*normal, selected, activated*).

Slideshows: Sequence still images and set them to display at timed intervals.

Advanced Settings

Additional functions are available in mid-level to high-end authoring applications. You'll still be dealing with the same basic video, audio, and still image assets, but you'll have even more control.

Advanced asset attributes

Video angles: Assign up to eight alternate camera angles to your main video tracks. Keep in mind that the alternate video tracks must be exactly the same length as the main video track.

Subtitles: Add subtitles to video tracks and designate their language. Some authoring software lets you add subtitles within the program instead of importing an external file.

Enhanced interactivity features

Menu compositing: Some of the newer authoring software allows you to create menus and buttons within the program itself.

Button routing: More advanced authoring software provides controls so you can set the button routing paths. A routing path is the order in which buttons are highlighted (see Chapter 6, page 124).

Scripting: Advanced authoring software allows you to write scripts that control many aspects of disc playback and interactivity. Scripts can store playback information in a DVD player's SPRM and GPRM registers (storage areas for numeric disc values). This can make the player "remember" certain previous viewer functions, such as which menu clips have already been played, and display only the alternates.

Remote functions: For consistency, take the time to assign the appropriate navigation features on your DVD to the standard buttons on a player's remote. This means the *Title* button should link to your disc's *main menu*, the *Angle* button should switch between available *video angles* on a track, and so on with the others. Viewers expect these buttons to work predictably, so don't let them down.

End or jump actions: Whether your application calls them *end actions* or *jump actions*, you can assign this command to motion menus, transitions, or video clips so the player knows which menu or video clip to jump to after a segment finishes playing.

Advanced disc settings

Disc size: Choose 4.7 GB single-layer or 9 GB double-layer. Keep in mind that a double-layered disc can't be burned on your own equipment; you'll need to save it to DLT tape and replicated (manufactured; see Chapter 17).

Region code: If you intend to create a region restricted disc, you can assign the appropriate numeric region code (see page 17).

Parental controls: Commercial discs that require age-based restrictions must be authored in an advanced application that can set parental control codes.

Copy protection: For discs that require copy protection, you need to designate the type of encryption in your authoring software. Choose either CSS or Macrovision. CCS encrypted discs must be written to DLT tape and then replicated (not burned). See Chapter 17 for further details about replication.

Troubleshooting

Despite what the marketing hype says, authoring software doesn't always work as expected. Even the best applications have their own unique glitches that you'll have to around.

If you're having a problem with your authoring software, there's a good chance that others are experiencing the same thing.

You can compare notes and get the answers you seek by joining a free Internet email newsgroup focused on DVD authoring. There may even be a group dedicated to your brand of authoring software.

Subscription information for some of the most popular DVD groups is listed at the end of this book. You can also find this information by visiting www.MotionMenu.com.

DVD File Tools

After a DVD project has been assembled and muxed into a collection of VOBs, IFOs, and BUPs, it would seem that it's a done deal and the files are locked and forever uneditable. But despite their "carved in granite" appearance, remember: if VOB files can be muxed, they can also be de-muxed if necessary. The same goes for IFO files—they can be edited if you know how.

Specialized tools allow you to split or append MPEG-2 files, edit the stored values in an IFO file, or even demux a VOB into its elementary video and audio streams.

There are many post-authoring tools available for download as free or shareware utilities. The following site is a good place to start: www.Doom9.org

Authoring Software Levels

As you've seen, there's a wide variety of features and options available in DVD authoring. While the options may be plentiful, most authoring software doesn't provide access to every feature contained in the DVD specification. Companies that create DVD software have wisely chosen to provide different feature sets—each appropriate to a specific type of customer.

Entry-level software is inexpensive and provides only the basic features that *novice* DVD authors and *home users* are most likely to care about. If you're new to DVD authoring, software in this range is a good starting point. The software is designed to do the job in the least amount of steps possible. This kind of application usually doesn't accept pre-encoded elementary video and audio streams, preferring to capture the source files and encode internally.

DVD authoring software is available for nearly every budget, ranging from inexpensive entry-level to affordable mid-range to high-end applications costing thousands of dollars.

Mid-range software is aimed at the *more advanced author* doing *professional-level work*. This kind of author wants access to most of the DVD features, but can't afford to spend a small fortune to get them. Mid-range DVD software is the logical choice for many video and design professionals who want to do high-quality work, but prefer to use an application with a user-friendly interface.

High-end software is designed for a smaller, more elite group of *authoring professionals*. This level of DVD software is most often used by companies doing commercial Hollywood movie work. They need the most feature-rich tools available and are willing (and able) to pay big bucks to get it. The most expensive and full-featured authoring software is likely to have a steep learning curve. If you're eyeing software in this range, don't forget to budget for the time and cost of training.

Choosing Your Software

The next few pages showcase user interfaces and features of several popular authoring applications. With so many applications available, it's a buyer's market, with options at every price level. Our category divisions are based mainly on price, but a few products in the list defy their entry-level and mid-range category and offer pro features usually found only in high-end software.

You probably won't base your choice on price alone, but if you're like most independent designers, budget will be a factor. If a product costs less than $500, there's little financial risk if you make the wrong choice. But at the high-end, you and your bank account might regret a bad purchase for years to come.

Buying considerations

Here's a short list of things to consider when choosing your DVD authoring software.

- ▼ Are the type of projects you'll produce for personal or professional use?
- ▼ What kind of user interface do you prefer: simple abstraction layer or spec?
- ▼ What platform do you prefer: PC or Mac?
- ▼ Do you require software that provides ultra high-end features?
- ▼ Do you need software that integrates with special hardware like an MPEG-2 encoder?
- ▼ Do you need authoring software that integrates closely with your NLE software?
- ▼ Do you need the largest feature set available?
- ▼ Does the software have a steep learning curve?
- ▼ Is your budget modest, unlimited, or in-between?
- ▼ Is there adequate support and training available?
- ▼ What is the cost of an upgrade?

Entry-level

Advantages

- ▼ Low cost
- ▼ Easiest to learn
- ▼ Built-in encoding
- ▼ Fast development time
- ▼ Menu and button templates

Disadvantages

- ▼ Limited menu template options
- ▼ Limited number of buttons per screen
- ▼ Lower-quality MPEG-2 encoding
- ▼ Long encode times
- ▼ Cannot import elementary MPEG-2 streams
- ▼ Cannot import Dolby audio
- ▼ No double-layered discs
- ▼ No advanced features

Mid-range

Advantages

- ▼ Affordable
- ▼ Intuitive user interface
- ▼ Import of elementary MPEG-2 video streams, both 4:3 and 16:9
- ▼ Encoding control with external MPEG-2 software of your choice
- ▼ Full control of menu appearance
- ▼ Double-layered disc authoring
- ▼ Writes to DLT
- ▼ Allows for copy protection
- ▼ Scripting control
- ▼ Access to many advanced features (multi-angles, more soundtracks)

Disadvantages

- ▼ More complex
- ▼ No hardware encoding integration
- ▼ Does not provide full access to all DVD features

High-end

Advantages

- ▼ Offers highest degree of authoring control over DVD specification.
- ▼ Arguably provides superior multiplexing, making the resulting DVDs more compatible with set-top players.
- ▼ Integrates with MPEG-2 hardware encoders to achieve fast encode times
- ▼ Allows high-end commercial features like DTS soundtracks, karaoke, parental block, full SPRM and GPRM control.

Disadvantages

- ▼ Expensive
- ▼ Less intuitive user interface
- ▼ Steep learning curve
- ▼ May require professional training

Sonic MyDVD

Type: Entry-level DVD authoring application

Platform: Windows

Manufacturer: Sonic

Input Formats: MPEG-2, DV, AVI, QuickTime

Output: DVD-R/+R

Noted Features: Basic menu templates, nice slideshow transitions, direct import of MPEG-2 video files.

Price: $79.99

Web Site: www.Sonic.com

Sonic MyDVD Plus

Sonic's MyDVD makes it easy to quickly put video content and photographs onto a DVD. It allows you to directly import video from your camcorder, and comes bundled with ArcSoft's video editing software. The two work nicely together to capture, edit, and then burn to DVD. It also allows you to import pre-encoded MPEG-2 files, a feature usually reserved for more advanced applications.

MyDVD offers a limited selection of pre-designed menu templates, but you can also import your own artwork if you need something more unique.

The slideshow feature is outstanding, with the ability to gracefully crossfade from one photo to another.

MyDVD is a great choice for home users or novice authors to dip their toes into the DVD authoring pool without a large investment.

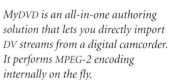

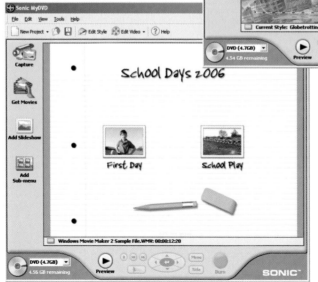

MyDVD is an all-in-one authoring solution that lets you directly import DV streams from a digital camcorder. It performs MPEG-2 encoding internally on the fly.

MyDVD is extremely simple to use and easy to learn. All functions are available within the main viewing area, including menu layout, slideshow assembly, and disc preview.

Web Links:

For a list of links to the software mentioned in this chapter, go to our site at:
www.MotionMenu.com

Apple iDVD

If you follow the philosophy of "whatever you do—do it with style," then Apple's **iDVD** is the perfect entry-level authoring software for you. With probably the most intuitive user interface in this category, iDVD doesn't try to provide every possible feature, but what it does, it does extremely well.

You can easily import your own still or motion menu background by dragging an image file or video clip into the *Settings* panel, but don't overlook the template options. If you must use menu templates, iDVD has, hands down, the best of the bunch. The designs are outstanding, but the best part is *drop zones*, irregularly shaped hotspots on selected templates where you can place your own video clips or photos. Just drag a file over the hotspot and violà—instant compositing!

A part of Apple's iLife suite of applications, iDVD is tightly integrated with iPhoto, iTunes, and iMovie. This means any media type that's archived in one of these other applications can be instantly accessed from within iDVD itself. Note the left-hand pane above which displays all the images locally contained in iPhoto. To use an image from iPhoto, simply drag a thumbnail image from the left pane over into the main display window.

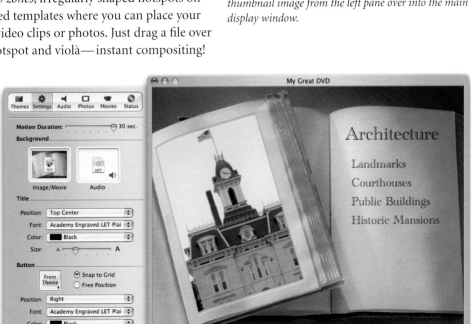

Apple iDVD

Type: Entry-level DVD authoring application

Platform: Mac

Manufacturer: Apple Computer

Input Formats: DV, QuickTime

Output: DVD-R

Noted Features: Sophisticated motion menu templates with drop zones. Imports chapter markers from iMovie. Internal MPEG-2 encoding. Integrated support for iTunes, iMovie, iPhoto. Requires a Mac with internal Apple SuperDrive.

Price: Bundled with selected Mac computers or can be purchased in the $49 iLife application suite.

Web Site: www.Apple.com

This conceptual menu design template has been customized by placing a short video clip in the designated drop zone over the book page.

Pinnacle
Impression
DVD-Pro

Type: Advanced entry-level DVD authoring application

Platform: Windows

Manufacturer: Pinnacle

Input Formats: DV, AVI, MPEG-2, MPEG-1, Dolby Digital

Output: DVD-R/RW, DVD+R/RW, DLT

Noted Features: Menu creation, Dolby Digital support

Price: $199

Web Site:
www.PinnacleSys.com

Pinnacle Impression DVD-Pro

Pinnacle Systems is well-known and respected in the video industry for their professional and consumer NLE video software.

Impression DVD is a solid addition to the Pinnacle consumer product line, providing a well-rounded set of DVD features that fit the needs of most consumers and even a few professionals.

The user interface is characteristically gray and subdued with few color icons, similar to Pinnacle's *Edition* video editing software. This low-key setting keeps the focus squarely on the imported assets and provides a familiar environment to authors who are accustomed to using other Pinnacle software.

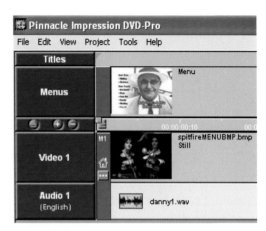

Impression DVD uses a drag-and-drop timeline interface to display related video, audio, and menu assets.

Impression DVD has a simple and efficient interface, with ever-present windows for imported assets, timeline displays and playback proofing.

Sonic DVDit (PE)

Another solid entry in the Sonic DVD product line, DVDit PE is geared towards the needs of corporate users and those who create presentations on DVD.

It has all the requisite features of entry-level authoring software, but goes beyond the expected with the ability to handle widescreen video, import Dolby Digital audio files, and write to DLT tape for replicated projects.

DVDit also comes with a large collection of attractive menu buttons and backgrounds with themes for both corporate and home projects.

The DVDit preview screen provides a generous area to indicate how your DVD will function after the project is burned to a disc.

Sonic DVDit

Type: Advanced entry-level DVD authoring application

Platform: Windows

Manufacturer: Sonic

Input Formats: DV, AVI, QuickTime, Dolby Digital

Output: DVD-RW/+RW

Noted Features: Wide selection of menu backgrounds and buttons, internal MPEG-2 encoding, widescreen support

Price: DVDit PE $399 DVDit SE $299

Web Site: www.Sonic.com www.DVDit.com

The DVDit user interface has a distinct, clean look that makes it easy to identify your options.

The "themes" panel circled in red at the right contains a collection of photographic backgrounds and buttons, many customized for use in corporate presentations.

Ulead DVD Workshop AC-3

Type: Advanced entry-level DVD authoring application

Platform: Windows

Manufacturer: Ulead

Input Formats: MPEG-2, MPEG-1, DV, AVI, QuickTime, Dolby Digital 2.0 and 5.1

Output: DVD-R/RW, DVD+R/RW

Noted Features: Direct capture from DV camcorder. Internal MPEG-2 encoding, chapter markers. Can encode Dolby Digital 2.0 audio.

Price: $299 (box) $279 (download)

Web Site: www.Ulead.com

Ulead DVD Workshop AC-3

Ulead's DVD Workshop AC-3 is a powerful authoring solution at a modest price. While it can be used for professional or corporate work, it still has the features and ease-of-use that consumers appreciate.

It's an all-in-one application, which allows you to capture video, encode, create menus, author, and burn discs all from within the same interface. It also has the advanced ability to import Dolby Digital audio tracks.

DVD Workshop provides a wide selection of useful menu backgrounds, buttons, and templates for motion video—enough to keep amateur authors busy for a long time.

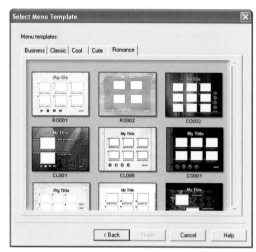

DVD Workshop provides a variety of menu templates in which you can place motion video clips.

DVD Workshop's user interface has five different modes of appearance: Start, Capture, Edit, Menu, and Finish, each of which can be selected at top of the screen.

Switching between modes changes the available options in the left-hand tool panel.

Adobe Encore DVD

Adobe Encore DVD is a strong contender in the emerging mid-range of DVD authoring applications. This category is characterized by a combination of professional-level features, a non-threatening user interface, and affordable pricing.

Encore DVD, Adobe's first effort in DVD authoring software, is a worthy companion to their other professional video products such as Premiere Pro and After Effects. It's a natural choice for video editors who are already comfortable with Premiere Pro and need to extend their video abilities to DVD.

Encore DVD is tightly integrated with Adobe Photoshop to facilitate custom menu design, but it also provides tools for menu production

Adobe Encore DVD may have an unassuming user interface, but don't underestimate the program—there's a lot of custom control under this hood.

within the application itself. In addition, Encore contains a library full of pre-designed professional menu templates.

Encore's internal encoding capabilities allow you to create MPEG-2 and Dolby Digital files from imported Windows AVI Video assets.

Adobe Encore DVD

Type: Mid-range DVD authoring application

Platform: Windows

Manufacturer: Adobe Systems

Input Formats: AVI, MPEG-2, PCM, Dolby Digital

Output: DVD-R/+R, DLT

Noted Features: Built-in menu editing features, tight integration with Photoshop. High-end menu templates and buttons. Integrated subtitling, MPEG-2 and Dolby Digital encoding. DVD-9 capable.

Price: $549

Web Site: www.Adobe.com

Encore DVD is a comfortable fit for video editors already familiar with Premiere and doing things "the Adobe way." The tabbed palettes and standardized interface will appeal to anyone who already uses Adobe products.

Integrated advanced features like video encoding and subtitling make Encore an appealing value for Windows-based design and corporate professionals.

Apple DVD Studio Pro 2.0

Type: Advanced mid-range DVD authoring application

Platform: Mac

Manufacturer: Apple Computer

Input Formats: QuickTime, MPEG-2, MPEG-1, Dolby Digital 5.1

Output: DVD-R, DLT

Noted Features: Three levels of user interface from basic to advanced. Built-in menu editing features, high-end menu templates with drop-zones, Line 21 data, comprehensive control of DVD spec. Bundled with Compressor for MPEG-2 encoding and A.Pack for Dolby Digital encoding.

Price: $499

Web Site: www.Apple.com

Apple DVD Studio Pro 2.0

Apple has upped the ante for affordable yet powerful DVD authoring with DVD Studio Pro 2.0. This version is so radically different from the previous one that it's effectively a new (and much better) application altogether.

It's clear that Apple has taken the concept of abstraction layer software to heart—DVD Studio Pro (DVDSP) provides no less than three interface configurations. The Basic, Extended, and Advanced modes provide choices for a comfortable user environment, regardless of your level of expertise.

The value of great menu design has not been overlooked. Like Adobe Encore DVD, DVDSP offers integrated menu creation capabilities, plus a collection of the most well-designed menu templates that we've ever seen in a commercial software package. Borrowing a page from the iDVD book, DVDSP's templates contain *drop zones* that allow you to make customized template designs with instant video and image compositing. Of course, you can still easily import your own custom Photoshop-created menus.

Apple bundles Compressor and A.Pack with DVDSP, two encoding applications that provide high-quality compressed video and audio streams. See Chapter 14 for more information on each.

DVDSP also provides several high-end features like integrated subtitling, scripting, DVD-9 custom layer break, Line 21 data import, access to GPRM variables (storage areas for numeric disc values), and parental block.

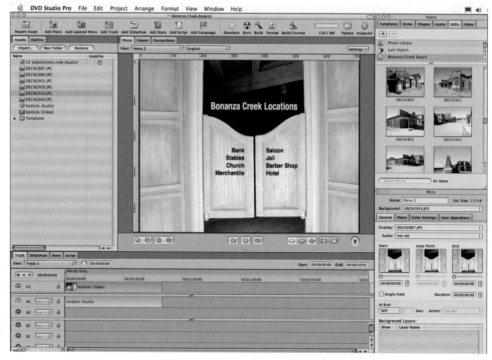

DVD Studio Pro's Advanced user environment is shown here with timeline-based editing and an abundance of control palettes for the benefit of advanced users.

Sonic ReelDVD

ReelDVD is Sonic's mid-range product aimed at authors such as videographers who need an application with some, but not all, of the high-end professional features found in more expensive software.

ReelDVD is built on the same formatting technology used in Sonic's highest-powered authoring package Scenarist. As a result, you can even export ReelDVD projects to be opened later in Scenarist.

The ReelDVD interface contains features similar to those found in high-end software like Scenarist and Creator, such as a storyboard view that displays icons representing the various assets and their relationships. It also provides the familiar timeline editing function so you can enjoy the best of both worlds.

ReelDVD offers many advanced features you'd expect in software at this level, such as support for Dolby Digital, subtitles, and multiple audio tracks. It's a good choice for professionals who want an affordable authoring solution now, with a format that allows for future editing in Scenarist.

ReelDVD provides timeline-based editing, a standard feature in most popular mid-range authoring applications.

Sonic ReelDVD

Type: Advanced mid-range DVD authoring application

Platform: Windows

Manufacturer: Sonic

Input Formats: MPEG-2, MPEG-1, Dolby Digital

Output: DVD-R/RW, DVD+R/RW, DLT

Noted Features: Storyboard and track (timeline) editing, export files to Scenarist, auto transcoding of audio to Dolby Digital

Price: $699.99

Web Site: www.Sonic.com

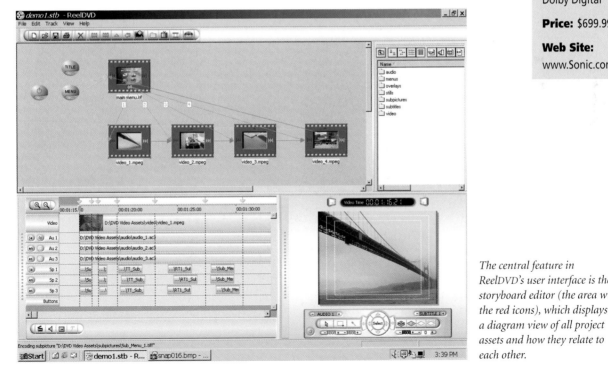

The central feature in ReelDVD's user interface is the storyboard editor (the area with the red icons), which displays a diagram view of all project assets and how they relate to each other.

Sonic DVD Producer

Type: mid-level (almost high-end) DVD authoring application

Platform: Windows

Manufacturer: Sonic

Input Formats: MPEG-2, MPEG-1, Dolby Digital, integrated hardware encoding

Output: DVD-R/RW, DVD+R/RW, DLT

Noted Features: Integrated hardware encoding, bit budget calculator, menu compositing, jacket picture creation

Price: $2499

Web Site: www.Sonic.com

Sonic DVD Producer

DVD Producer is a powerful authoring package at the upper end of the mid-range. It incorporates most of the popular mid-range level features, but adds integration with hardware encoders and other top-level capabilities.

It's aimed at multimedia producers who prefer a friendly user interface, but it's not for beginners—there's a wealth of advanced features beneath the streamlined surface. Among its many features are built-in menu compositing, a bit budget calculator, and the ability to create jacket pictures. It's also OpenDVD compliant, a Sonic technology that allows a completed burned DVD to be easily re-edited at a later date.

DVD Producer has an exceptionally simple outward appearance, with a minimal number of windows and palettes. The palette above displays a list of imported video and audio assets.

Although DVD Producer possesses most of the same features found in mid-range authoring software, it has the advanced ability to interface with the SD-1000 hardware encoder card to import video directly into the program.

Sonic Scenarist

When you author DVDs with Scenarist, you've definitely hit the big-time, baby. Equipped with the most robust feature set available, it's not a matter of asking what can it do—the real question is, "What *can't* it do?" Its vast abilities make Scenarist the number one choice for Hollywood-level authoring and it has been used to create the majority of mainstream movie DVDs. Sonic promotes Scenarist as having superior multiplexing capabilities, producing DVDs that are more compatible with DVD players.

Despite its amazing feature set, Scenarist isn't for everyone. Aside from its high price tag, the user interface is more difficult to master than those in the mid-range. Scenarist is not exactly what you'd call abstraction layer

software—it expects you to understand and manipulate DVD specification commands. As with ReelDVD, Scenarist has a storyboard-style interface, but not a timeline editor.

While it may have a steep learning curve, Scenarist is the only choice for creating DVDs that incorporate every feature available in the DVD specification.

Scenarist's powerful controls don't attempt to shield the user from the harsh realities of the DVD specification.

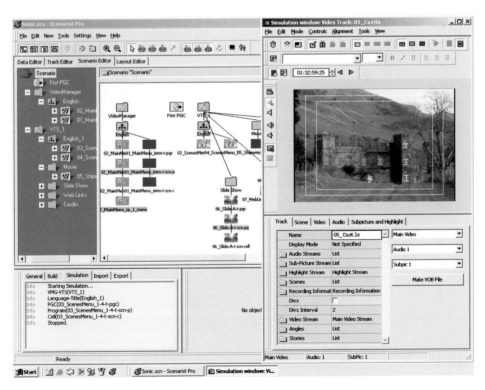

Sonic Scenarist

Type: High-end DVD authoring application

Platform: Windows

Manufacturer: Sonic

Input Formats: MPEG-2, MPEG-1, Dolby Digital, integrated hardware encoding

Output: DVD-R/RW, DVD+R/RW, DLT

Noted Features: Integrated hardware encoding, bit budget calculator, menu compositing, jacket picture creation. Full DVD specification support.

Price: $5000 to $35,000 depending upon configuration and hardware bundle.

Web Site: www.Sonic.com

Sonic Scenarist provides the highest degree of control of any DVD authoring software available, but its complex user interface might take a while to learn.

Sonic DVD Creator

Type: High-end DVD authoring application

Platform:
Mac OS 9 only

Manufacturer: Sonic

Input Formats:
MPEG-2, MPEG-1, Dolby Digital, integrated hardware encoding

Output: DVD-R, DLT

Noted Features:
Integrated hardware encoding, bit budget calculator, menu compositing, jacket picture creation. No OS X version available— OS 9 only.

Price: $14,999 (software only)

Web Site:
www.Sonic.com

Sonic DVD Creator

While Scenarist may be the most powerful Windows DVD authoring application, Sonic Creator is at the top of the heap in authoring features for the Mac platform.

Like Scenarist, Creator sports a storyboard editing interface with colorful icons representing the assets contained in the project. It also provides an intuitive editing time-line that shows video tracks with their associated audio and subtitles.

If Creator has any drawback, it would be that it's only available for Mac OS 9, which makes it difficult, if not impossible to function on the newest OS X optimized Mac hardware.

Sonic Fusion, *also for the Mac OS 9, is a feature-reduced version of Creator. It has the same user interface, but is not as powerful (or expensive) as Creator. Price: from $799 to $3999 depending upon the hardware bundle.*

Creator's colorful interface relies on a combination of storyboard and timeline asset editing.

Creator is definitely "Mac-like" and intuitive, but with advanced features that belie its user-friendly appearance.

Technical Testing

*Hardware and software techniques
for quality control testing*

16

Testing your project is critically important because a lot of things can go wrong when you develop something as complex as a DVD project. And the very last thing you want to happen is to find an error on a finished disc, especially one that has been reproduced in large quantities. At several stages throughout the development process you should burn the project onto a DVD disc and test for possible problems. This testing process is sometimes referred to as QC (Quality Check or Quality Control) and sometimes as QA (Quality Assurance).

If you've collected assets for your project from outside sources, don't assume that those assets have been prepared correctly. Take the time to preview all movies and audio files that will be included in your project, making sure the quality is acceptable and that everything plays as expected. If you've received video segments or graphics from another designer, check the file formats, sizes, and spelling accuracy of menu items.

Instead of using a new DVD-R disc every time you test your project, use a DVD-RW (rewritable) disc or a DVD+RW if you have a +RW drive. You'll have to erase the rewritable disc each time before you burn a new test, and the process is slow, but DVD-RWs can be erased and rewritten a thousand times, saving lots of money and many DVD-R discs. Note however, that *rewritable* discs have more compatibility problems with consumer set-top players than standard DVD-Rs (and DVD+Rs), so you should use RWs mainly for testing on computer DVD players. To test your project on consumer players, burn a standard recordable DVD disc (DVD-R or DVD+R). However, if you've determined that your own set-top player *does* play rewritables without a problem, don't hesitate to use rewritable discs for testing. See Chapter 1 for more information about existing disc formats.

Testing Tips

If you have a project that will be reproduced in large quantities, the replication facility will probably be able to offer some analysis and testing procedures.

Projects with large budgets can benefit from independent laboratory testing, such as the services offered by Intellikey Labs, (www.IntellikeyLabs.com), or by high-end, expensive software, such as Surveyor by Interra (www.Interra.com), that can check video streams, navigation data and commands, file structure, and more.

It's rumored that some designers who don't have a collection of different consumer players laying around for testing have been know to take their test disc to a large consumer electronics store to test it in as many players as possible. For some unknown reason, this technique has come to be known as sending your disc to the "Circuit City Labs."

Testing Methods

There are three methods you'll use for DVD project testing: *simulation, emulation,* and *check disc* testing.

Simulation

Simulation refers to testing your DVD project while it's open in the authoring software on your computer. With this method you test your project using the built-in preview feature of your authoring software. Pages 273 and 274 show examples of simulation testing.

You can use simulation to check that menus function correctly and to check for spelling errors in graphics, subtitles, and captions. You can check for audio and video synchronization problems, but don't judge audio and video quality by what you hear and see in simulation testing because your computer is just *simulating* the final product.

Emulation

Emulation refers to testing multiplexed (see page 231 for an explanation of multiplexing) project files by playing them in the *software* DVD player application on your computer.

Use emulation to check audio/video quality and synchronization. Test the menus to see that mouse navigation and arrow keys behave correctly in selecting menu buttons. If you programmed content to return to a certain menu when the "Return" or "Enter" key is pressed, test to make sure all key commands are working.

Look for video quality problems such as color bleeding and interlace flickering (see Chapter 4 for more about problem-video issues).

The example below shows how to test a project in Apple's DVD Player application:

1. From the "File" menu, choose "Open VIDEO_TS Folder...."
2. In the "Open Folder" window that appears, select a VIDEO_TS folder from one of your DVD project folders.
3. Click the "Play" button (the right-facing triangle) on the software remote controller.

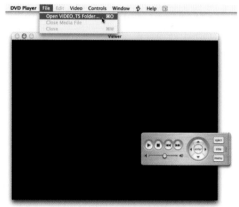

Emulation testing involves playing the final formatted files (multiplexed files) in your software DVD player.

Check disc

The final method of testing before you start duplicating copies of your project is to burn it onto a DVD-R disc (or DVD+R) using your DVD burner. This disc is called a *check disc.* Test the disc to see that it plays correctly on computers, both Macs and PCs. Test it in as many consumer players as possible. Of the large number of players that are available, there are a lot of inconsistencies in how well they play DVDs and how accurately they interpret menu commands. Test the disc for worst-case scenarios by viewing with a player that's connected to a cheap TV.

Simulation Testing

DVD authoring software features a preview command that simulates what your project will look like, and how it will behave after it has been multiplexed and burned onto a disc.

The following two pages show software preview simulation as seen in a couple of popular authoring programs, Apple's DVD Studio Pro and Adobe Encore DVD.

DVD Studio Pro

DVD Studio Pro's Graphical View window shows the folders that serve as containers for your project's content (shown top-right). The various color-coded folders can hold video and audio (green "Track" folders), menu graphics (blue folder), and slideshow photos (gray folder).

To run a simulation test of a folder's content (or the entire project):

1. Select a folder. If you want to preview and test the project as it would play in a player, select the folder that contains the content that will play when the disc is inserted into a player.

2. Click the "Preview" button in the lower-right corner of the "Graphical View" window.

3. Use the controller buttons at the bottom of the preview window to simulate navigation in a player.

The examples on this page show DVD Studio Pro 1.5. Version 2.0, a major version upgrade, was expected to be released just as our book went to press.

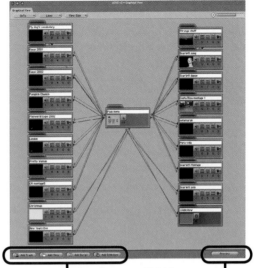

If testing reveals errors:

▼ Test the disc in other DVD players to see if it's an isolated problem in a specific player.

▼ Try burning the project onto another, better-quality disc.

▼ Try burning a disc at the slowest speed your software allows.

▼ Try lowering the combined data rate in your authoring software and re-encoding the project. See "Data rate budgeting" on page 229.

These buttons add folders that hold video/audio files, menus, and slideshows.

Select a folder, then click the "Preview" button in the bottom-right corner of the Graphical View window to open the project in a preview window (below).

These buttons simulate the buttons on a DVD player and can be used to test the project navigation and content.

Adobe Encore DVD

Adobe's DVD authoring program, Encore, provides the Project Preview window (shown below) to preview your project.

To run a simulation test of how your project will behave in a DVD player:

1. Open a project in Encore.

2. From the File menu, choose the "Preview" option.

3. Preview your project in the preview window that opens. The controller buttons in the bottom-right corner of the preview window let you test the menus for usability and check to see that buttons link to the correct movies or submenus. In addition to testing the menu buttons with your mouse, also test using the arrow keys on your computer keyboard.

Testing a DVD-9

If your project is large enough to require a DVD-9 disc (a disc with two layers of content) for final reproduction, how do you test it with a single layer DVD-R or DVD+R?

The answer is simple, but takes a little extra work. In your DVD authoring program, replace large video tracks with *small* placeholder videos so the project content fits onto a single layer disc.

If you have large amounts of data planned for the DVD-ROM storage of the disc, temporarily remove most of it to reduce the amount of content.

After adjusting the amount of content in the project, burn a test disc. Even though the actual video content has been substituted, the menus will work the same and you can test the DVD's architecture and functionality.

Mac DVD-RW Testing Tip

DVD Studio Pro does not officially support burning a project directly to a DVD-RW disc in the Macintosh SuperDrive (Mac's internal DVD burner). But you can trick the Mac and burn a DVD-RW disc directly from DVD Studio Pro (or from iDVD, Apple's entry-level DVD authoring software): Launch DVD Studio Pro (or iDVD) with a DVD-R disc in the internal SuperDrive, then eject the DVD-R disc and replace it with a DVD-RW disc. You should now be able to burn your project from within the authoring application, if you choose.

Encore's Project Preview window provides remote control buttons for simulating playback on a set-top player.

Duplication & Replication

Reproducing your project on DVD media

After you've finished authoring your DVD project and you've tested it to make sure all the menus are working as you intend, you transfer the final files onto a DVD disc. For personal projects you may need only one or two discs; other projects may need hundreds or thousands of copies.

There are two different processes to make multiple copies from a DVD master: **duplication** and **replication.** In this chapter we'll discuss the differences between these two processes and when to use one over the other.

Our discussion will assume you're using a common type of DVD disc media, DVD-R, officially known as **DVD-R for General.** "General" means the format is intended for a broad base of consumer use. General media is available in 1X (one times) speed and also 4X (four times) speed. This refers to the speed at which a disc can be recorded. A 1X disc records in real time; that is, 40 minutes of video takes 40 minutes to record onto the disc. A 4X disc is four times faster; 40 minutes of video takes 10 minutes to record. Obviously 4X is better, but 4X media will not record at 4X speed unless you have a DVD drive capable of burning at 4X speed. Both 1X and 4X discs will play normally in a DVD player.

You may find DVD-R discs labeled as **DVD-R for Authoring.** Don't buy "for Authoring" discs unless you have a DVD drive that can write to this type of disc (and you probably don't). The *for Authoring* media format is officially designated as "for professional use." Don't be confused by the words "Authoring" or "professional." You can "author" a professional DVD project without using Authoring media. The General format is more recent, and according to a DVD White Paper from Pioneer New Media Technologies, Inc. (one of the creators of the DVD format), "future drives will most likely be General type drives."

Authoring media & General media:

Because "Authoring" media and "General" media use different laser wavelengths, each one must be recorded in a corresponding type of drive. You cannot record (burn) General media in a DVD drive that's compatible with the Authoring media format, and you cannot record Authoring media in a DVD drive that's compatible with the General media format.

Duplication services

If you need to make hundreds of duplicates and you don't want to tie up your DVD drive for several days, you can search the Internet for "duplication services" and you'll find an amazing number of professional DVD and CD facilities that offer duplication services at reasonable rates.

The Duplication Process

When you use the DVD drive connected to your computer to burn a DVD, you're using the **duplication** method. Duplication is a *laser burning* process that uses laser technology to make copies of DVDs. This process is appropriate when several conditions are present:

▼ Relatively small quantities of discs are needed (generally up to 100 or 200 copies).

▼ The project contents will fit on a single-sided, single-layer disc (a DVD-R).

▼ The project does not use encryption technology (CSS: Content Scrambling System) that can't be handled by DVD-R.

Duplication is affordable and convenient for producing limited quantities of discs. If you need just one disc to put in a display booth kiosk, or if you need to make a dozen copies to give a sales team, duplicating the discs with your DVD drive is a good solution. But it's slow, especially if you need to burn a large number of discs.

Limited-quantity duplicators

If you need quantities in the range of 25 to 100, you're probably duplicating DVDs for a client and you need a more efficient workflow. You should consider investing in a duplicator designed for small offices and small-to-medium quantities. These duplicators connect to your computer and, depending on the model, can hold from 25 to 100 blank DVD discs on a spindle, and automatically load and burn them. Some duplicators can also print custom label graphics on your discs. Printable discs are white and have a special, printable coating on the top surface.

Primera Technology's Bravo Disc Publisher (shown below) can automatically duplicate up to 25 discs and print graphics on them. This is a great solution for duplicating small quantities of professional-looking DVDs for friends, relatives, associates, or clients. Other Primera models hold up to 50 or 100 discs, but do not include an integrated printer. Check out their printers and duplicators at www.PrimeraTechnology.com. We've included a Bravo Disc Publisher PDF brochure in the ROM section of the attached DVD disc.

You can find additional information about other duplicators and printers when you search the Internet for "DVD duplicators."

The Bravo Disc Publisher from Primera Technology automatically duplicates and prints up to 25 DVD-Rs. An optional attachment increases the capacity to 50 discs.

Do-It-Yourself Duplication

Let's say you need to duplicate a DVD project and you need just a few copies, or perhaps a dozen, to deliver to your client. Some entry-level DVD authoring programs (such as Apple's iDVD) automatically assemble your project into the proper multiplexed format and burn the files straight to a DVD disc without creating a copy of the multiplexed files on your hard disk.

We prefer authoring software that assembles the multiplexed files and saves them to the computer's hard disk. That makes it easy to drag and drop the multiplexed files to DVD burning software (as shown below) whenever you need to make a duplicate. And it makes it easy to access the files when using an automated duplicator such as the Bravo Disc Publisher shown on the previous page.

To burn a DVD using Roxio's Toast (Mac):

1. Open Toast, then click the "Other" icon. The info bar displays "DVD" to indicate Toast is set to create a DVD disc.

2. Drag your multiplexed DVD project folder (the folder that contains the AUDIO_TS and VIDEO_TS folders) to the Toast Window.

3. Click the "Record" button in the bottom-right corner (circled below).

Some of the most popular Windows DVD-burning applications include Sonic's RecordNow Max, Ahead Software's Nero Burning ROM (below), Roxio's Easy CD & DVD Creator (shown below, bottom), and Pinnacle's Instant CD/DVD.

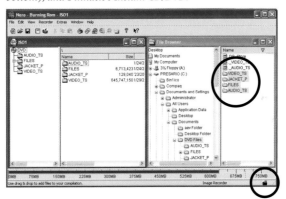

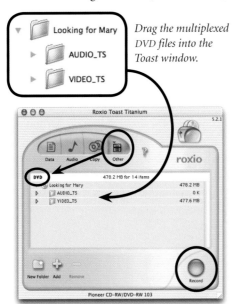

Drag the multiplexed DVD files into the Toast window.

Nero Burning ROM: Select the DVD file folders to burn, then click the "Burn" icon in the lower-right corner.

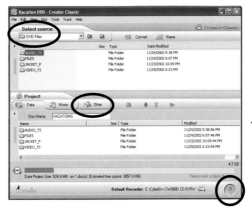

Easy CD & DVD Creator: Select your DVD project as the "source," choose "Other" from the "Project" tabs, then click the Roxio icon in the bottom-right corner to burn a DVD.

Verification Tip

Avoid disc errors by verifying your disc before you send it to a replicator. If there are any kind of playback errors in the final DVD-R disc (or DLT tape, if used to deliver final files to a replication facility), the replicator will not be able to correct them. Deliver a back-up disc along with the original, just in case an error is encountered on the original.

Choosing a Format

Most readers of this book will probably produce smaller, less complex DVD projects that won't require replication. But if your project does require a lot of content, you'll determine exactly how much and which disc format is needed in the planning stage of your project when you do the "bit budgeting" explained in Chapter 13.

The Replication Process

Replication is an *injection molding* process used to reproduce large quantities of discs, usually more than one or two hundred. Replication is mandatory when disc content won't fit on a single-sided, single-layer disc. Since the *duplication* process can only make single-sided, single-layer DVD-Rs, any project whose storage capacity exceeds one layer of data (4.37 GB) must be *replicated*.

The replication process involves sending your master files to a replication facility, either on DLT tape (see the following page) or on a master DVD-R disc. If your project uses more than one layer, you must put the content for each layer on a separate DLT. At the replication facility a glass master is made from your data and a mold is made from the glass master. An injection molding process is then used to make copies of your DVD from the mold.

If you're going to reproduce a single-sided, single-layered DVD, most replication facilities will accept your files on a DVD-R disc that you burned on your computer's DVD burner. Some facilities may require that you supply your files on a DLT tape. If you authored your DVD project to contain more than one layer of content, or if you incorporated CSS (Content Scrambling System) encryption in your files, delivery of your data on DLT tape is your only option.

Replication Formats

When you replicate a DVD project, it's possible to have content on both sides of a disc, and each side can have two layers of content. The amount of content contained in your DVD project will determine which disc size format is used in the replication process.

The most popular disc size formats available for replication are:

DVD-5
Single-sided with a single layer. This format can hold up to 4.37 GB.

DVD-9
Single-sided with two-layers. This format holds up to 7.95 GB.

Several other formats exist, but they're not very common or popular:

DVD-10
Two-sided with a single layer on each side. This format holds up to 8.75 GB.

DVD-10 is considered a "dated" format and few new titles are published in it. Some replicators no longer produce DVD-10s and recommend using a single DVD-9 or two DVD-5 discs instead.

DVD-14
Two-sided with two layers on one side and one layer on the other side. This format holds up to 12.3 GB.

DVD-18
Two-sided with two layers on each side. This format holds up to 15.9 GB. This is not a commonly used format.

What is DLT?

Digital Linear Tape is a common archival system that uses half-inch magnetic tape and requires a separate DLT drive. DLT drives use a SCSI connection (Small Computer System Interface, pronounced "scuzzy") which is not provided on newer computers. If you have an empty slot in your computer, you can install a third-party SCSI card and then connect a DLT drive. Or you may be able to find a friend or a local service bureau who can copy your files to a DLT for you.

DLT has the advantage of being very reliable compared to DVD-R and less likely to be written with errors.

Because technical requirements vary from place to place, check with the replication facility you choose to get detailed information about their specific requirements and how they want the project delivered. The site www.DVDdemystified.com is a great resource for finding information about replication facilities (and just about anything else concerning DVD). You can also conduct a search on the Internet for "DVD replication services."

Realistically, if you've just recently taken up DVD design and production, it's a long-shot that your projects will be so large or complex that you'll need DLT delivery *or* replication. Personal projects certainly don't need huge quantities, and even professional projects that you may produce for clients (anything from wedding videos to promotional DVDs) don't usually demand the thousands of copies that are necessary for Hollywood movie DVDs.

Replication Legal Issues

When you choose a replicator, check to make sure they are a fully licensed manufacturer that pays royalties to the various patent owners of DVD technologies. If you use an unlicensed replication facility, you could risk legal actions, fines, or seizure of your discs.

Royalties that are due are charged per disc and per technology patent. Although the fees are small, the business of DVD manufacturing is big and getting bigger, providing a revenue stream for the patent owners that is worth protecting. Think "legal hassle."

The Philips Corporation web site lists all licensed disc manufacturers in the United States and worldwide: www.Licensing.philips.com /licensees/database/licensees.html.

A DLT tape drive is an external device that holds an ejectable half-inch tape cartridge. DLT, which requires a SCSI connection, provides extremely large storage capacities, ranging from 20 GB to over 50 TB (a terabyte is roughly a thousand gigabytes).

To DLT or not to DLT. That's the replication.

Delivery of your project on a DLT is not necessary unless your project is too large to fit on a single-sided, single-layer disc, or unless you've used features that require DLT delivery, such as CSS encryption (Content Scrambling System). Always consult with your replication facility to verify what media type you can use to deliver your project.

Disc Printing Tip

To avoid wasting DVD discs, buy inexpensive cardboard discs to test print label designs. Search the Internet for "cardboard templates" or visit one of these sites:

www.CDrom2go.com

www.PrimeraTechnology.com

Label Design Tip

Disc printers that you buy usually include software templates for designing disc labels. For projects that require labeling a large quantity of discs, the commercial printer you choose can provide templates or design services.

More disc printers

Epson makes affordable printers that are specially designed to print single CDs and DVDs:

Epson Stylus Photo 900 (about $200) and Epson Stylys Photo 960 (about $350).

Visit www.Epson.com for more information. The Epson CD print software is not supported by Mac OS X.

First Impressions

Even after you've poured your heart and soul into producing a great DVD with beautiful video, snazzy editing, and flawless menus, the first impression of your work is going to be the **labeling** and **packaging.**

Labeling

If you have a small office and want all duplicating and labeling to stay in-house, you can choose from several kinds of printers that print directly onto CDs or DVDs. Inkjet disc printers can print full-color graphics on discs that have a specially coated, white surface made for printing. Thermal disc printers can print one and two color graphics on ordinary silver discs, simulating the standard screen printing technique often used on discs.

The more affordable disc printers range between $1,500 and $3,000, and are well worth the price if you want to deliver a professional looking product (see page 276 for one example of a disc printer).

You can search the Internet for "disc printers" or "DVD printers" and find many sources for disc printers. Visit the Primera Technology web site (www.PrimeraTechnology.com) to see a great line of printers and accessories for both Macs and PCs.

Avoid using printed adhesive labels on your DVDs. The thickness of the label or an uneven coat of adhesive may cause a disc to play improperly in some DVD players. Stick-on labels can even peel off inside players or drives. A printed disc looks more professional than a disc with a stick-on label.

Packaging

DVD packaging is available in a variety of styles. For many projects the jewel case is most efficient because the printed disc label shows through the transparent lid and serves as a self-cover graphic. The most common types of DVD packages are:

▼ Paper, cardboard, vinyl, or Tyvek sleeves (Tyvek is made of polyethelene fibers bonded under heat and pressure).

▼ Cardboard mailers with an insert.

▼ Single and dual Amaray cases (plastic book-style cases). The Amaray case design is a result of the DVD Forum's recommendation that DVD packaging be unique and distinguishable from CD packaging. The DVD Forum is an international organization that promotes and establishes standards for the DVD format (www.DVDforum.com).

▼ Standard and Slim-Line jewel cases.

Paper sleeve.

Cardboard mailer.

Amaray case.

Jewel case.

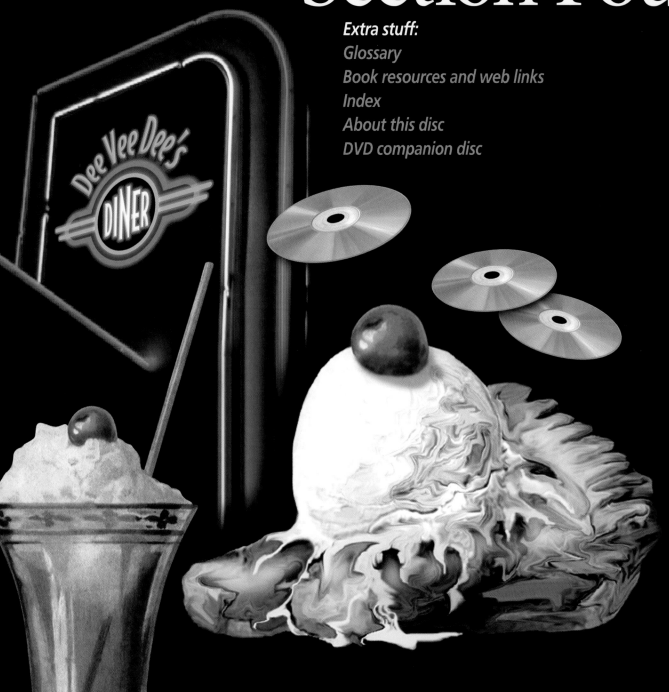

Section Four

Extra stuff:
Glossary
Book resources and web links
Index
About this disc
DVD companion disc

**You might be a DVD designer if you
make up new words and phrases such as . . .**

▼ Take it to the Mux.

▼ Don't let your babies grow up to be muxers.

▼ Muxa la vista, baby.

▼ Hasta la muxa, baby.

▼ Hasta la vista, muxer.

▼ Buenas muxas.

▼ Born to mux.

▼ Muxable.

▼ Just mux it!

▼ DVDs kick mux!

▼ Muxadelic!

▼ Muxalicious!

▼ Don't mux with Texas.

▼ You gotta be muxin' me!

▼ I don't muxing think so.

▼ I'm in a state of mux.

▼ Well I'll be demuxed!

▼ Inmuxication.

▼ Mux happens.

▼ Come on baby, do the mux.

▼ Discover your inner muxer.

▼ Adios mi aMuxo.

▼ Mi muxa es su muxa.

Glossary

abstraction layer: Refers to the graphical user interface provided by most DVD authoring applications (or any other kind of software) in that the abstraction layer determines the degree to which the user is "shielded" from the most technical aspects of the DVD specification.

AC3: See Dolby Digital

anamorphic: A widescreen video format that has a native aspect ratio of 16:9, but is horizontally squeezed into a 4:3 aspect ratio to fit within the allowable video dimensions on a DVD. Anamorphic video is expanded to its full width upon playback.

AUDIO_TS (Audio_Title Set): All finished DVD projects contain a VIDEO_TS folder, but the folder is always empty and only contains data when it's on a DVD-Audio formatted disc. It serves no purpose on a DVD-Video disc, but most DVD set-top players need it to be present in order to play the disc correctly.

AVI: Audio Video Interleaved. A popular Windows video format developed by Microsoft. An uncompressed AVI file is often used as the source file to encode video into the MPEG-2 format.

authoring application: Software used to assemble edited video and audio assets into a DVD structure—a menu system that is navigable and provides easy access to any part of the content.

background: The part of a menu design that serves as a background for buttons or graphics. Menu backgrounds can be static images, flat solid colors, or motion video clips.

B-frame (Bi-directional Frame): Video compression software and hardware compresses video by analyzing every single frame of a movie, deciding what digital information to throw away based upon *previous* and *next* frame information. B-frames are created using digital information from the video frames on either side of them.

bit rate: The rate at which data is transferred. Video encoding software lets you adjust the bit rate at which video is encoded into the MPEG-2 format. High bit rate settings make larger, higher-quality files, and low bit rate settings make smaller, lower-quality files. DVD specifications allow MPEG-2 files to have a maximum bit rate setting of 9.8 Mbps.

bit resolution: The number of bits (digital pieces of information) in an audio sample. Audio can be 8-bit, 16-bit, 24-bit, or 32-bit. Larger bit numbers mean higher fidelity and better quality. The bit resolution determines the audio's "dynamic range," the number of steps for describing the audio level from quiet to loud. To determine the dynamic range in decibels, multiply the bit rate by 6. An 8-bit recording has a dynamic range of 48 decibels.

Blu-Ray: Upcoming DVD technology that will increase the single-layer disc capacity of a DVD from 4.7 GB to 27 GB.

BUP: An abbreviation for "back up." .BUP (pronounced *dot bup*) files are backups of IFO files (information files created when a DVD project is multiplexed). A DVD player looks for .BUP files if an IFO file is damaged or if some other error occurs while reading a disc.

burner, DVD burner: A hardware device that writes authored DVD data to a DVD disk. Current models can support variable burn speeds from 1x to 4x and DVD-RW or DVD+RW formats. High-end burners can accommodate DVD-R authoring discs.

button: A graphical element on a DVD menu that provides a link to content or other menus.

CBR (Constant Bit Rate): A type of MPEG-2 encoding that applies the same bit rate compression to video segments regardless of their degree of motion.

CCD (Charge-Coupled Device): A technology used to build light-sensitive electronic devices such as video cameras.

Closed Captions: Text display of spoken dialog and sound effects in a video. Developed to make video content accessible to viewers who are hard of hearing. Closed Caption data is embedded on line 21 of an MPEG-2 video stream. It's often referred to as Line 21 data.

Compositing: The process of overlaying and arranging several video or graphic elements into a single composite video.

Compressionist: A professional whose specialty is encoding video and audio.

Content: Usually refers to the edited video, audio, and slideshows that are presented on a DVD. It is often referred to as main content (the feature movie or video on the disc) and bonus content (additional video segments that support the main content).

CSS (Content Scrambling System): An encryption technology available for use on DVDs.

D1: A high-quality, uncompressed professional digital video (DV) format with a pixel dimension of 720 x 486.

de-mux: The process of undoing the multiplex process used by authoring software that combines various project files (audio, video, menu graphics, captions) into one file. De-muxing is helpful when you need a specific file from a project, such as an audio file, but no longer have access to the original, separate project files.

Dolby Digital: Compressed Dolby Digital audio stream. Also known as AC3 format. Based on a source PCM audio file, it retains the quality of the original but the digital file is compressed on the average of 8:1. The use of AC3 audio files allows more room for MPEG-2 video and other assets on a DVD.

DSP (Digital Signal Processing): Audio editing software can use DSP tools to modify volume levels of audio selections, change the duration of a selection without changing the pitch, change the pitch of a selection, change the sample rate, convolve a sound (apply the characteristics of one sound onto another sound), fade sound in or out, convert sound between mono and stereo, and more.

DTS (Digital Theater Systems): High-end audio 5.1 digital surround format provided as an alternate track on many high-end movie DVDs. It competes with Dolby Digital.

Duplication: A process of reproducing discs by burning data onto them with laser beams.

DV: Digital Video. A popular consumer video format that provides high-quality video.

DVCPRO: A high-quality professional video format.

DVD (Digital Versatile Disc *or* Digital Video Disc): A popular, consumer disc format designed specifically for the storage and delivery of audio and video content in a highly compressed, high-quality format. DVDs are available in several different, competing formats: DVD-R, DVD+R, DVD-RW, and DVD+RW.

DVD-5: The most common professionally replicated DVD format. The single-side, single-layer disc holds up to 4.37 GB of data.

DVD-9: A high-capacity professional DVD format that contains a double layer on a single-sided disc. It holds up to 7.95 GB of data.

DVD-ROM: A standardized format for placing data files onto a DVD disc.

DVD+R (pronounced *DVD plus R*): A popular write-once disc format for consumer DVD authoring. Competes with the DVD-R format. Labeled as having a 4.7 GB capacity, but actually holds only 4.37 GB of data. DVD+R is based upon the professional DVD-5 disc format.

DVD+RW (pronounced *DVD plus RW*): A popular rewritable consumer disc format. Its label claims a storage capacity of 4.7 GB, but it actually holds only 4.37 GB of data. It competes with the DVD-RW format.

DVD-R (pronounced *DVD dash R*): A popular write-once disc format for consumer DVD authoring. Competes with the DVD+R format. DVD-R disc labels claim a storage capacity of 4.7 GB, but actually hold only 4.37 GB of data. DVD-Rs are based on the professional DVD-5 disc format.

DVD-RW: (pronounced *DVD dash RW*): A popular rewritable consumer disc format. Although DVD-RWs have a labeled capacity of 4.7 GB, they actually hold only 4.37 GB of data. DVD-RW Competes with the DVD+RW format.

DVD-Video: A standardized format for authoring video and audio onto a disc.

encoder: A hardware card or a software program that can analyze and compresses video. Each encoder employs its own proprietary algorithms to make quality versus file-size decisions.

file extensions:

.ac3: The Dolby Digital audio file format.

.aiff: Mac audio file format.

.avi: PC video format.

.m2v: MPEG-2 video file format.

.mov: QuickTime multimedia format.

.pct: PICT, a Mac image file format.

.psd: Native Photoshop file format.

.tif: Tagged Image File Format primarily used for printing.

.wav: PC audio file format.

first play: A DVD authoring term for the content that plays when a disc is first inserted into a set-top player. The first play is often an FBI warning about illegal copying of copyrighted material.

format, logical: The format used for data on a DVD, such as DVD-Video or DVD-Audio.

format, physical: The type of disc media used to record DVD projects, such as DVD-R, DVD+R, DVD-RW, DVD+RW, and DVD-ROM.

frame rate: Refers to the number of frames per second shown (or recorded) in film or video.

GOP (Group of Pictures): A GOP is the sequence of similar compressed video frames within an MPEG-2 file. It consists of I, B, and P frames. A GOP is commonly 15 frames in length, one-half of a second.

hardware encoder: A special card in a computer that communicates with encoding software. Hardware encoders are faster and often better quality than software encoders.

HD-DVD: High-definition DVD intended for widescreen high-definition video screens with pixel dimensions of 1280 x 720 or higher.

highlights: A visual device to indicate that a menu item is *selected*. Menu highlights can also be created to indicate when a selected item is *activated* (the remote's Select button is pressed).

hybrid DVD: A video-DVD with an added DVD-ROM directory that contains computer data files. Hybrid DVDs can be used in either a set-top player or software player, but the ROM files are only accessible and visible on a computer.

IEEE 1394: A serial bus interface standard adopted by the Institute of Electrical and Electronics Engineers for high-speed communication between devices. IEEE 1394 is also known as FireWire and i.Link.

I-frame (intraframe): A video frame that contains all of the video information for a GOP. It's the point in an MPEG-2 video stream where chapter markers can be placed.

IFO (Information File Object): IFO files are created automatically when authoring software multiplexes a DVD project. They contain commands and instructions that enable DVD players to play a DVD and provide menu behavior as the author intended.

Indeo: A software-only codec (compression/decompression technology) developed by Intel for digital video, based on the hardware-only codec, DVI (Digital Video Interactive).

interlaced scan: The video display technology used by most TV sets (except for HDTV—newer high-definition TVs), Interlacing displays each frame of video as two separate fields, even and odd numbered horizontal scan lines. The TV screen alternately displays each field at a rate of 30 times per second for NTSC TVs, or 25 times per second for PAL TVs. At any point in time only half of the image in a single frame is visible.

Line 21 data: Refers to Closed Caption technology. NTSC DVDs store Closed Caption data on Line 21 of the MPEG-2 video stream.

LPCM audio (Linear Pulse Code Modulation): An uncompressed audio format, usually implemented as AIFF or WAV files. Commonly referred to as PCM format.

Macrovision: An analog DVD encryption system.

main menu: The graphical interface of a DVD that provides access to the main areas of content included on the disc. It's usually the first menu that appears on a DVD.

mastering: A process that replication facilities use to create the master disc (glass master) needed to reproduce large quantities of a DVD title.

menu: A graphical interface that provides selection choices for navigating the contents of a DVD title.

menu environment: A themed menu design created to emulate either a real or imagined 3D space.

menu system: A collection of integrated motion, still, and audio elements that provide disc navigation and establish a unified theme for a DVD.

miniDV: A compressed high-quality digital capture format used widely in consumer digital camcorders. MiniDV has a pixel dimension of 720 x 480.

motion graphics: Animation and special effects that are created with video compositing software such as Adobe After Effects.

motion menu: A DVD menu that includes motion video, either as a background or as small, inset movie clips.

MP3: A popular compressed audio format for computer audio files, but not natively allowed in DVD.

MPEG-1: A first-generation compressed video format developed by the Moving Picture Experts Group. Roughly comparable to VHS quality, it's about half the resolution of MPEG-2. It is accepted within the DVD specifications, but is not capable of the high-quality possible when using the more advanced MPEG-2 format.

MPEG-2: A high-quality, compressed video format developed by the Motion Picture Experts Group. It's the primary compressed video format accepted by the DVD specification. MPEG-2 files can be almost six times smaller than the original video stream without noticeable image degradation.

MPEG-4: A compressed video format designed for efficient streaming over the Internet. This format cannot be used for DVD authoring.

multiplex: A process performed by DVD authoring software that reformats the files of a DVD project into a structure that DVD players understand.

muxing: Shorthand for *multiplex,* destined to become the buzz word of the decade.

NLE (Non-Linear Editor): Digital video editing software that enables non-linear manipulation of digital files, compared to old-school editing techniques that required cutting and pasting strips of film together in the order they were to appear on a screen.

non-square pixels: Pixels that are rectangular, such as those used by broadcast television monitors. By comparison, computers use square pixels.

NTSC (National Television System Committee): The standard interlaced video format used in North America and Japan. NTSC has a frame rate of 29.97 fps. Some people call NTSC "Never The Same Color."

PAL: Phase Alternate Line. The standard interlaced video format used in much of Europe, Hong Kong, and the Middle East. PAL has a frame rate of 25 fps.

PCM: See LPCM Audio.

P-frame (Predicted Frame): A single frame of video that has been derived from the difference in previous frames, based on the I Frame of a GOP.

pixel: The smallest singular unit of color (or gray) on a computer screen or television monitor that combines with other pixels to create an image.

program chain (PCG): Programmed instructions that set the parameters for VOB playback on a DVD.

progressive scan: Video display technology that displays all horizontal scan lines of a single frame at once, instead of showing alternating fields of scan lines as in interlaced video. NTSC progressive scan video has one field per frame that displays the entire frame at 30 times per second. PAL progressive scan video displays each frame 25 times per second.

QuickTime: Apple Computer's infrastructure for viewing video and other types of multimedia on a computer.

recorder: A device that encodes and writes to a DVD disc directly from a video source with no authoring involved and intended for the consumer market.

region coding: A security technique meant to deter pirating and illegal copying of DVD titles. DVD players manufactured and sold in different parts of the world can play only discs that have been authored with that region's code number. DVDs can be authored to be playable only with a region-specific player.

remote functions: DVD features that can be controlled by using the buttons on a remote control, including arrow buttons, the menu button, the return button, etc.

replication: A process of reproducing DVD titles with a manufacturing procedure that requires a glass master and a stamping process.

royalty-free: A system of selling content (motion graphics, soundtracks, or photos) for a one-time fee and permission to use the items for allowable purposes (allowable purposes may vary from among different vendors).

sample rate: The number of times per second that a digital audio sample is taken. Audio on a CD, recorded at 44,100 samples each second, is known as 44.1 kHz (kiloHerz). DVD audio requires a sample rate of 48 kHz.

seamless transition: A brief video clip between menus that makes the transition appear to be one uninterrupted motion, not an abrupt cut.

set-top DVD player: A consumer hardware device that provides DVD playback on television systems.

software DVD player: A software application that plays DVDs on desktop computers equipped with a DVD drive.

software encoder: A software application that analyzes, compresses, and converts digital video files into the MPEG-2 format.

square pixels: Pixels that are square, such as the ones used by computer screens to display images. TVs use non-square (rectangular) pixels.

still menu: A DVD menu made from a still photo or a static graphic.

submenu: A menu that is accessed from another menu higher up in the organization of the project architecture.

subpicture overlay: A bitmap graphic that overlays a DVD video image (or still image) to provide emphasis to a portion of the screen, as in a menu button highlight. Subpictures are also used to display subtitles and karaoke text.

subtitles: Text display of spoken dialog in a video. Used primarily to translate spoken dialog into the DVD viewer's native language. Subtitles are a type of subpicture overlay. Unlike Closed Captions, subtitles are not embedded in a video stream, b-ut exist as separate overlayed elements.

SVCD (Super Video CD): An extension of the VCD format that supports higher-quality MPEG-2 compression. SVCD plays on very few set-top DVD players, but will usually play on a computer DVD player.

transition: A short video clip that plays when a menu item is selected to provide an interesting visual connection between the menu and the selected content.

UDF (Universal Disc Format): The underlying standard format for all DVD discs.

VBR (Variable Bit Rate): A type of MPEG-2 encoding that selectively varies the bit rate compression to video segments based on their complexity and degree of motion.

VCD (Video on CD): A video format that utilizes MPEG-1 compression to achieve a picture quality similar to that of a VHS video and plays on a wide selection of DVD set-top players.

VIDEO_TS (Video_Title Set): In a DVD project, the authoring software *multiplexes* the project files and places them in a new folder named "Video_TS." The multiplexed files contain the project menus and video.

VOB (Video Object): A special MPEG-2 video file combined with audio files and subtitles.

VST (Virtual Studio Technology) **plug-Ins:** A standard audio plug-in technology for realtime audio effects.

Resources

DVD-related web links   *Visit www.MotionMenu.com for clickable links to the web addresses in this list of resources.*

General DVD and DV Information

The following sites provide information about DVD authoring and digital video.

www.DVDdemystified.com

www.DVDrHelp.com

www.Recipe4DVD.com

www.tfDVD.com

www.2-pop.com

www.BenWaggoner.com

www.Doom9.org

www.PostForum.com/forums

www.DV.com

www.CybMotion.com

www.JoeClark.org

www.MotionMenu.com

Organizations

A list of professional and corporate organizations that support the DVD format.

www.DVDforum.org

www.DVDfllc.co.jp

www.DVDa.org

www.DVDplusrw.org

www.DVDrw.com

www.Blu-rayDisc.info

Vendor Links

Links to selected DVD and video software/hardware vendors

NLE Video Editing

Premiere Pro: www.Adobe.com

Final Cut Pro: www.Apple.com

Avid Xpress DV: www.Avid.com

Edition: www.PinnacleSys.com

Vegas: www.SonicFoundry.com

MovingPicture: www.stagetools.com

Videowave: www.Roxio.com

DVD Authoring

Adobe Encore DVD: www.adobe.com

DVD Studio Pro: www.apple.com

Impression DVD:
www.PinnacleSys.com

myDVD to Scenarist: www.Sonic.com

DVD Workshop: www.Ulead.com

Video Compositing

After Effects: www.Adobe.com

Combustion: www.Discreet.com

Image Editing

Photoshop: www.Adobe.com

3D animation

Maya: www.Alias.com

Lightwave 3D: www.NewTek.com

3ds max: www.Discreet.com

Soft Image: www.SoftImage.com

Electric Image: www.ElectricImage.com

Digital Audio

ProTools: www.DigiDesign.com

Sonicfire: www.SmartSound.com

Peak: www.Bias-Inc.com

Audition: www.Adobe.com

MPEG-2 encoding

Compressor: www.Apple.com

Cleaner: www.Discreet.com

TMPGEnc Plus: www.TMPGEnc.com

Cinema Craft Basic:
www.CinemaCraft.com

ProCoder: www.Canopus.com

BitVice: www.Innobits.com

Dolby Digital and DTS encoders

A.Pack: www.Apple.com

Surcode: www.Surcode.com

Besweet: DSPguru.NoTrace.dk/

DVD disc burning

CD/DVD Creator: www.Roxio.com

Toast: www.Roxio.com

Nero Burning ROM: www.Nero.com

Primera Technology, Inc.
www.PrimeraTechnology.com

Subtitling

FAB Subtitle Editor:
www.FAB-Online.com

CCaption: www.CCaption.com

Subtitle Workshop:
Viplay.divx-digest.com

Eva: www.Instrumentality.org

Software DVD players

CinePlayer: www.Sonic.com

PowerDVD: www.GoCyberlink.com

WinDVD: www.InterVideo.com

VLC Player: www.VideoLAN.org
(VLC open-source VOB player)

Interactual Player:
www.Interactual.com

Stock video, audio, and images

www.12inchDesign.com

www.ArtBeats.com

www.AnimationsForVideo.com

www.Eyewire.com

www.Veer.com

Selected designers

Selected links to the web sites for the designers who contributed their work and expertise to this book.

The Pavement:
www.The-Pavement.com

MPL Media: www.MPLmedia.com

Finishing Post:
www.Finishing-Post.co.uk

Tiz Beretta: www.BerettaDesigns.com

Stanford Creative:
www.Stanford-Creative.com

Marek Doszla: www.LaFaktory.com

Stream AV (Mark Kimonides):
www.StreamAV.com.au

Internet newsgroups about DVD authoring

One of the best ways to learn about DVD authoring is to subscribe to one or all of these DVD newsgroups.

Geoffrey Tully's DVD list:
DVDlist.tully.com/mailman/listinfo/
dvdlist

Bruce Nazarian's DVD List:
www.Recipe4DVD.com/register.html

Apple DVD list: lists.Apple.com/
mailman/listinfo/dvdlist

General DVD books

If you need to go deeper into the DVD specification and authoring, we recommend these other fine books.

DVD Demystified
by Jim Taylor
McGraw-Hill Professional

DVD Authoring and Production
by Ralph LaBarge
CMP Books

DVD Production
by Philip De Lancie and Mark Ely
Focal Press

DVD software books

DVD Studio Pro 1.5 for Macintosh: Visual QuickPro Guide
by Martin Sitter
Peachpit Press

DVD Studio Pro 2.0 : The Complete Guide to DVD Authoring with Macintosh
by Bruce C. Nazarian
McGraw-Hill/TAB Electronics

Other Books

After Effects in Production
by Trish and Chris Meyer
CMP Books

Creating Motion Graphics wth After Effects, Volume 1 and Volume 2
by Trish and Chris Meyer
CMP Books

Nonlinear Editing: Storytelling, Aesthetics & Craft
by Bryce Butto, CMP Books

Photoshop for Nonlinear Editors
by Richard Harrington
CMP Books

Index

Examples used in this book

A

About this DVD

You can view this disc using a DVD-equipped computer or a set-top DVD player and television set.

The disc also contains DVD-ROM data (extra files we've made available for you) which you can access using any Macintosh or Windows computer with a DVD-ROM drive. Just insert the disc in your DVD drive and open the folder named EXTRAS to access the DVD-ROM content inside. You can drag any of the items from the EXTRAS folder to your Desktop.

The "ReadMeFirst" file in the EXTRAS folder gives detailed information about the DVD and the DVD-ROM content. It's available as a PDF and as a text file.

The DVD contains:

▼ Examples of many of the professional menus featured in this book.

▼ Examples of personal menus shown in Chapter 5.

▼ Encoding examples that show high-motion and low-motion video encoded with seven different popular encoders.

The EXTRAS folder contains:

▼ A Title-Safe and Action-Safe Photoshop template to use for menu design.

▼ Two sample soundtrack files in AIFF and WAV formats, created with Apple Soundtrack software.

▼ Two QuickTime movies featuring Clan Tynker and two large-format images to demonstrate DVD-ROM's unique ability to deliver large files and a variety of content and file types.

▼ From TriLab Productions: two royalty-free motion video clips and a PDF brochure for the *Digital Hotcakes* collection of royalty-free video clips.

▼ From Primera Technology: a PDF brochure for *Bravo Disc Publisher,* a combination disc duplicator and disc printer.